Street by Street

G000293561

CROYDON, SUTTON,
BECKENHAM, EPSOM,
MITCHAM, PURLEY

Banstead, Carshalton, Caterham, Chipstead, Coulsdon,
Ewell, Merton, Morden, New Addington, Penge, Selsdon,
Warlingham, Wimbledon, Woldingham

2nd edition September 2004
© Automobile Association Developments
Limited 2004

Original edition printed September 2002

Ordnance Survey® This product includes map data
licensed from Ordnance Survey ®
with the permission of the Controller of Her Majesty's
Stationery Office. © Crown copyright 2004.
All rights reserved. Licence number 399221.

Published by AA Publishing (a trading name of
Automobile Association Developments Limited, whose
registered office is Southwood East, Apollo Rise,
Farnborough, Hampshire, GU14 0JW. Registered
number 1878835).

Mapping produced by the Cartography Department of
The Automobile Association. (A02245)

A CIP Catalogue record for this book is available from
the British Library.

Printed by GRAFIASA S.A., Porto, Portugal

The contents of this atlas are believed to be correct at
the time of the latest revision. However, the publishers
cannot be held responsible for loss occasioned to any
person acting or refraining from action as a result of
any material in this atlas, nor for any errors, omissions
or changes in such material. This does not affect your
statutory rights. The publishers would welcome
information to correct any errors or omissions and to
keep this atlas up to date. Please write to Publishing,
The Automobile Association, Fanum House (FH17),
Basing View, Basingstoke, Hampshire, RG21 4EA.

Ref: ML167sz

Key to map pages	ii-iii
Key to map symbols	iv-1
Enlarged map pages	2-3
Main map pages	4-61
Index – towns & villages	62
Index – streets	63-76
Index – featured places	76-78
Acknowledgements	79

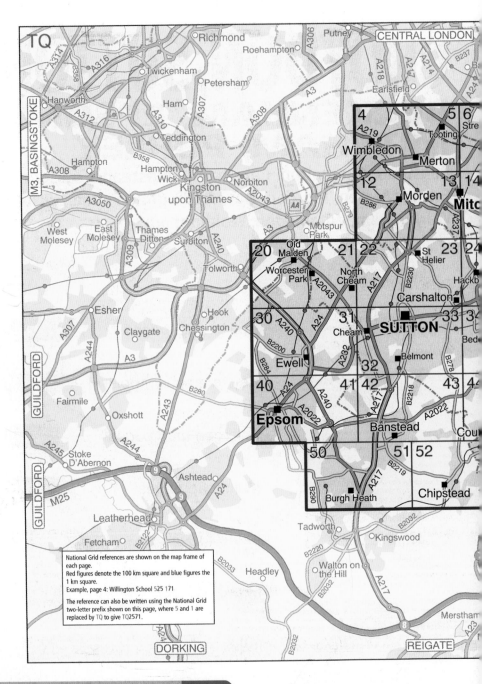

TQ

Richmond
Roehampton
CENTRAL LONDON
Putney
Twickenham
Petersham
Earlsfield
Hanworth
Ham
Teddington
Hampton
Hampton Wick
Norbiton
Kingston upon Thames
Wimbledon
Merton
Tooting
Stre

4 | **5** | **6**

West Molesey
East Molesey
Thames Ditton
Surbiton
Motspur Park
Morden
12 | **13** | **14**
Mitc

Tolworth
Old Malden
Worcester Park
North Cheam
St Helier
Hackb
Carshalton
20 | **21** | **22** | **23** | **24**

Esher
Claygate
Chessington
Hook
Cheam
SUTTON
Bed
30 | **31** | **33** | **3**

Fairmile
Oxshott
Ewell
Belmont
40 | **41** | **42** | **43** | **4**

Stoke D'Abernon
Ashtead
Epsom
Banstead
Cou
50 | **51** | **52**

Leatherhead
Fetcham
Burgh Heath
Chipstead

Tadworth
Kingswood
Headley
Walton on the Hill
Merstham

DORKING
REIGATE

M3, BASINGSTOKE
GUILDFORD
GUILDFORD

National Grid references are shown on the map frame of each page.
Red figures denote the 100 km square and blue figures the 1 km square.
Example, page 4: Willington School 525 171

The reference can also be written using the National Grid two-letter prefix shown on this page, where 5 and 1 are replaced by TQ to give TQ2571.

Scale of enlarged map pages 1:10,000   6.3 inches to 1 mile

1/4   miles   1/2
1/4   1/2   kilometres   3/4   1

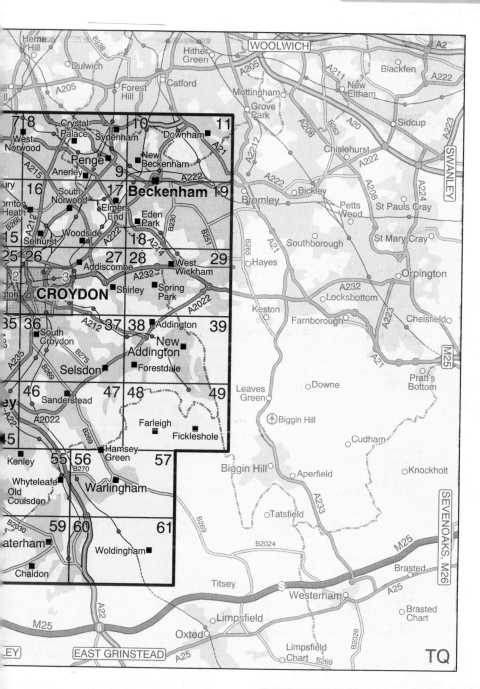

Herne Hill
Dulwich
A205
Forest Hill
Catford
Hither Green
WOOLWICH
A205
Mottingham
Grove Park
A20
A211
Blackfen
New Eltham
Sidcup
A2
A222
A223
SWANLEY

B238
Crystal Palace
Sydenham
Downham
A21
Chislehurst
A222

7 | 8
West Norwood
Penge
Anerley
A215
New Beckenham
A2212
Bromley
A208
A224
A222

10 | 11

9

16 | 17
Beckenham | 19
Bickley
Petts Wood
St Pauls Cray
A208

South Norwood
Thornton Heath
B266
A212
Elmers End
Eden Park
B230
A21
Southborough
St Mary Cray

15 | 18
Woodside
Selhurst
A222
A214
B251
B265
Hayes

25 | 26 | 27 | 28 | 29
Addiscombe
A232
West Wickham
A232
Locksbottom
Orpington
A223
Chelsfield
M25

CROYDON
Shirley
Spring Park
A2022
Keston
Farnborough
A21

35 | 36 | 37 | 38 | 39
South Croydon
A212
B275
Addington
New Addington
Forestdale
Pratt's Bottom

A235
B269
Selsdon
Leaves Green
Downe
A21

46 | 47 | 48 | 49
Sanderstead
A2022
B269
Farleigh
Fickleshole
Biggin Hill
Cudham
Knockholt

Kenley
55 | 56 | 57
Hamsey Green
B270
Whyteleafe
Old Coulsden
Warlingham
Biggin Hill
Aperfield
SEVENOAKS, M26

B2030
59 | 60 | 61
Caterham
Woldingham
Tatsfield
M25
Brasted

Chaldon
B2024
Westerham
A25
Brasted Chart

M25
6
A22
Titsey
Limpsfield
Oxted
Limpsfield Chart
B2026
B269
TQ

EAST GRINSTEAD
A25

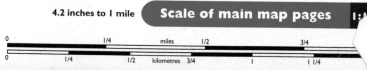

4.2 inches to 1 mile | **Scale of main map pages** | 1:

0 ... 1/4 ... miles 1/2 ... 3/4

0 ... 1/4 ... 1/2 ... kilometres 3/4 ... 1 ... 1 1/4

iv

Junction 9	Motorway & junction	⊖	Underground station
Services	Motorway service area	⊖	Light railway & station
	Primary road single/dual carriageway	++++++++	Preserved private railway
Services	Primary road service area	*LC*	Level crossing
	A road single/dual carriageway	•—•—•—•—•	Tramway
	B road single/dual carriageway	- - - - - - -	Ferry route
	Other road single/dual carriageway	....	Airport runway
	Minor/private road, access may be restricted	— · — · — · —	County, administrative boundary
← ←	One-way street	ⱱⱱⱱⱱⱱⱱ	Mounds
	Pedestrian area	**17**	Page continuation 1:15,000
============	Track or footpath	**3**	Page continuation to enlarged scale 1:10,000
	Road under construction		River/canal, lake
⌐ - - - - ⌐	Road tunnel		Aqueduct, lock, weir
AA	AA Service Centre	465 ▲ Winter Hill	Peak (with height in metres)
P	Parking		Beach
P+🚌	Park & Ride		Woodland
🚌	Bus/coach station		Park
	Railway & main railway station		Cemetery
	Railway & minor railway station		Built-up area

	Featured building		Abbey, cathedral or priory
	City wall		Castle
A&E	Hospital with 24-hour A&E department		Historic house or building
PO	Post Office	Wakehurst Place NT	National Trust property
	Public library		Museum or art gallery
	Tourist Information Centre		Roman antiquity
	Seasonal Tourist Information Centre		Ancient site, battlefield or monument
	Petrol station, 24-hour Major suppliers only		Industrial interest
†	Church/chapel		Garden
	Public toilets		Garden Centre Garden Centre Association Member
	Toilet with disabled facilities		Garden Centre Wyevale Garden Centre
PH	Public house AA recommended		Farm or animal centre
	Restaurant AA inspected		Zoological or wildlife collection
Madeira Hotel	Hotel AA inspected		Bird collection
	Theatre or performing arts centre		Nature reserve
	Cinema		Aquarium
	Golf course	V	Visitor or heritage centre
	Camping AA inspected		Country park
	Caravan site AA inspected		Cave
	Camping & caravan site AA inspected		Windmill
	Theme park		Distillery, brewery or vineyard

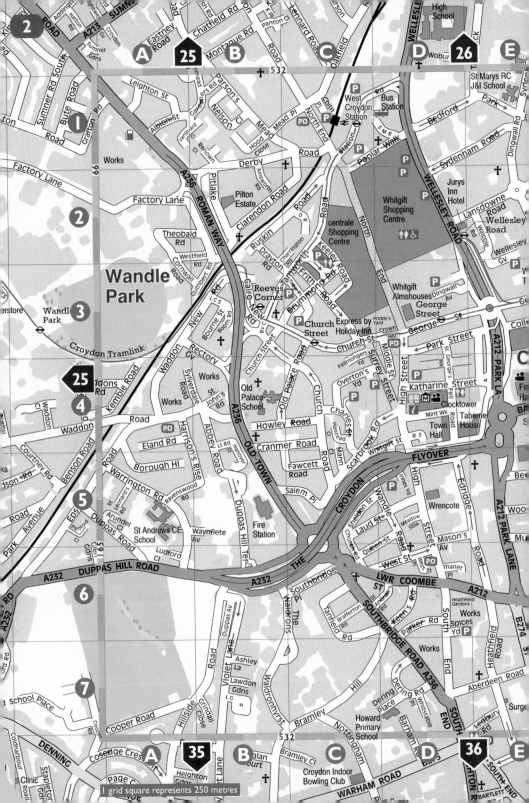

I grid square represents 500 metres

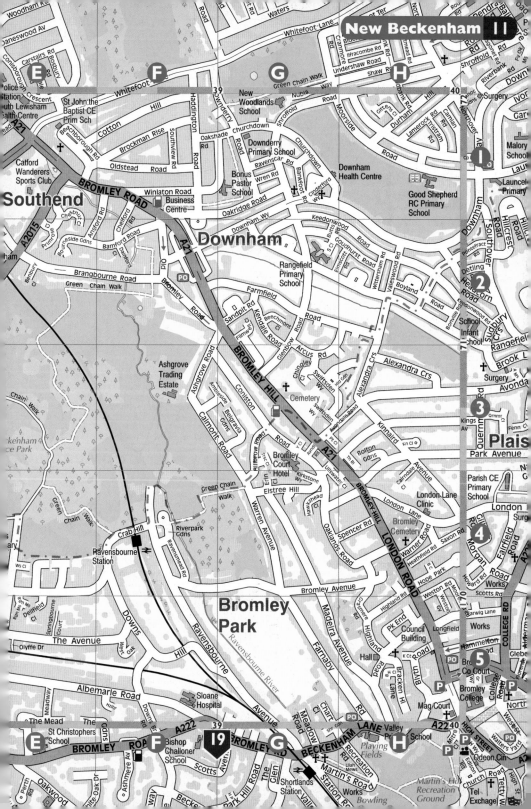

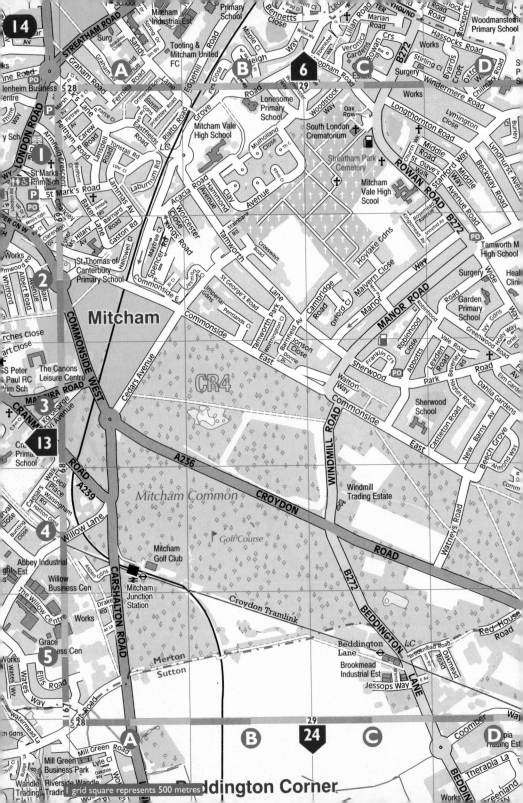

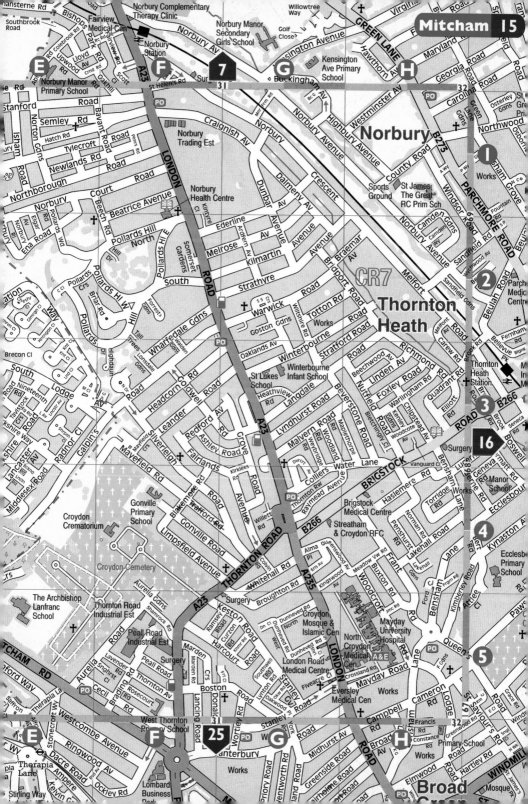

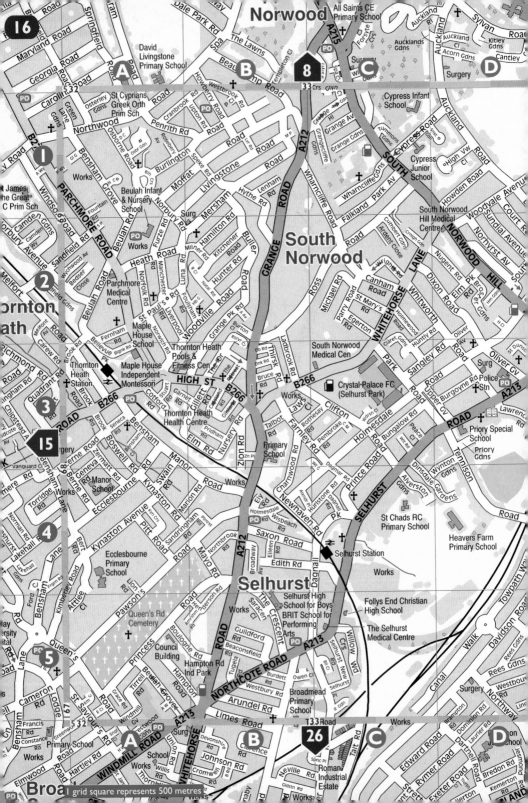

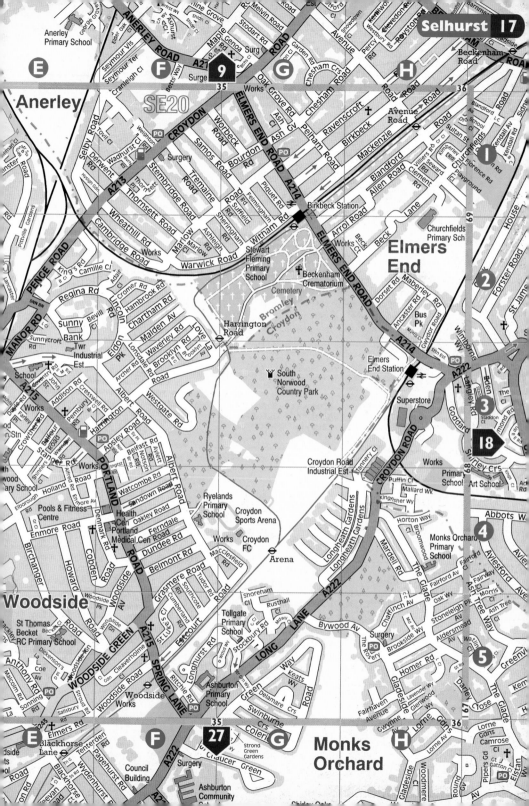

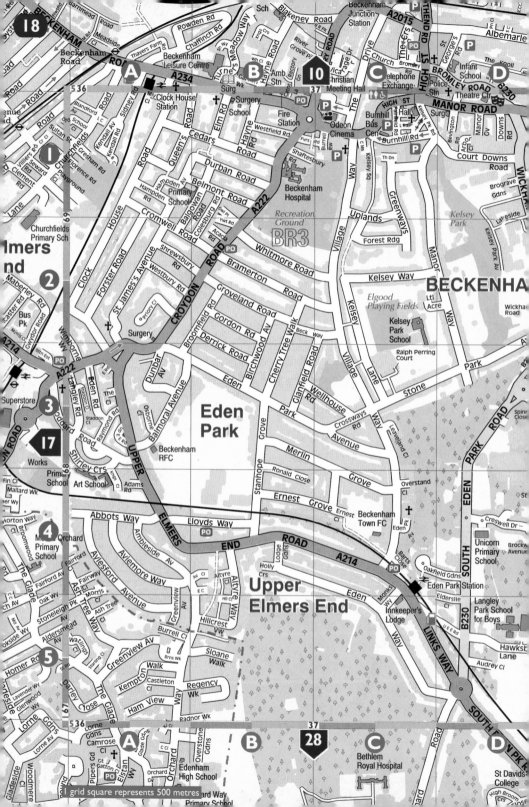

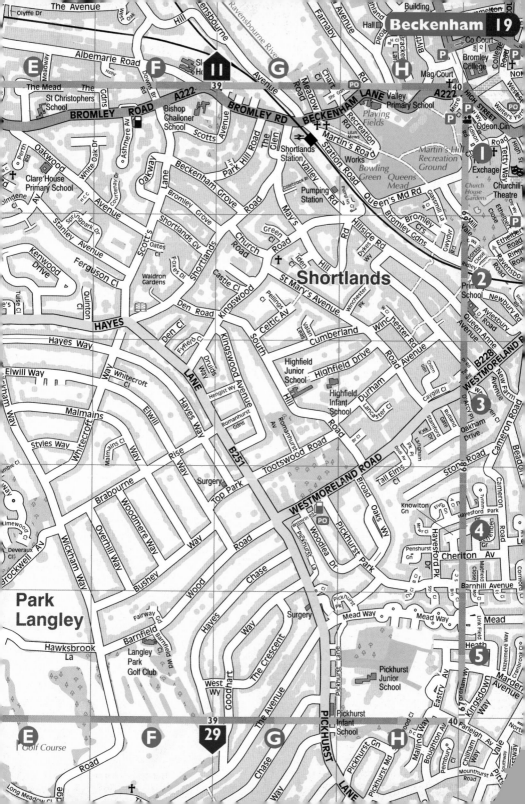

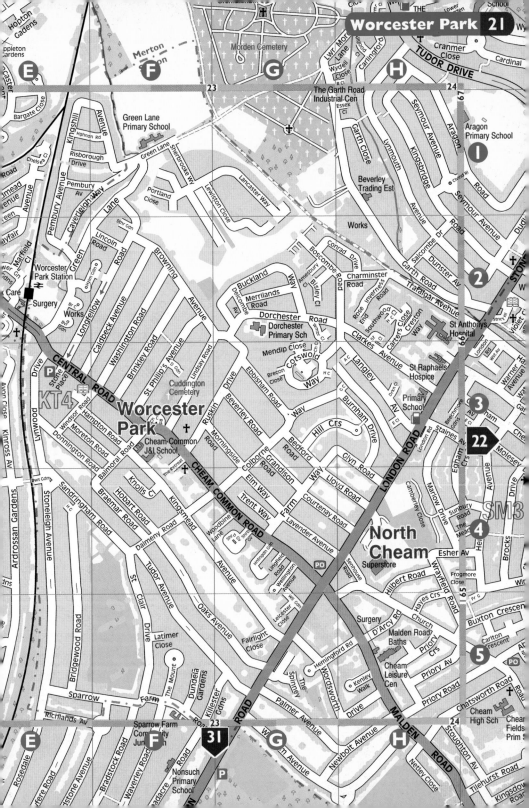

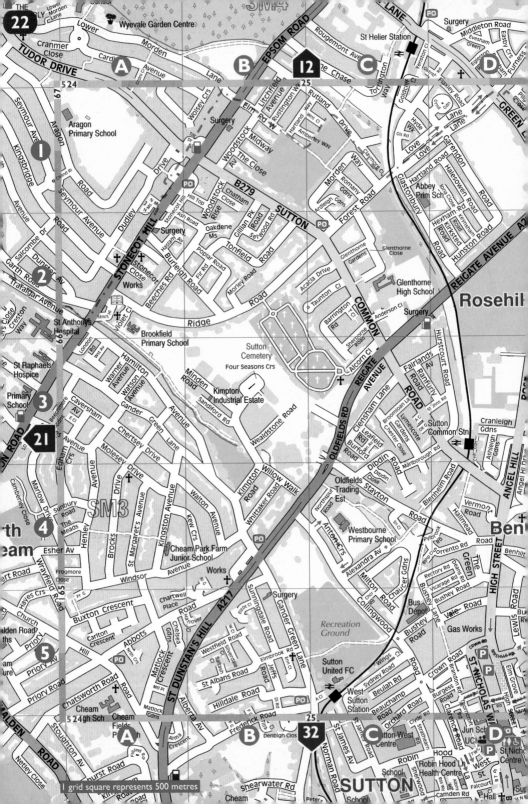

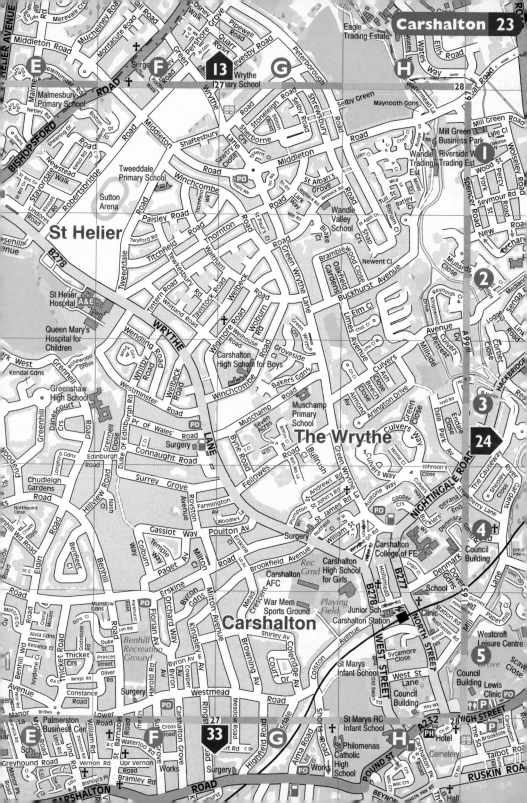

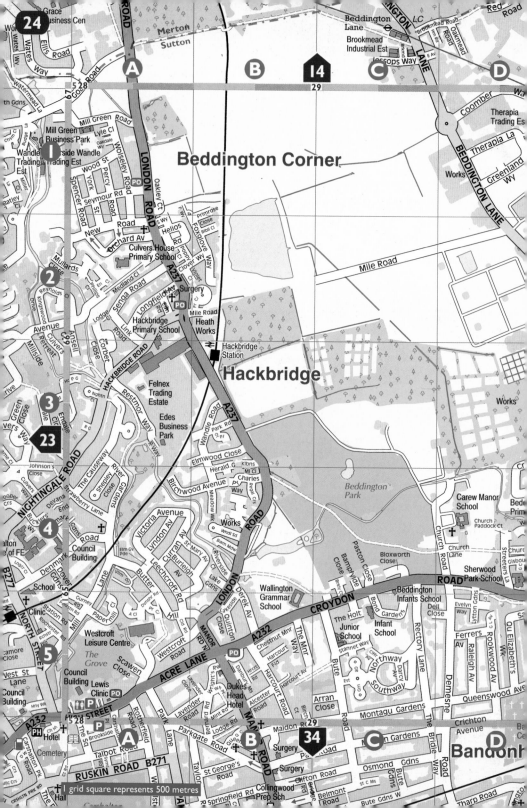

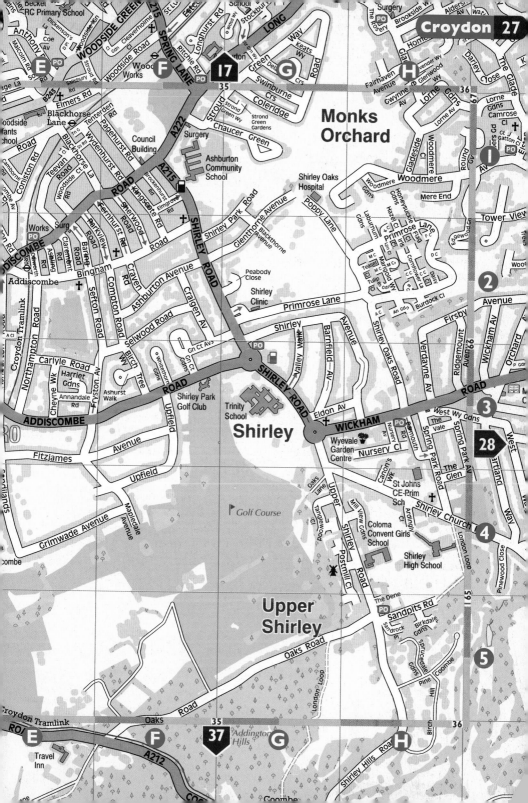

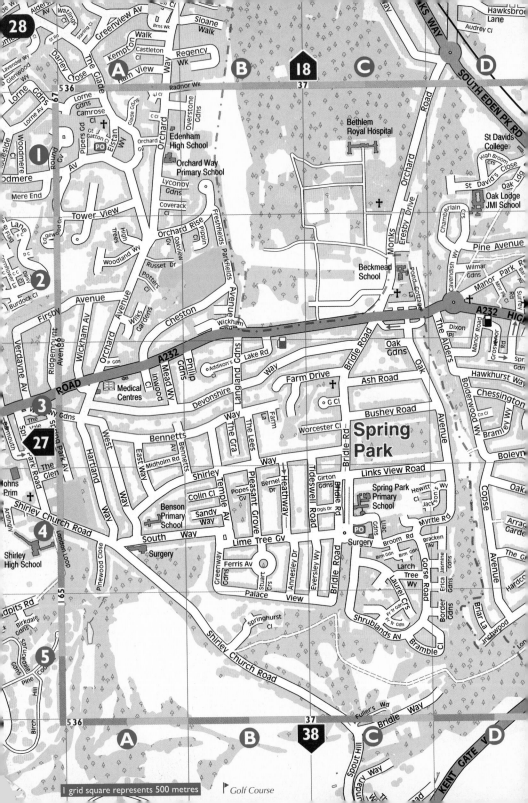

Golf Course

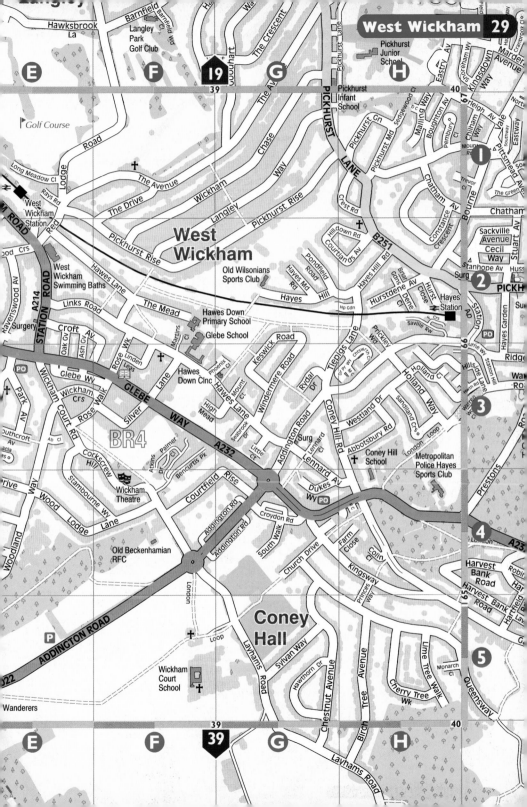

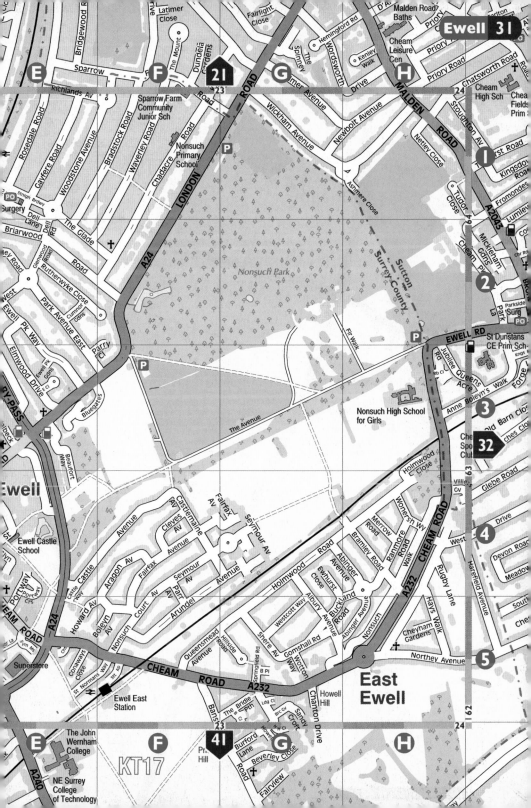

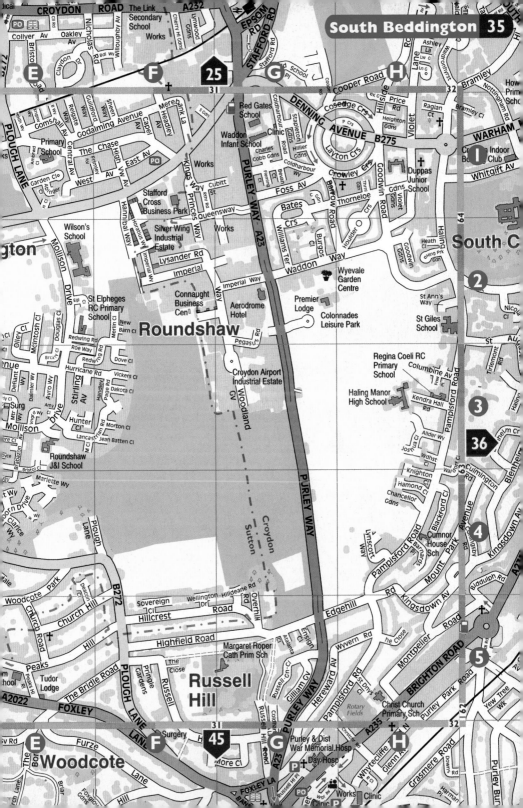

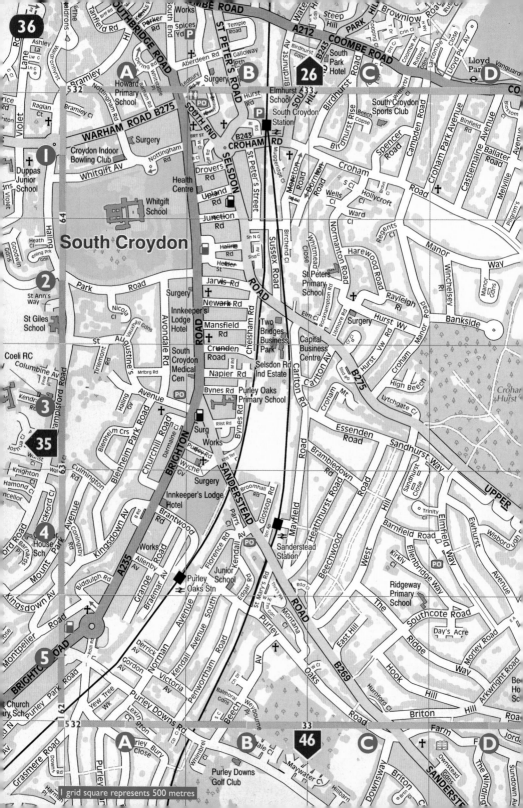

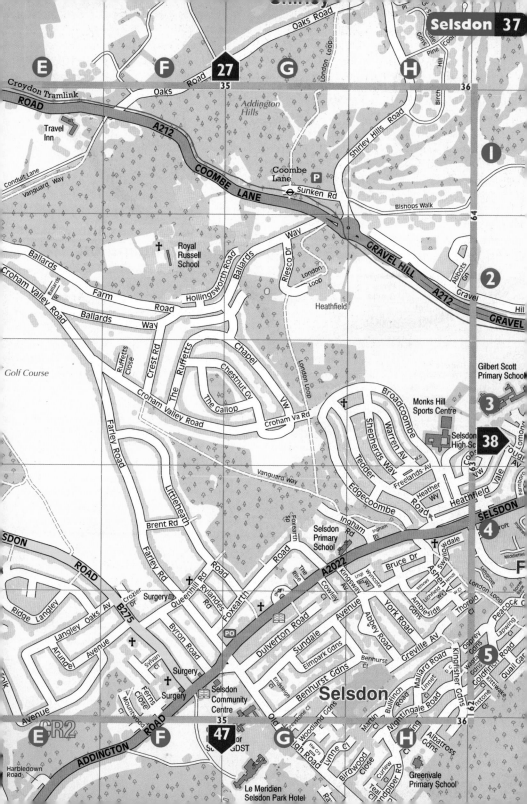

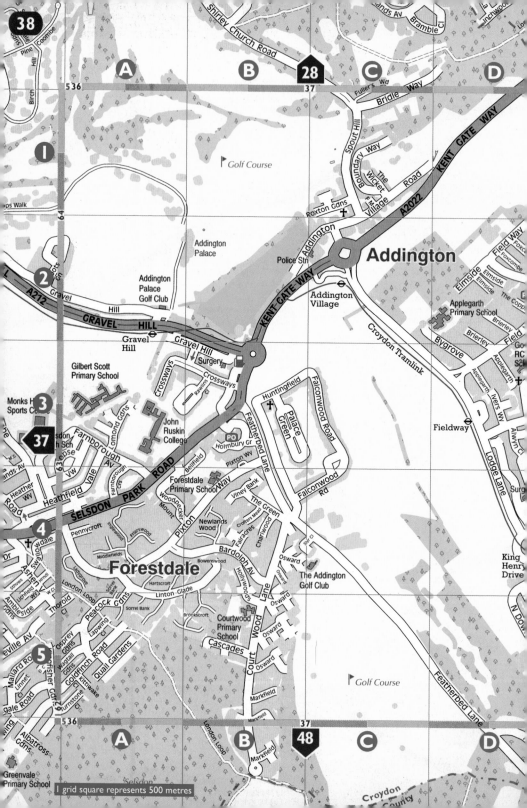

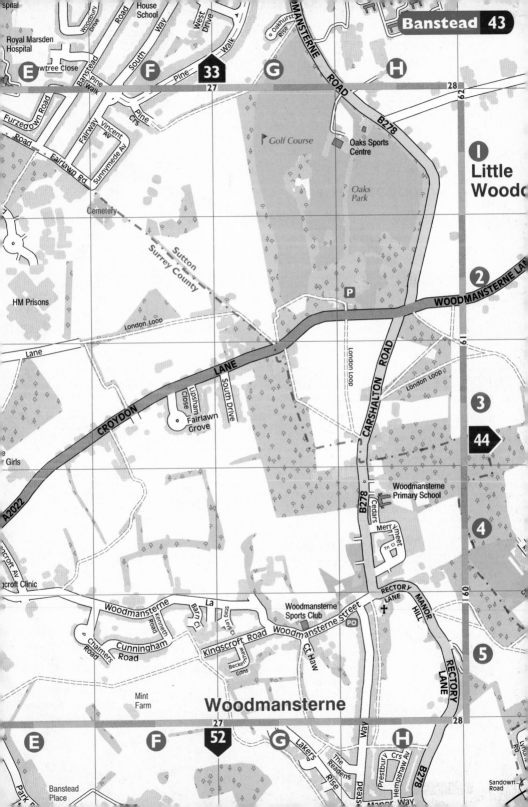

Royal Marsden Hospital

spital

awtree Close

House School

West Drive

South Way

Pine Walk

Woodbury Drive

Road

Banstead Pine Walk

Furzedown Road

Road

Fairway

Fairlawn Rd

Vincent AV

Sunnymede AV

Pine Crs

E **F** **33** **G** **H**

27 28

Oakhurst Rise

MANSTERNE ROAD

B278

29

I

Little Woodd

Golf Course

Oaks Sports Centre

Oaks Park

Cemetery

Sutton Surrey County

2

WOODMANSTERNE LANE

HM Prisons

London Loop

P

London Loop

London Loop

3

Lane

CROYDON LANE

Lipsham Close

Fairlawn Grove

South Drive

CARSHALTON ROAD

44

A2022

Girls

Woodmansterne Primary School

B278

Cedars

Merr

meet Tn

4

croft AV

croft Clinic

Woodmansterne Road

Kenneth Road

Chalmers Road

Cunningham Road

La Barn Ct

Stag Leys Ct

Kingscroft Road

Becket Gdns

Woodmansterne Sports Club

Woodmansterne Street

Ct Haw

PO

RECTORY LANE

MANOR HILL

RECTORY LANE

5

Mint Farm

Woodmansterne

E **F** **52** **G** **H**

27 28

Lakers Rise

The Readens

stead

Way

Prestbury Crs AV

Hempshaw Way

B278

Rd

Sandown Road

Banstead Place

Park

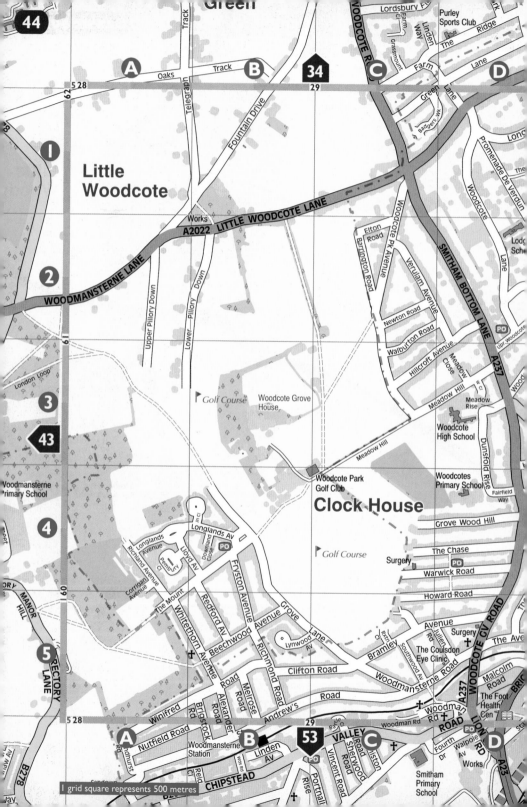

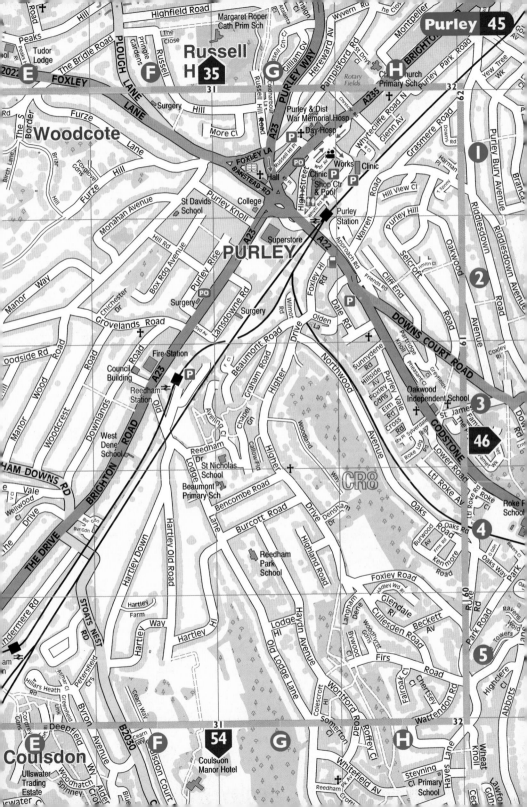

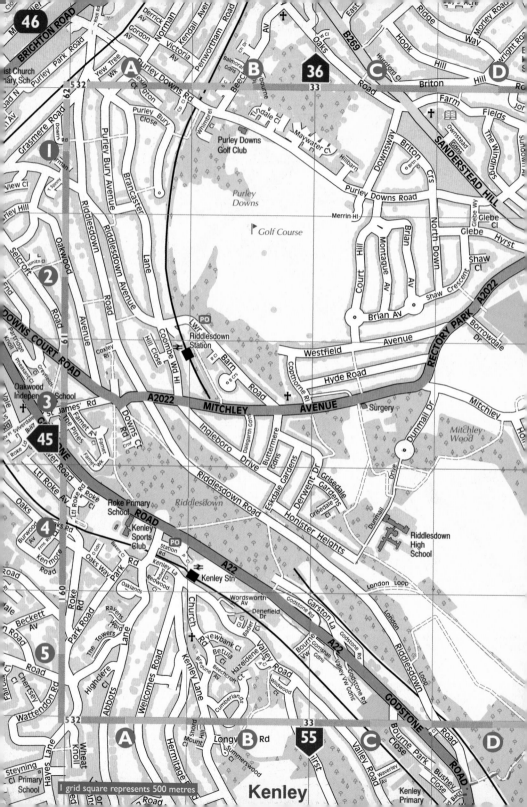

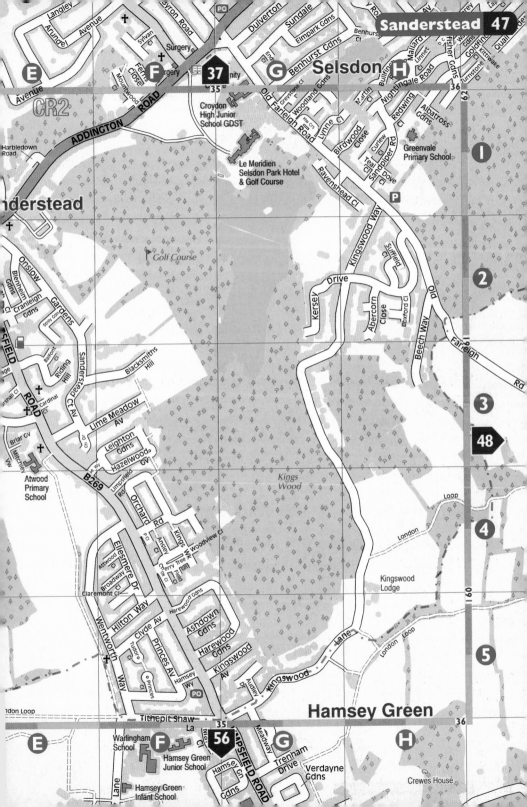

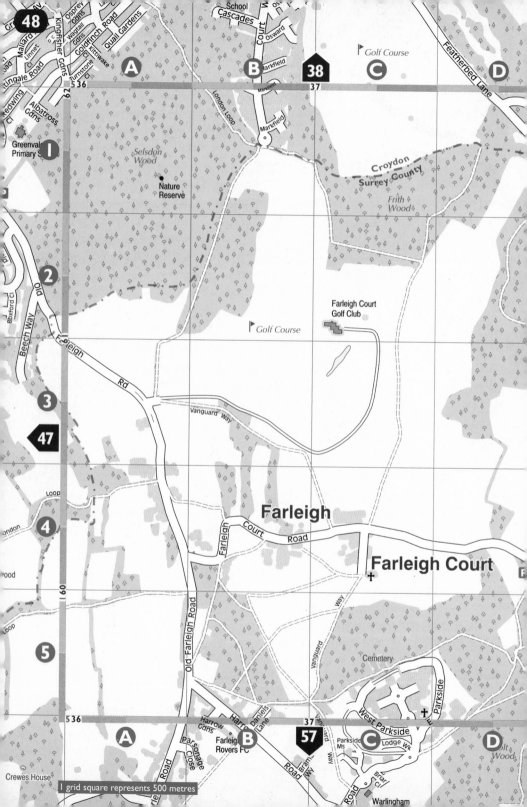

48

Greenvale Primary S

Selsdon Wood

Nature Reserve

A **B** **38** **C** **D**

Golf Course

Croydon
Surrey County

Frith Wood

Featherbed Lane

School Cascades

Osward

Court

Markfield

London Loop

Markfield

Mallard

Kingfisher Gdns

Osprey Gdns

Wagtail Gdns

Goldfinch Road

Kittiwake

Turnstone

Quail Gardens

Limnet

Redwing Cl

Albatross Gdns

Nightingale Road

1

2

Old Farleigh

Beech Way

Bbxford Cl

3

47

Rd

Golf Course

Farleigh Court
Golf Club

Vanguard Way

London Loop

4

Loop

Farleigh

Farleigh Court Road

Farleigh Court

Vanguard Way

5

Old Farleigh Road

Cemetery

Parkside

West Parkside

Lodge Wk

Parkside
Ms

A **B** **57** **C** **D**

Crewes House

Parsonage Close

Harrow Gdns

Farleigh Rovers FC

Daniels Lane

Harrow

Farleigh Road

Vanguard Way

Bram Wy

Briar Cl

Holt Wood

Warlingham

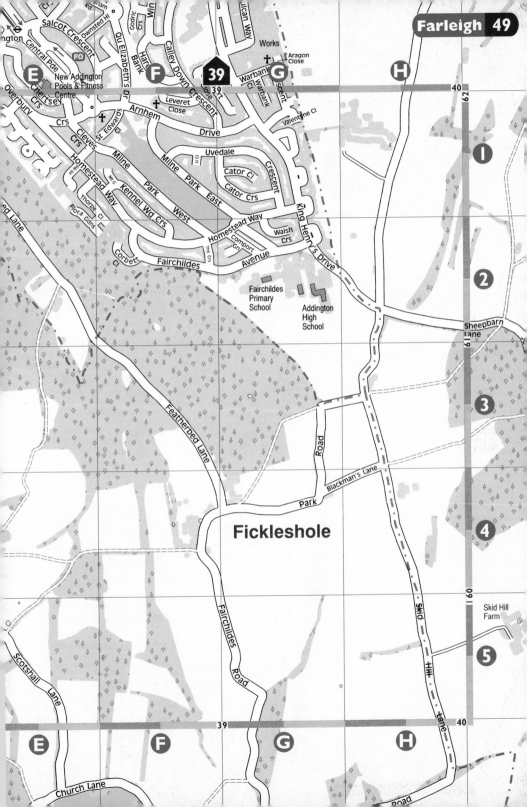

Fickleshole

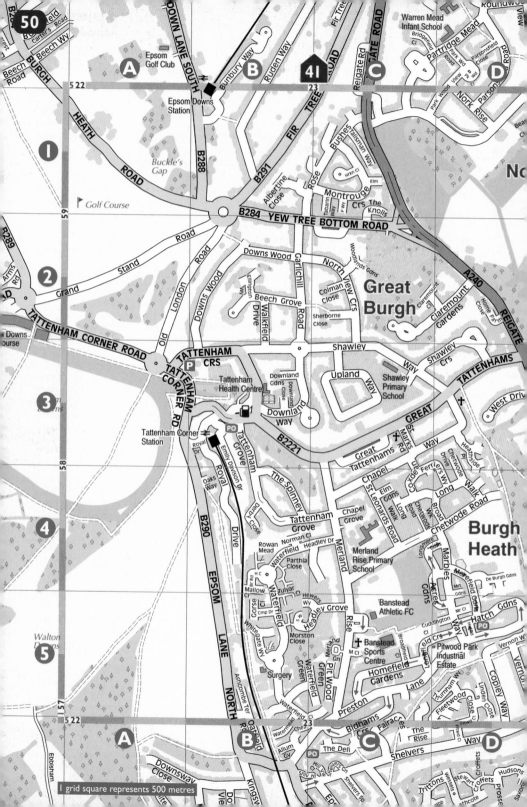

1 grid square represents 500 metres

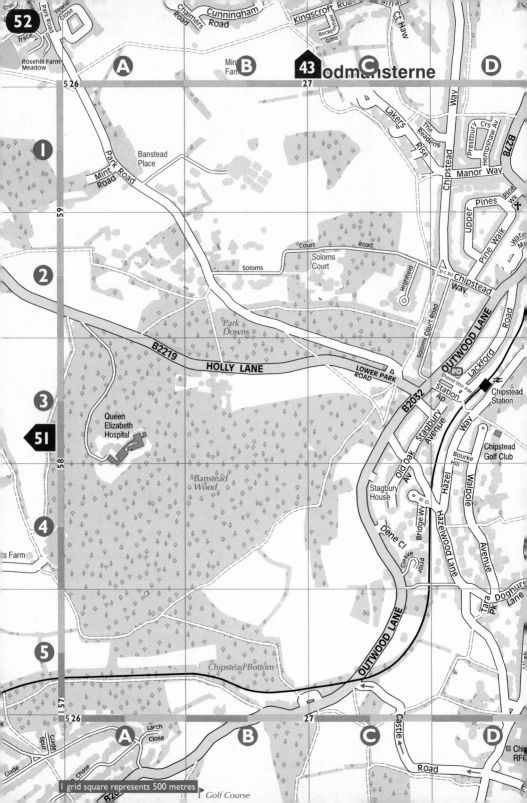

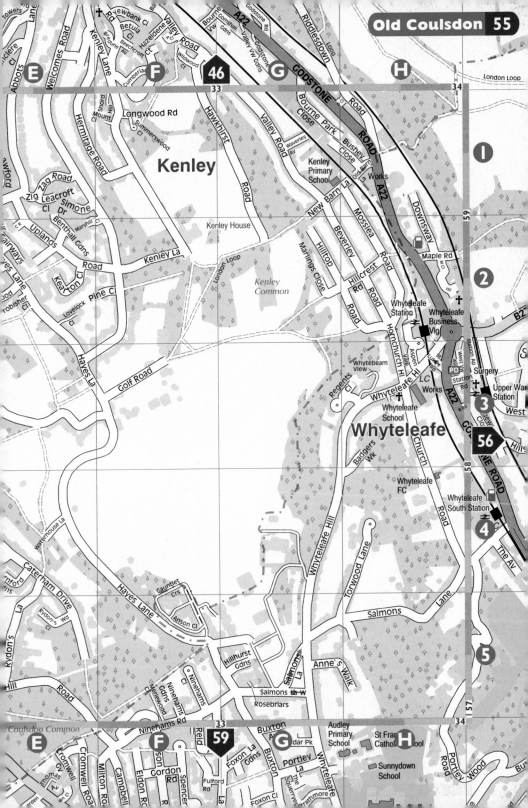

E F **48** G H

Old Farleigh

Cemetery

Parkside

West Parkside

Harrow Gdns

Parsonage Close

Farleigh Rovers FC

Daniels Lane

Harrow Road

Vanguard

Vanguard Way

Parkside Ms

Lodge Wk

Holt Wood

Farleigh Road

Bramber Wy

Chesham Road

Briar Cl

Warlingham Park School

Ledgers Road

Warlingham Park School

I

59

Chelsham

Greenhill Lane

Chesham Road

Cranmer Gdns

Alexandra Rd

Alexandra Av

Sunny Bank

Cranmer

Manor Cl

Albert Rd

Fern

Crowborough Dr

Winston Dr

Marks Rd

Elise Road

Vanguard Way

2

Rogers Lane

Chelsham Place Farm

Washpond

3

58

B269

The Ct

Blanchman's Rd

Gresham Av

Eden Wy

High La

Farm Road

Cedar GV

Larch

Lane

LIMPSFIELD

Slines Oak Road

Slines Oak

Barnard Road

Vanguard Way

Worms Heath

ROAD

4

B269

Golf Course

High Lane

Slines New Road

Slines New Road

Slines New Road

Butlers Dene Road

Slines Oak Road

5

Dukes Hill

Beulah Wk

Beulah Walk

Hilltop Walk

Upland Rd

Vanguard Way

57

38

E F **61** G H

Woldingham Garden Village

Lunghurst Road

Long Hill

Rd

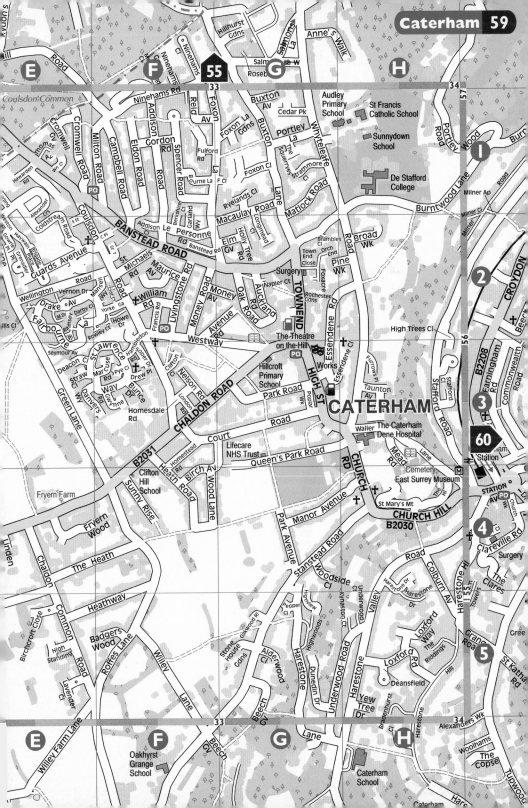

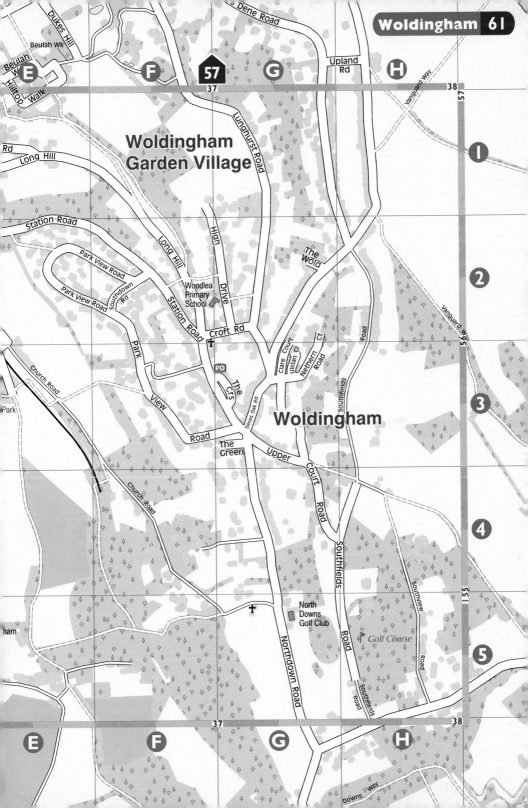

Dene Road

Dukes Hill

Beulah Wk

Beulah Wk

E

Hilltop

Walk

F

57

37

G

Upland Rd

H

Vanguard Way

38

57

Rd

Long Hill

1

Woldingham
Garden Village

Lunghurst Road

Station Road

The Wold

2

Park View Road

Long Hill

High Drive

Vanguard Way

Southdown Rd

Park View Road

Station Road

Woodlea Primary School

Croft Rd

Clare Court

Ulstan Cl

Nethern Ct

Road

Road

3

Park

View

PO

The Crs

Southfields

Woldingham

Slines Oak Rd

Church Road

Road

The Green

Upper

Court Road

Southfields

4

Park

Church Road

155

ham

North Downs Golf Club

Southfields Road

Southview Road

Golf Course

5

Northdown Road

37

38

E

F

G

H

Downs Way

Addington	38 C2	Clock House	44 C4	Lower Sydenham	9 H1	St Helier	23 E2	Upper Norwood
Addiscombe	26 D1	Collier's Wood	5 F4	Merton	4 C5	Sanderstead	47 E1	Upper Shirley
Anerley	17 E1	Coney Hall	29 G5	Merton Park	12 B1	Selhurst	16 B4	Upper Sydenham
Bandonhill	34 D1	Coulsdon	54 A1	Mitcham	14 A2	Selsdon	37 G5	Waddon
Banstead	51 G1	Croydon	2 E4	Monks Orchard	27 G1	Shirley	27 G3	Wallington
Beckenham	18 C2	Crystal Palace	9 E3	Morden	12 C3	Shortlands	19 G2	Wandle Park
Beddington	25 E3	Downham	11 F2	Morden Park	12 A5	South Beddington	34 D2	West Ewell
Beddington Corner	24 A1	East Ewell	31 H5	New Addington	39 F3	South Croydon	35 H2	West Norwood
Bellingham	10 C1	Eden Park	18 B3	New Beckenham	10 A3	Southend	11 E1	West Wickham
Belmont	32 C4	Elmers End	17 H2	Norbury	15 H1	South Norwood	16 B2	Whyteleafe
Benhilton	22 D4	Epsom	40 A4	Nork	50 D1	South Wimbledon	5 E2	Wimbledon
Broad Green	25 H1	Ewell	31 E4	North Cheam	21 H4	Spring Park	28 C3	Woldingham
Bromley Park	11 G5	Farleigh	48 B4	North Looe	41 G3	Stoneleigh	30 D1	Woldingham Garden Village
Burgh Heath	50 D4	Farleigh Court	48 C4	Norwood New Town	8 B3	Streatham	7 E2	Woodcote
Carshalton	23 G5	Fickleshole	49 G4	Old Coulsdon	54 D5	Streatham Park	6 B1	Woodcote Green
Carshalton Beeches	33 G4	Forestdale	38 A4	Old Malden	20 B1	Streatham Vale	6 B4	Woodmansterne
Carshalton on the Hill	33 H5	Furzedown	6 B1	Park Langley	19 E5	Sutton	32 C1	Woodside
Caterham	59 G3	Great Burgh	50 C2	Penge	9 G4	Sydenham	9 H2	Worcester Park
Chaldon	58 D4	Hackbridge	24 B3	Purley	45 G2	Thornton Heath	15 H2	The Wrythe
Cheam	32 A1	Hamsey Green	47 G5	Rosehill	22 D2	Tooting	5 H2	
Chelsham	57 G2	Kenley	55 F1	Roundshaw	35 F2	Tooting Graveney	5 F2	
Chipstead	53 E4	Little Woodcote	44 A1	Russell Hill	35 F5	Upper Elmers End	18 B4	

USING THE STREET INDEX

Street names are listed alphabetically. Each street name is followed by its postal town or area locality, the Postcode District, the page number, and the reference to the square in which the name is found.

Standard index entries are shown as follows:

Abbey Dr *TOOT* SW17 ....6 A2

Street names and selected addresses not shown on the map due to scale restrictions are shown in the index with an asterisk:

Albemarle Pk *BECK* BR3 *.............10 D5

GENERAL ABBREVIATIONS

ACC	ACCESS	CTYD	COURTYARD	HLS	HILLS	MWY	MOTORWAY	SE
ALY	ALLEY	CUTT	CUTTINGS	HO	HOUSE	N	NORTH	SER
AP	APPROACH	CV	COVE	HOL	HOLLOW	NE	NORTH EAST	SH
AR	ARCADE	CYN	CANYON	HOSP	HOSPITAL	NW	NORTH WEST	SHOP
ASS	ASSOCIATION	DEPT	DEPARTMENT	HRB	HARBOUR	O/P	OVERPASS	SKWY
AV	AVENUE	DL	DALE	HTH	HEATH	OFF	OFFICE	SMT
BCH	BEACH	DM	DAM	HTS	HEIGHTS	ORCH	ORCHARD	SOC
BLDS	BUILDINGS	DR	DRIVE	HVN	HAVEN	OV	OVAL	SP
BND	BEND	DRO	DROVE	HWY	HIGHWAY	PAL	PALACE	SPR
BNK	BANK	DRY	DRIVEWAY	IMP	IMPERIAL	PAS	PASSAGE	SQ
BR	BRIDGE	DWGS	DWELLINGS	IN	INLET	PAV	PAVILION	ST
BRK	BROOK	E	EAST	IND EST	INDUSTRIAL ESTATE	PDE	PARADE	STN
BTM	BOTTOM	EMB	EMBANKMENT	INF	INFIRMARY	PH	PUBLIC HOUSE	STR
BUS	BUSINESS	EMBY	EMBASSY	INFO	INFORMATION	PK	PARK	STRD
BVD	BOULEVARD	ESP	ESPLANADE	INT	INTERCHANGE	PKWY	PARKWAY	SW
BY	BYPASS	EST	ESTATE	IS	ISLAND	PL	PLACE	TDG
CATH	CATHEDRAL	EX	EXCHANGE	JCT	JUNCTION	PLN	PLAIN	TER
CEM	CEMETERY	EXPY	EXPRESSWAY	JTY	JETTY	PLNS	PLAINS	THWY
CEN	CENTRE	EXT	EXTENSION	KG	KING	PLZ	PLAZA	TNL
CFT	CROFT	F/O	FLYOVER	KNL	KNOLL	POL	POLICE STATION	TOLL
CH	CHURCH	FC	FOOTBALL CLUB	L	LAKE	PR	PRINCE	TPK
CHA	CHASE	FK	FORK	LA	LANE	PREC	PRECINCT	TR
CHYD	CHURCHYARD	FLD	FIELD	LDG	LODGE	PREP	PREPARATORY	TRL
CIR	CIRCLE	FLDS	FIELDS	LGT	LIGHT	PRIM	PRIMARY	TWR
CIRC	CIRCUS	FLS	FALLS	LK	LOCK	PROM	PROMENADE	U/P
CL	CLOSE	FLS	FLATS	LKS	LAKES	PRS	PRINCESS	UNI
CLFS	CLIFFS	FM	FARM	LNDG	LANDING	PRT	PORT	UPR
CMP	CAMP	FT	FORT	LTL	LITTLE	PT	POINT	V
CNR	CORNER	FWY	FREEWAY	LWR	LOWER	PTH	PATH	VA
CO	COUNTY	FY	FERRY	MAG	MAGISTRATE	PZ	PIAZZA	VIAD
COLL	COLLEGE	GA	GATE	MAN	MANSIONS	QD	QUADRANT	VIL
COM	COMMON	GAL	GALLERY	MD	MEAD	QU	QUEEN	VLG
COMM	COMMISSION	GDN	GARDEN	MDW	MEADOWS	QY	QUAY	VLS
CON	CONVENT	GDNS	GARDENS	MEM	MEMORIAL	R	RIVER	VW
COT	COTTAGE	GLD	GLADE	MKT	MARKET	RBT	ROUNDABOUT	W
COTS	COTTAGES	GLN	GLEN	MKTS	MARKETS	RD	ROAD	WD
CP	CAPE	GN	GREEN	ML	MALL	RDG	RIDGE	WHF
CPS	COPSE	GND	GROUND	ML	MILL	REP	REPUBLIC	WKS
CR	CREEK	GRA	GRANGE	MNR	MANOR	RES	RESERVOIR	WKS
CREM	CREMATORIUM	GRG	GARAGE	MS	MEWS	RFC	RUGBY FOOTBALL CLUB	WD
CRS	CRESCENT	GT	GREAT	MSN	MISSION	RI	RISE	WY
CSWY	CAUSEWAY	GTWY	GATEWAY	MT	MOUNT	RP	RAMP	YD
CT	COURT	GV	GROVE	MTN	MOUNTAIN	RW	ROW	YHA
CTRL	CENTRAL	HGR	HIGHER	MTS	MOUNTAINS	S	SOUTH	
CTS	COURTS	HL	HILL	MUS	MUSEUM	SCH	SCHOOL	

POSTCODE TOWNS AND AREA ABBREVIATIONS

BECK	Beckenham	COUL/CHIP	Coulsdon/Chipstead	HOR/WEW	Horton/West Ewell	PUR/KEN	Purley/Kenley	TOOT
BELMT	Belmont	CROY/NA	Croydon/New Addington	KWD/TDW/WH	Kingswood/	REDH	Redhill	WARL
BMLY	Bromley	CTHM	Caterham		Tadworth/	RYNPK	Raynes Park	WIM/MER
BNSTD	Banstead	DUL	Dulwich		Walton on the Hill	SAND/SEL	Sanderstead/Selsdon	WLCTN
BRYLDS	Berrylands	EPSOM	Epsom	MRDN	Morden	SNWD	South Norwood	WNWD
CAR	Carshalton	EW	Ewell	MTCM	Mitcham	STRHM/NOR	Streatham/Norbury	WPK
CAT	Catford	FSTH	Forest Hill	NRWD	Norwood	SUT	Sutton	WWKM
CHEAM	Cheam	GDST	Godstone	NWMAL	New Malden	SYD	Sydenham	
CHSGTN	Chessington	HAYES	Hayes	PGE/AN	Penge/Anerley	THHTH	Thornton Heath	

BELMT SM2	32	C5
SNWD SE25	17	F4
WLGTN SM6	34	C1
Belsize Gdns SUT SM1	22	D5
Belvedere Av WIM/MER SW19	4	A2
Belvedere Dr WIM/MER SW19	4	A2
Belvedere Rd NRWD SE19	8	A2
Belvedere Sq WIM/MER SW19	4	A2
Benbury Cl BMLY BR1	12	D5
Bench Fld SAND/SEL CR2	36	D2
Bencombe Rd PUR/KEN CR8	45	G4
Bencroft Rd STRHM/NOR SW16	6	E4
Bencurtis Pk WWKM BR4	29	F4
Benedict Rd MTCM CR4	13	F2
Benedict Wharf MTCM CR4	13	G2
Benett Gdns STRHM/NOR SW16	15	E1
Benfleet Cl SUT SM1	23	E5
Benham Cl COUL/CHIP CR5	54	D5
Benhill Av SUT SM1	22	D5
Benhill Rd SUT SM1	23	E5
Benhill Wood Rd SUT SM1	23	E5
Benhilton Cl SAND/SEL CR2	37	H5
Benhurst Cl SAND/SEL CR2	37	H2
Benhurst La STRHM/NOR SW16	7	G2
Bennetts Av CROY/NA CR0	28	A3
Bennetts Cl MTCM CR4	6	B5
Bennetts Wy CROY/NA CR0	28	A3
Bensham Cl THHTH CR7	16	A3
Bensham Gv THHTH CR7	16	A1
Bensham La CROY/NA CR0	25	H1
THHTH CR7	15	H3
Bensham Manor Rd THHTH CR7	16	A3
Benson Rd CROY/NA CR0	25	G4
Benthall Gdns PUR/KEN CR8	55	E1
Benton's La WNWD SE27	8	A1
Benton's Ri WNWD SE27	8	B1
Benwood Ct SUT SM1	23	E4
Beresford Rd BELMT SM2	32	B3
Berkeley Cl WLGTN SM6	24	C4
Berkeley Pl EPSOM KT18	40	B5
The Berkeleys SNWD SE25 *	17	E3
Berkshire Cl CTHM CR3	59	F2
Berkshire Wy MTCM CR4	15	E3
Bernard Gdns WIM/MER SW19	4	B1
Bernard Rd WLGTN SM6	34	B1
Bernel Dr CROY/NA CR0	28	B4
Berne Rd THHTH CR7	16	A4
Berney Rd CROY/NA CR0	26	B1
Berridge Rd NRWD SE19	8	B2
Berry La DUL SE21	8	B1
Berryman's La SYD SE26	9	H1
Bertal Rd TOOT SW17	5	F1
Bertie Rd SYD SE26	9	H3
Bert Rd THHTH CR7	16	A4
Besley St STRHM/NOR SW16	6	C3
Betchworth Cl SUT SM1	33	F1
Betchworth Wy CROY/NA CR0	39	E4
Bethersden Cl BECK BR3	10	B4
Betjeman Cl COUL/CHIP CR5	54	B2
Betony Cl CROY/NA CR0	27	H5
Betts Cl BECK BR3	18	A1
Betts Wy PGE/AN SE20	17	F1
Betula Cl PUR/KEN CR8	46	B5
Beulah Av THHTH CR7	16	A1
Beulah Crs THHTH CR7	16	A1
Beulah Gv CROY/NA CR0	16	A5
Beulah Hl NRWD SE19	7	H5
THHTH CR7	16	A2
Beulah Wk WIM SW19	4	B4
Beulah Wk CTHM CR3	57	E5
Bevan Ct CROY/NA CR0	35	G1
Bevan Pk EW KT17	40	D1
Beverley Av WIM/MER SW19	5	F3
Beverley Cl EW KT17	41	G1
Beverley Gdns WPK KT4	21	G1
Beverley Rd CTHM CR3	55	G2
MTCM CR4	14	D3
PGE/AN SE20	17	F1
WPK KT4	21	G3
Beverstone Rd THHTH CR7	15	G5
Bevill Cl SNWD SE25	17	E2
Bevington Rd BECK BR3	18	D1
Bewley St WIM/MER SW19	5	E1
Bewlys Rd WNWD SE27	7	H2
Beynon Rd CAR SM5	33	H1
Bickersteth Rd TOOT SW17	5	H3
Bickley St TOOT SW17	5	G2
Bicknoller Cl BELMT SM2	32	D5
Bidborough Cl HAYES BR2	19	H4
Biddulph Rd SAND/SEL CR2	36	A4
Biggin Av MTCM CR4	5	H5
Biggin Hl NRWD SE19	7	H4
Biggin Wy NRWD SE19	7	G4
Bigginwood Rd		
STRHM/NOR SW16	7	H4
Binfield Rd SAND/SEL CR2	36	D1
Bingham Rd CROY/NA CR0	27	F2
Birchanger Rd SNWD SE25	17	E4
Birch Av CTHM CR3	59	H3
Birch Ct WLGTN SM6	24	B5
Birchcroft Cl CTHM CR3	58	C5
Birchcroft Cl SAND/SEL CR2	45	F4
Birches Cl EPSOM KT18	40	C5
MTCM CR4	13	H2
Birchfield Cl COUL/CHIP CR5	54	D5
Birchfield Gv EW KT17	31	G5
Birch Hl CROY/NA CR0	37	H1
Birch La PUR/KEN CR8	45	E1
Birch Tree Av WWKM BR4	39	H1
Birch Tree Wy CROY/NA CR0	27	F2
Birch Wk MTCM CR4	6	A5
Birch Wy WARL CR6	57	E3
Birchwood Av BECK BR3	18	B3
WLGTN SM6	24	A4
Birchwood Cl MRDN SM4	12	D3
Birchwood La WARL CR6	58	D5
Birchwood Rd TOOT SW17	6	B1
Birdhurst Av SAND/SEL CR2	26	D4
Birdhurst Gdns SAND/SEL CR2	3	F7
Birdhurst Ri SAND/SEL CR2	36	C1
Birdhurst Rd SAND/SEL CR2	36	C1
WIM/MER SW19	5	G3

Birdwood Cl SAND/SEL CR2	47	G1
Birkbeck Rd BECK BR3	17	H1
WIM/MER SW19	5	E1
Birkdale Gdns CROY/NA CR0	27	H5
Bisenden Rd CROY/NA CR0	3	J3
Bisham Cl MTCM CR4	23	H1
Bishop's Cl COUL/CHIP CR5	54	C3
SUT SM1	22	C4
Bishopsford Rd MRDN SM4	23	F1
Bishopsmead Cl		
HOR/WEW KT19	30	B5
Bishops Park Rd		
STRHM/NOR SW16	7	E5
Bishop's Pl SUT SM1	33	E1
Bishop's Rd CROY/NA CR0	26	A1
Bishopsthorpe Rd SYD SE26	9	G1
Bishops Wk CROY/NA CR0	37	H1
Bisley Cl WPK KT4	21	G2
Blackbush Cl BELMT SM2	32	D5
Blackenham Rd TOOT SW17	5	F3
Blackford Cl SAND/SEL CR2	35	H4
Blackhorse La CROY/NA CR0	26	D2
Blacklands Rd CAT SE6	11	E1
Blackman's La WARL CR6	49	G4
Blacksmiths Hl SAND/SEL CR2	47	F3
Blackthorne Av CROY/NA CR0	27	G2
Blake Cl CAR SM5	23	G2
Blakehall Rd CAR SM5	33	H2
Blakemore Rd THHTH CR7	16	A3
Blakeney Av BECK BR3	10	B5
Blakeney Cl HOR/WEW KT19	30	A5
Blakeney Rd BECK BR3	10	B5
Blake Rd CROY/NA CR0	3	K2
MTCM CR4	13	G2
Blake's Gn WWKM BR4	29	E1
Blanchland Rd MRDN SM4	12	D4
Blanchman's Rd WARL CR6	57	E3
Blandford Av BECK BR3	17	H2
Blandford Cl CROY/NA CR0	25	E4
Blandford Rd BECK BR3	17	H1
Blean Gv PGE/AN SE20	9	G4
Blegborough Rd		
STRHM/NOR SW16	6	C3
Blenheim Cl WLGTN SM6	34	C3
Blenheim Gdns SAND/SEL CR2	36	A3
WLGTN SM6	34	C2
Blenheim Park Rd		
SAND/SEL CR2	36	A4
Blenheim Rd HOR/WEW KT19	40	B1
PGE/AN SE20	9	H4
SUT SM1	22	C4
Bletchingly Cl THHTH CR7	15	H3
Bloomhall Rd NRWD SE19	8	B2
Bloomsbury Ct HOR/WEW KT19	30	B5
Blossom Cl SAND/SEL CR2	26	D5
Bloxworth Cl WLGTN SM6	24	C4
Bluebell Cl SYD SE26	8	D1
WLGTN SM6	24	B2
Blueberry Gdns COUL/CHIP CR5	54	B1
Blue Cedars BNSTD SM7	41	H4
Bluegates EW KT17	31	E5
Blue Riband Est CROY/NA CR0 *	2	A2
Blunt Rd CROY/NA CR0	3	J5
Blyth Rd BMLY BR1	11	H5
Blytheswood Pl		
STRHM/NOR SW16	7	G1
Bodiam Rd STRHM/NOR SW16	6	D5
Bodmin Gv MRDN SM4	12	D3
Bolderwood Wy WWKM BR4	28	D3
Boleyn Av EW KT17	31	E5
Boleyn Gdns WWKM BR4	28	D3
Bolstead Rd MTCM CR4	6	B5
Bolters La BNSTD SM7	42	A5
Bolton Dr MRDN SM4	23	E1
Bolton Gdns BMLY BR1	11	H3
Bonchurch Cl BELMT SM2	32	D5
Bond Gdns WLGTN SM6	24	C5
Bond Rd MTCM CR4	13	H1
WARL CR6	56	D3
Bonville Rd BMLY BR1	11	H2
Booth Rd CROY/NA CR0	2	C4
Border Crs SYD SE26	9	F2
Border Ga MTCM CR4	5	G5
Border Rd SYD SE26	9	F2
Bordesley Rd MRDN SM4	12	D3
Borough Hl CROY/NA CR0	2	A7
Borough Rd MTCM CR4	13	G1
Borrowdale Cl SAND/SEL CR2	46	D3
Borrowdale Dr SAND/SEL CR2	46	D2
Boscombe Rd TOOT SW17	6	A1
WIM/MER SW19	4	C5
WPK KT4	21	G2
Boston Rd CROY/NA CR0	15	F5
Boswell Rd THHTH CR7	16	A3
Bothwell Rd CROY/NA CR0	39	E5
Botsford Rd RYNPK SW20	12	A1
Boughton Av HAYES BR2	19	H5
Boulogne Rd CROY/NA CR0	16	A5
Boundary Rd WIM/MER SW19	5	F3
WLGTN SM6	34	A4
Boundary Wy CROY/NA CR0	38	C1
Bourdon Rd PGE/AN SE20	17	G1
Bourke Hl COUL/CHIP CR5	53	H3
Bourne Dr MTCM CR4	13	F1
Bournefield Rd CTHM CR3	55	H3
Bourne La CTHM CR3	59	F1
Bournemouth Rd		
WIM/MER SW19	4	C5
Bourne Park Cl PUR/KEN CR8	55	C1
Bourneside Gdns CAT SE6	11	E2
Bourne St CROY/NA CR0	2	B3
Bournevale Rd		
STRHM/NOR SW16	7	E1
Bourne Vw PUR/KEN CR8	46	B5
Bourne Wy HOR/WEW KT19	30	A4
SUT SM1	32	B1
Bouverie Gdns COUL/CHIP CR5	45	E4
Bouverie Rd COUL/CHIP CR5	53	E3
Bowenswood CROY/NA CR0	38	B4
Bowens Wd CROY/NA CR0 *	38	B4
Bowley Cl NRWD SE19 *	8	D3

Bowley La NRWD SE19	8	D2
Bowman's Meadow		
WLGTN SM6	24	B4
Boxford Cl SAND/SEL CR2	47	H1
Boxley Rd MRDN SM4	13	E4
Box Ridge Av PUR/KEN CR8	45	F2
Boxwood Wy WARL CR6	56	D2
Boyd Rd WIM/MER SW19	5	F3
Boyland Rd BMLY BR1	11	H2
Brabazon Av WLGTN SM6	35	E3
Brabourne Ri BECK BR3	19	F4
Bracewood Gdns CROY/NA CR0	3	J4
Bracken Av CROY/NA CR0	28	C4
Bracken Hill Cl BMLY BR1	11	H5
Bracken Hill La BMLY BR1	11	H5
Brackley Cl WLGTN SM6	35	E3
Brackley Rd BECK BR3	10	B4
Bradford Cl SYD SE26	9	F1
Bradford Dr HOR/WEW KT19	30	D2
Brading Rd CROY/NA CR0	15	F5
Bradley Cl BELMT SM2	32	D5
Bradley Rd NRWD SE19	7	H3
Bradmore Wy COUL/CHIP CR5	54	A3
Bradshaw Cl WIM/MER SW19	4	C3
Bradshaws Cl SNWD SE25	17	E2
Bradstock Rd EW KT17	31	E2
Braemar Av SAND/SEL CR2	36	A5
THHTH CR7	15	H2
Braemar Gdns WWKM BR4	29	E2
Braemar Rd WPK KT4	21	F4
Braeside BECK BR3	10	C2
Braeside Av WIM/MER SW19	4	A1
Braeside Rd STRHM/NOR SW16	6	C4
Brafferton Rd CROY/NA CR0	2	C6
Brailsford Cl WIM/MER SW19	5	G4
Brair Bank CAR SM5	34	A4
Bramber Wy WARL CR6	57	F1
Bramble Acres Cl BELMT SM2	32	C5
Bramble Banks CAR SM5	34	A5
Bramble Cl BECK BR3	19	E4
CROY/NA CR0	28	C5
Brambledown Cl HAYES BR2	19	G5
Brambledown Rd SAND/SEL CR2	36	A3
SAND/SEL CR2	34	A3
Brambles Cl CTHM CR3	59	G2
The Brambles SUT SM1	23	F3
WIM/MER SW19 *	4	B2
Bramblewood Cl CAR SM5	23	G2
Bramcote Av MTCM CR4	13	H3
Bramerton Rd BECK BR3	18	B2
Bramley Av COUL/CHIP CR5	44	C5
Bramley Cl SAND/SEL CR2	35	H1
Bramley Hl SAND/SEL CR2	2	C7
Bramley Hyrst SAND/SEL CR2 *	36	A1
Bramley Rd BELMT SM2	31	H4
SUT SM1	33	F1
Bramley Wy WWKM BR4	28	D3
Brampton Rd CROY/NA CR0	26	D1
Bramston Rd TOOT SW17	5	H4
Brancaster La PUR/KEN CR8	46	A1
Brancker Cl WLGTN SM6	35	E3
Brandon Rd SUT SM1	22	D5
The Brandries WLGTN SM6	24	D5
Brandy Wy BELMT SM2	32	C5
Brangbourne Rd BMLY BR1	11	E2
Brangwyn Crs WIM/MER SW19	5	H5
Branksome Rd WIM/MER SW19	4	C5
Brantwood Rd SAND/SEL CR2	36	A4
Brasted Cl BELMT SM2	32	C5
SYD SE26	9	G1
Braxted Pk STRHM/NOR SW16	7	F3
Braybrooke Gdns NRWD SE19	8	C3
Breakfield COUL/CHIP CR5	54	C1
Brecon Cl MTCM CR4	15	E5
WPK KT4	21	H2
Bredhurst Cl PGE/AN SE20	9	G3
Bredon Rd CROY/NA CR0	26	D1
Bredune PUR/KEN CR8	46	B5
Brenchley Cl HAYES BR2	19	H4
Brenley Cl MTCM CR4	14	A2
Brent Rd SAND/SEL CR2	37	E5
Brettgrave HOR/WEW KT19	30	A5
Brian Av SAND/SEL CR2	46	D1
Briane Rd HOR/WEW KT19	30	A5
Briar Av STRHM/NOR SW16	7	F4
Briar Cl CROY/NA CR0	28	C4
Briar Gdns HAYES BR2	29	H1
Briar Gv SAND/SEL CR2	47	E5
Briar Hl PUR/KEN CR8	45	E1
Briar La CAR SM5	34	A4
CROY/NA CR0	28	D5
Briarwood Ct WPK KT4 *	21	E2
Briarwood Rd EW KT17	31	E2
Brickfield Rd CROY/NA CR0	15	H5
WIM/MER SW19	4	D1
Brickfield Vls SUT SM1 *	23	G4
Bridgefield Cl CROY/NA CR0	3	G2
Bridgefield Rd SUT SM1	32	C2
Bridgelands Cl BECK BR3	10	C5
Bridge Pde STRHM/NOR SW16 *	7	E2
Bridge Pl CROY/NA CR0	2	F3
Bridge Rd BECK BR3	10	B4
EW KT17	41	H1
SUT SM1	22	D2
WLGTN SM6	34	B3
Bridge Rw CROY/NA CR0 *	26	B2
Bridges La CROY/NA CR0	25	E5
Bridgetown Cl NRWD SE19 *	8	C2
Bridge Vls WIM/MER SW19 *	4	C1
Bridge Wy COUL/CHIP CR5	52	C1
Bridgewood Pl PGE/AN SE20	9	F4
Bridgewood Rd		
STRHM/NOR SW16	6	D4
WPK KT4	21	H5
Bridle Cl HOR/WEW KT19	30	A1
Bridle Pth CROY/NA CR0	25	E4
The Bridle Pth EW KT17	31	G5
Bridle Rd CROY/NA CR0	28	C3
EW KT17	41	H1
The Bridle Rd PUR/KEN CR8	35	E5
Bridle Wy CROY/NA CR0	38	C1

Bridleway Cl EW KT17	31	G5
The Bridle Wy WLGTN SM6	24	C5
Bridport Rd THHTH CR7	15	G3
Brierley CROY/NA CR0	38	D2
Brierley Cl SNWD SE25	17	E3
Brier Rd KWD/TDW/WH KT20	50	B4
Brigade Pl CTHM CR3	59	E2
Briggs Cl MTCM CR4	6	B5
Brighton Rd BELMT SM2	33	E3
BNSTD SM7	42	B4
COUL/CHIP CR5	53	C3
PUR/KEN CR8	45	F4
SAND/SEL CR2	36	A4
Brightwell Cl CROY/NA CR0	25	C2
Brightwell Crs TOOT SW17	5	H2
Brigstock Rd COUL/CHIP CR5	44	B5
THHTH CR7	15	H4
The Brindles BNSTD SM7	51	F2
Brinkley Rd WPK KT4	21	F3
Brisbane Av WIM/MER SW19	4	D5
Briscoe Rd WIM/MER SW19	5	F3
Bristol Cl WLGTN SM6	35	E4
Bristol Rd MRDN SM4	13	E4
Bristow Rd CROY/NA CR0	25	E5
NRWD SE19	8	C2
Briton Cl SAND/SEL CR2	46	C1
Briton Crs SAND/SEL CR2	46	C1
Briton Hill Rd SAND/SEL CR2	36	C5
Broadcombe SAND/SEL CR2	37	H5
Broadeaves Cl SAND/SEL CR2	36	C1
Broadfield Cl		
KWD/TDW/WH KT20	50	C5
Broad Green Av CROY/NA CR0	25	H1
Broadlands Dr WARL CR6	56	C4
Broadmead Av WPK KT4	21	E3
Broad Oaks Wy HAYES BR2	19	H4
Broadview Rd		
STRHM/NOR SW16	6	D3
Broad Wk CTHM CR3	59	H2
EPSOM KT18	40	C5
Broadwater Rd TOOT SW17	5	G3
Broadway Av CROY/NA CR0	16	B5
Broadway Rd SAND/SEL CR2	47	F4
Broadway Cl SAND/SEL CR2	47	F4
Broadway Gdns WIM/MER SW19 *	4	C3
Broadway Gdns MTCM CR4	13	G4
The Broadway CHEAM SM3	32	A2
WIM/MER SW19	4	B2
Brockenhurst Av WPK KT4	20	C2
Brockenhurst Rd CROY/NA CR0	27	F1
Brockenhurst Wy		
STRHM/NOR SW16	14	D1
Brockham Cl WIM/MER SW19	4	C2
Brockham Crs CROY/NA CR0	39	F3
Brocklesby Rd SNWD SE25	17	F3
Brockman Ri BMLY BR1	11	F1
Brocks Dr CHEAM SM3	22	A4
Brockwell Av BECK BR3	18	D4
Brograve Gdns BECK BR3	18	D1
Bromley Av BMLY BR1	11	C4
Bromley Crs HAYES BR2	19	H1
Bromley Gdns HAYES BR2	19	H1
Bromley Gv HAYES BR2	19	F1
Bromley Hl BMLY BR1	11	G4
Bromley Rd BECK BR3	19	E1
BECK BR3	10	D5
CAT SE6	11	E1
Brook Cl HOR/WEW KT19	30	C4
Brook Ct BECK BR3 *	10	B5
Brookfield Av SUT SM1	23	G4
Brookfields Av MTCM CR4	13	G4
Brooklands Av WIM/MER SW19	5	H3
Brooklyn Cl CAR SM5	23	H5
Brooklyn Gv SNWD SE25	17	F3
Brooklyn Rd SNWD SE25	17	F3
Brook Md HOR/WEW KT19	30	C4
Brookmead MTCM CR4	14	C5
Brookmead Rd CROY/NA CR0	14	D5
Brook Rd THHTH CR7	16	B3
Brookscroft CROY/NA CR0	38	B5
Brookside CAR SM5	34	A1
Brookside Crs WPK KT4	21	E2
Brookside Wy CROY/NA CR0	27	H4
Brookview Rd		
STRHM/NOR SW16	6	C2
Brookwood Cl HAYES BR2	19	H3
Broomfield Rd BECK BR3	18	A3
Broomfield Cl CROY/NA CR0	39	E4
Broomhall Rd SAND/SEL CR2	36	B3
Broomloan La SUT SM1	22	C3
Broom Rd CROY/NA CR0	28	A3
Broomwood Cl CROY/NA CR0	17	H4
Broseley Gv SYD SE26	10	A2
Broster Gdns SNWD SE25	16	D2
Broughton Rd THHTH CR7	15	G5
Brown Cl WLGTN SM6	35	E3
Browning Av SUT SM1	23	G5
WPK KT4	21	F2
Brownlow Rd CROY/NA CR0	3	J7
Bruce Dr SAND/SEL CR2	37	H4
Bruce Rd MTCM CR4	6	A4
SNWD SE25	16	B3
Brumfield Rd HOR/WEW KT19	30	A1
Brunel Cl NRWD SE19	8	D3
Brunswick Ms STRHM/NOR SW16	6	D3
Brunswick Pl NRWD SE19	8	E3
Brunswick Rd SUT SM1	23	E5
Bruton Rd MRDN SM4	13	E3
Bryden Cl SYD SE26	10	A2
Buckfast Rd MRDN SM4	12	D3
Buckhurst Av CAR SM5	23	G4
Buckingham Av THHTH CR7	15	G5
Buckingham Cl BELMT SM2 *	32	C4
Buckingham Gdns THHTH CR7	15	H1
Buckingham Rd MTCM CR4	14	D3
Buckland Rd BELMT SM2	31	H4
Buckland Wk MRDN SM4	13	E3
Buckleigh Av RYNPK SW20	12	B2
Buckleigh Rd STRHM/NOR SW16	6	D4
Buckleigh Wy NRWD SE19	8	D4
Bucklers' Wy CAR SM5	23	H4
Buckles Wy BNSTD SM7	51	E1

Bucknall Wy BECK BR3		
Bucknills Cl EPSOM KT18		
Budge La MTCM CR4		
Buff Av BNSTD SM7		
Bug Hl WARL CR6		
Bulganak Rd THHTH CR7		
Buller Rd THHTH CR7		
Bullfinch Rd SAND/SEL CR2		
Bullrush Cl CAR SM5		
CROY/NA CR0		
Bunbury Wy EW KT17		
Bunce Dr CTHM CR3		
Bungalow Rd SNWD SE25		
The Bungalows		
STRHM/NOR SW16		
Bunting Cl MTCM CR4		
Burcott Rd PUR/KEN CR8		
Burdett Rd CROY/NA CR0		
Burdock Cl CROY/NA CR0		
Burdon La BELMT SM2		
Burdon Pk BELMT SM2		
Burfield Cl TOOT SW17		
Burford Dr WARL CR6		
Burford La EW KT17		
Burford Rd SUT SM1		
WPK KT4		
Burgess Rd SUT SM1		
Burgh Heath Rd EW KT17		
Burghill Rd SYD SE26		
Burghley Pl MTCM CR4		
Burghley Rd WIM/MER SW19		
Burgh Mt BNSTD SM7		
Burgos Cl CROY/NA CR0		
Burgoyne Rd SNWD SE25		
Burleigh Av WLGTN SM6		
Burleigh Gdns SUT SM1		
Burley Cl STRHM/NOR SW16		
Burlington Rd THHTH CR7		
Burma Ter NRWD SE19 *		
Burnell Rd SUT SM1		
Burnet Gv HOR/WEW KT19		
Burnham Dr WPK KT4		
Burnham Gdns CROY/NA CR0		
Burnham Rd MRDN SM4		
Burnham Wy SYD SE26		
Burnhill Rd BECK BR3		
Burns Cl CAR SM5		
WIM/MER SW19		
Burns Dr BNSTD SM7		
Burntwood Cl CTHM CR3		
Burntwood La CTHM CR3		
Burntwood Vw NRWD SE19 *		
Burrell Cl CROY/NA CR0		
Burrell Rw BECK BR3		
Burstow Rd RYNPK SW20		
Burton Cl THHTH CR7		
Burtwell La WNWD SE27		
Burwood Av PUR/KEN CR8		
Bury Gv MRDN SM4		
Bushey La SUT SM1		
Bushey Rd CROY/NA CR0		
Bushey Wy BECK BR3		
Bute Gdns WLGTN SM6		
Bute Gdns West WLGTN SM6		
Bute Rd CROY/NA CR0		
WLGTN SM6		
Butlers Dene Rd CTHM CR3		
Butterfly Wk WARL CR6		
Butter Hl WLGTN SM6		
Buttermere Gdns PUR/KEN CR8		
Butts Rd BMLY BR1		
Buxton Av CTHM CR3		
Buxton Crs CHEAM SM3		
Buxton La CTHM CR3		
Byards Cft STRHM/NOR SW16		
Bycroft St PGE/AN SE20		
Bygrove CROY/NA CR0		
Bygrove Rd WIM/MER SW19		
Byland Cl CAR SM5		
SYD SE26		
Byne Rd CAR SM5		
SYD SE26		
Byron Av SAND/SEL CR2		
Byron Av East SUT SM1		
Byron Cl PGE/AN SE20 *		
SYD SE26 *		
Byron Gdns SUT SM1		
Byron Rd SAND/SEL CR2		
Byton Rd TOOT SW17		
The Byways HOR/WEW KT19		
The Byway BELMT SM2		
Bywood Av CROY/NA CR0		
Bywood Cl PUR/KEN CR8		

C

Cadogan Ct BELMT SM2		
Caernarvon Cl MTCM CR4		
Caesars Wk MTCM CR4		
Cairndale Cl BMLY BR1		
Cairo New Rd CROY/NA CR0		
Caithness Dr EPSOM KT18		
Caithness Rd MTCM CR4		
Caldbeck Av WPK KT4		
Calder Rd MRDN SM4		
Caledon Rd WLGTN SM6		
Calley Down Crs CROY/NA CR0		
Callow Fld PUR/KEN CR8		
Calmont Rd BMLY BR1		
Calthorpe Gdns SUT SM1		
Calverley Cl BECK BR3		

...ley Rd EW KT17 ....31 E2
...erley Cl CHEAM SM3 ....21 H4
...orne Rd BELMT SM2 ....32 C3
OY/NA CRO..........................27 E1
...idge Gv PGE/AN SE20 * 9 F5
...idge Rd CAR SM5 ....24 C4
E/AN SE20 ....17 E2
...en Gdns SUT SM1 ....32 D1
...TH CR7 ....32 C3
...en Hill Rd NRWD SE19 ....8 C3
...en Rd SAND/SEL CR2 ....23 H5
' SM1 ....32 D1
...en Wy THHTH CR7 ....15 H2
...ot Cl WIM/MER SW19 ....4 A2
...on Rd CROY/NA CRO.................15 H5
...e Cl SNWD SE25 ....17 E2
...n RMLY BR1 ....11 H1
...mile Av MTCM CR4 ....5 H5
...bell Cl STRHM/NOR SW16 * 6 D2
...bell Cots MTCM CR4 ....14 A1
...bell Rd CROY/NA CRO...............59 F1
IM CR3 ....59 F1
...en Rd SAND/SEL CR2 ....36 C1
...on Cl SAND/SEL CR2 ....3 H7
...re Gdns
HM/NOR SW16 ....6 C4
...ng Rd CROY/NA CRO.................3 J2
...'s Rd COUL/CHIP CR5 ....54 C3
...s La KWD/TDW/WH KT20..............51 E4
...'s Wk CROY/NA CRO.................17 H4
...bury Cl BECK BR3..................10 D5
...bury Rd CROY/NA CRO...............3 H4
DN SM4 ....13 E5
...y Gdns NRWD SE19 ....35 F1
...Av WLGTN SM6 ....35 F1
...Rd CROY/NA CRO....................26 D2
...ay Pl WLGTN SM6 * 24 B4
...an Rd NRWD SE19 ....5 E3
...al Av MRDN SM4 ....14 A5
...al Cl MRDN SM4 ....12 A5
...ID/SEL CR2 ....47 E3
...KT4 ....21 E5
...l Cl COUL/CHIP CR5 ....54 D4
...d Rd MTCM CR4 ....14 D1
...TH CR7 ....15 H2
...GTN SM6 ....32 C2

Cecil Rd CROY/NA CRO................15 E5
SUT SM1 ....32 B2
WIM/MER SW19 ....4 D4
Cedar Cl CAR SM5...................33 H2
EW KT17 ....40 D4
Cedar Gdns BELMT SM2 ....57 E3
Cedar Hi EPSOM KT18 ....40 A5
Cedarhurst BMLY BR1 * 11 G4
Cedar Pk CTHM CR3 ....59 G1
Cedar Rd BELMT SM2 ....33 G2
CROY/NA CRO.........................3 G2
Cedars BNSTD SM7 ....43 H4
Cedars Av MTCM CR4 ....14 A3
Cedars Rd BECK BR3..................18 A1
CROY/NA CRO.........................25 E4
MRDN SM4 ....12 C3
Cedar Tree Gv WNWD SE27............7 H2
Cedarville Gdns
STRHM/NOR SW16 * 7 F3
Cedar Wk PUR/KEN CR8...............55 E1
Celtic Av HAYES BR2.................19 G2
Central Av WLGTN SM6 ....35 E1
Central Hi NRWD SE19 ....8 A2
Central Pde CROY/NA CRO............39 E5
PGE/AN SE20 * 9 E5
STRHM/NOR SW16 * 7 E1
Central Pl SNWD SE25 * 17 E3
Central Rd MRDN SM4 ....12 D4
Central Ter BECK BR3 * 21 E3
Central Wy CAR SM5 ....33 G4
Centurion Cl WLGTN SM6 * 24 B3
Cerne Rd MRDN SM4 ....13 E5
Chadacre Rd EW KT17 ....31 F1
Chadwick Av WIM/MER SW19 ....4 C3
Chaffinch Av CROY/NA CRO...........17 H4
Chaffinch Cl CROY/NA CRO...........17 H4
Chaffinch Rd BECK BR3..............10 A5
Chalcot Cl BELMT SM2 ....32 C3
Chaldon Common Rd
CTHM CR3...........................59 E4
Chaldon Rd CTHM CR3 ....59 F3
Chaldon Wy COUL/CHIP CR5 ....54 A2
Chalfont Cl SNWD SE25 ....16 D2
Chalford Rd DUL SE21...............8 B1
Chalgrove Av MRDN SM4 ....12 C4
Chalgrove Rd BELMT SM2 ....33 F3
Chalice Cl WLGTN SM6...............34 D2
Chalkenden Cl PGE/AN SE20..........9 G5
Chalkley Cl MTCM CR4 ....13 H1
Chalk Paddock EPSOM KT18 ....40 B5
Chalk Pit Rd BNSTD SM7.............51 G2
Chalk Rd SUT SM1...................33 E1
Challin St PGE/AN SE20.............9 G2
Chalmers Rd BNSTD SM7 ....44 A5
Chamberlain Crs WWKM BR4 ....28 D2
Champion Crs SYD SE26 ....10 A1
Champion Rd SYD SE26 ....10 A1
Champneys Cl MRDN SM4 * 32 B5
Champneys Cl BELMT SM2 ....32 B3
Chancellor Gdns SAND/SEL CR2 ......35 H4
Chancery La BECK BR3...............18 D1
Chanctonbury Gdns
BELMT SM2 ....32 D3
Chandler Dr BELMT SM2 ....31 G5
Chantry Hurst EPSOM KT18...........40 A5
Chantry Wy MTCM CR4 ....13 F2
Chapel La PUR/KEN CR8 ....45 G3
Chapel Gv EPSOM KT18...............50 C4
Chapel Rd WARL CR6.................56 D3
WNWD SE27 * 7 H1
Chapel Vw SAND/SEL CR2 ....37 E5
Chapel Wy EPSOM KT18...............50 C4
Chapman Rd CROY/NA CRO............25 G2
Charles Cobb Gdns
CROY/NA CRO.........................35 G1
Charles Dickens Ter
PGE/AN SE20 * 9 G4
Charles St CROY/NA CRO.............2 C5
Charleville Circ SYD SE26 ....9 E2
Charlmont Rd TOOT SW17 ....5 G3
Charlotte Rd WLGTN SM6 ....34 C2
Charlton Gdns COUL/CHIP CR5 ....53 G5
Charlwood CROY/NA CRO 38 B4
Charminster Av
WIM/MER SW19 ....12 C1
Charminster Rd WPK KT4 ....21 H2
Charnwood Av WIM/MER SW19 ....12 C1
Charnwood Rd SNWD SE25 ....16 B4
Charrington Rd CROY/NA CRO.........2 C4
Chart Cl CROY/NA CRO...............17 G5
HAYES BR2 ....11 G5
MTCM CR4 ....13 H3
Charters Cl NRWD SE19 ....8 C2
Chartham Rd SNWD SE25.............17 F2
Chartwell Cl CROY/NA CRO...........16 D5
Chartwell Pl CHEAM SM3 ....22 A5
EPSOM KT18 ....40 C4
Chartwell Wy PGE/AN SE20..........9 F5
Charwood STRHM/NOR SW16 *.........7 G1
Chase End EW KT17 ....40 B3
Chase Rd HOR/WEW KT19..............1 H1
Chasefield Rd TOOT SW17............5 H1
Chaseley Dr SAND/SEL CR2...........36 B5
Chasemore Cl MTCM CR4 ....23 H1
Chasemore Gdns CROY/NA CRO........35 G1
Chase Rd HOR/WEW KT19.............40 B2
Chaseside Av RYNPK SW20 ....4 A5
The Chase COUL/CHIP CR5 ....44 C4
STRHM/NOR SW16 ....7 F4
WLGTN SM6 ....35 E1
Chatfield Ct CTHM CR3..............59 F2
Chatfield Rd CROY/NA CRO...........25 H2
Chatham Av HAYES BR2 ....28 B1
Chatham Cl CHEAM SM3 ....21 H4
Chatsfield EW KT17.................40 D5
Chatsworth Av WWKM BR4 ....29 H3
Chatsworth Pl MTCM CR4 ....13 H2
Chatsworth Rd CHEAM SM3 ....21 H5
CROY/NA CRO.........................3 F6
Chaucer Cl BNSTD SM7 ....42 A4

Chaucer Gdns SUT SM1...............22 C5
Chaucer Gn CROY/NA CRO.............27 F1
Chaucer Rd SUT SM1.................32 C5
Chave Cft EPSOM KT18 * 50 C4
Chavecroft Ter EPSOM KT18 * 50 C4
Cheam Common Rd WPK KT4...........21 F5
Cheam Man CHEAM SM1 * 32 A2
Cheam Park Wy CHEAM SM3...........31 H2
Cheam Rd SUT SM1...................32 D1
Chelford Rd BMLY BR1 ....11 F2
Chelmsford Cl BELMT SM2............32 C4
Chelsea Cl WPK KT4.................21 E1
Chelsea Gdns CHEAM SM3 ....22 A5
Chelsea Sq CAR SM5.................33 H4
Chelsham Rd SAND/SEL CR2 ....36 B3
Chelwood Cl COUL/CHIP CR5..........55 G4
EW KT17 ....40 D2
Chepstow Ri CROY/NA CRO............3 H4
Chepstow Rd CROY/NA CRO............3 H4
Cheriton Av HAYES BR2 ....19 H4
Cherry Cl CAR SM5 ....33 H3
EW KT17 ....41 H4
MRDN SM4 ....12 A3
Cherry Hill Gdns CROY/NA CRO.......25 E4
Cherry Orchard Gdns
CROY/NA CRO.........................3 F1
Cherry Orchard Rd CROY/NA CRO......3 F1
Cherry Tree Ct COUL/CHIP CR5.......54 B3
Cherry Tree Ter BECK BR3 * 47 F4
Cherry Tree Wk BECK BR3............29 H5
WWKM BR4 ....38 D1
Cherry Wy HOR/WEW KT19............30 B2
Cherrywood La MRDN SM4 ....12 A3
Chertsey Cl PUR/KEN CR8 ....45 H5
Chertsey Crs CROY/NA CRO...........39 E5
Chertsey St TOOT SW17 ....6 A2
Cherwell Ct HOR/WEW KT19..........20 A5
Chesham Cl BELMT SM2...............32 A5
Chesham Crs PGE/AN SE20...........9 G5
Chesham Rd PGE/AN SE20............9 G5
WARL CR6 ....57 G1
Cheshire Cl MTCM CR4 ....15 F1
Chesney Crs CROY/NA CRO............39 E3
Chessington Cl HOR/WEW KT19 ....30 A2
Chessington Rd
HOR/WEW KT19.......................30 A2
Chessington Wy WWKM BR4............38 D2
Chester Cl SUT SM1.................23 C5
Chesterfield Rd HOR/WEW KT19......30 D3
Chester Gdns MRDN SM4 ....13 E4
Chestnut Av HOR/WEW KT19..........20 C5
WWKM BR4 ....39 G1
Chestnut Cl CAR SM5................15 E1
CAT SE6 ....11 E1
STRHM/NOR SW16 ....7 G1
SAND/SEL CR2 ....37 F3
Chestnut Gv MTCM CR4 ....14 D4
SAND/SEL CR2 ....37 E3
Chestnut Mnr WLGTN SM6............24 B5
Chestnut Rd TOOT SW17..............5 H3
The Chestnuts BECK BR3 * 17 H2
Chestnut Ter SUT SM1 * 22 D5
Cheston Av CROY/NA CRO.............28 A1
Chetwode Dr EPSOM KT18............50 D3
Chetwode Rd EPSOM KT18............50 C4
Chevening Rd NRWD SE19 ....8 B4
Cheviot Cl BELMT SM2...............32 D5
BNSTD SM7 ....42 C5
Cheviot Rd WNWD SE27 ....7 H2
Cheyham Gdns BELMT SM2 ....31 H5
Cheyham Wy BELMT SM2 ....32 A5
Cheyne Ct BNSTD SM7 ....42 D5
Cheyne Wk CROY/NA CRO.............3 J1
Chichele Gdns CROY/NA CRO..........3 H6
Chichester Ct EW KT17 * 30 D4
Chichester Dr PUR/KEN CR8 ....45 F2
Chichester Rd CROY/NA CRO..........3 H5
Cleves Av CROY/NA CRO..............49 E1
Chiddingstone Cl BELMT SM2.........32 C5
Childs La NRWD SE19 * 8 A4
Chillerton Rd TOOT SW17............6 A2
Chilmark Rd STRHM/NOR SW16........14 D1
Chiltern Cl CROY/NA CRO............3 H5
WPK KT4 ....21 H3
Chiltern Gdns HAYES BR2............19 H5
Chiltern Rd BELMT SM2..............32 D5
The Chilterns BELMT SM2 * 32 D4
Chiltons Cl BNSTD SM7 ....42 D5
Chilworth Gdns SUT SM1............23 E4
Chingley Cl BMLY BR1 ....11 G3
Chipstead Av THHTH CR7.............15 H5
Chipstead Cl BELMT SM2.............32 D5
COUL/CHIP CR5 ....53 E2
NRWD SE19 ....8 D4
Chipstead Rd BNSTD SM7............51 F2
Chipstead Station Pde
COUL/CHIP CR5 * 53 F1
Chipstead Valley Rd
COUL/CHIP CR5 ....53 F1
Chipstead Wy BNSTD SM7............52 D1
Chisholm Rd CROY/NA CRO............3 H2
Chislet Cl BECK BR3................10 C4
Chiswick Cl CROY/NA CRO............25 F4
Christchurch Ct WIM/MER SW19 ......5 F4
Christchurch Pk BELMT SM2..........33 E3
Christ Church Rd BECK BR3 * 18 C1
Christchurch Rd PUR/KEN CR8........45 H1
WIM/MER SW19 ....5 F5
Christian Flds STRHM/NOR SW16 .....15 F2
Christie Dr SNWD SE25...............17 E4
Christie Wk COUL/CHIP CR5..........54 D4
Chucleigh Gdns SUT SM1.............23 H4
Chulsa Rd SYD SE26.................9 F2
Church Av BECK BR3.................18 A1
Churchdown BMLY BR1 ....10 D5
Church Dr WWKM BR4.................29 G4
Church Farm La CHEAM SM3...........32 A2
Churchfields BECK BR3..............17 H1
Church Hi CAR SM5..................33 H1
CTHM CR3 ....59 F5
PUR/KEN CR8 ....45 G4
WIM/MER SW19 ....4 C2
Church Hill Rd CHEAM SM3...........21 H5
Churchill Cl WARL CR6..............56 C2

Churchill Rd SAND/SEL CR2 ....36 A4
TOOT SW17 ....5 H1
WARL CR6 ....56 D2
WIM/MER SW19 ....12 C1
WLGTN SM6 ....24 D4
Churchley Rd SYD SE26..............9 F1
Churchmore Rd
STRHM/NOR SW16 ....6 C5
Church Paddock Ct WLGTN SM6........24 D4
Church Pth MTCM CR4................13 G2
CROY/NA CRO.........................2 C5
Church Ri CTHM CR3.................55 H5
Church Rd CHEAM SM3...............32 A2
CROY/NA CRO.........................2 C5
CTHM CR3............................55 H5
CTHM CR3............................59 G1
EW KT17.............................40 C5
HAYES BR2...........................19 H4
HOR/WEW KT19........................30 B3
MTCM CR4............................13 G3
NRWD SE19...........................8 C4
PGE/AN SE20.........................35 E5
PUR/KEN CR8.........................46 B5
WARL CR6............................56 D2
WIM/MER SW19........................4 D4
WLGTN SM6...........................24 C4
Church St CROY/NA CRO..............2 C5
STRHM/NOR SW16.....................6 C1
Church Wk CTHM CR3.................60 A4
STRHM/NOR SW16.....................14 B1
Church Wy SAND/SEL CR2............36 D5
Churters Gv EW KT17 * 3 G4
Cinderford Wy BMLY BR1.............11 F2
Cinnamon Cl CROY/NA CRO * 25 E1
Cintra Pk NRWD SE19................8 D4
Circle Gdns WIM/MER SW19...........12 C2
Clairvale Rd TOOT SW17.............6 B2
Clandon Cl EW KT17.................31 E4
Clare Ct CTHM CR3..................61 G5
Claremont Cl SAND/SEL CR2..........47 E4
Claremont Rd CROY/NA CRO...........3 J2
Claremont Cl EPSOM KT18............55 H1
Claremont Gdns EPSOM KT18..........50 C2
Clarence Rd CROY/NA CRO............26 D1
SUT SM1.............................23 E5
WIM/MER SW19.......................4 D5
WLGTN SM6..........................34 B1
Clarendon Gv MTCM CR4..............13 H2
Clarendon Rd CROY/NA CRO...........2 C4
WIM/MER SW19.......................5 E5
WLGTN SM6..........................34 B2
The Clares CTHM CR3................60 A4
Claret Gdns SNWD SE25..............16 C3
Clareville Rd CTHM CR3.............60 A4
Clarice Wy WLGTN SM6...............35 F4
Clarkes Av WPK KT4.................21 H2
Clay Av MTCM CR4...................14 B1
Clayton Dr CROY/NA CRO.............25 G2
Claygate Crs CROY/NA CRO...........39 E2
Claymore Cl MRDN SM4..............12 C4
Clayton Rd EW KT17.................40 C4
Cleave Prior COUL/CHIP CR5.........52 C4
Cleaverholme Cl SNWD SE25.........17 F5
Cleeve Wy SUT SM1.................22 D5
Clement Cl PUR/KEN CR8.............54 D1
Clement Rd BECK BR3...............17 G1
WIM/MER SW19.......................4 A2
Clensham La SUT SM1...............22 C5
Clevedon Rd PGE/AN SE20............9 H5
Cleveland Gdns WPK KT4.............20 D5
Cleveland Ri MRDN SM4.............21 H1
Cleveland Rd WPK KT4...............20 D5
Cleves Av EW KT17..................31 E4
Cleves Rd CROY/NA CRO..............49 E1
Cliff End PUR/KEN CR8..............45 G4
Cliffe Rd SAND/SEL CR2.............36 B1
Clifford Av WLGTN SM6..............34 C5
Clifford Rd SNWD SE25.............17 E3
Clifton Av BELMT SM2...............42 D1
Clifton Cl CTHM CR3................59 F5
Clifton Ct BECK BR3 * 17 H2
Clifton Ms SNWD SE25...............16 C5
Clifton Pl BNSTD SM7 * 42 D5
Clifton Rd COUL/CHIP CR5...........44 B5
SNWD SE25..........................16 C5
WLGTN SM6..........................34 B1
Clinton Ter SUT SM1 * 23 E5
Cliveden Rd WIM/MER SW19...........4 C3
Clive Rd WIM/MER SW19..............5 G3
Clock House Rd BECK BR3............17 F2
Cloister Gdns SNWD SE25............17 F5
The Close BECK BR3.................18 A3
CAR SM5.............................33 G4
CHEAM SM3...........................32 B1
MTCM CR4............................13 H3
PUR/KEN CR8.........................55 F5
SNWD SE25 * 17 E5
Clouston Cl WLGTN SM6..............35 E1
Clovelly Av WARL CR6...............56 D5
Clover Wy WLGTN SM6...............24 C3
Clowser Cl SUT SM1 * 33 E1
Clyde Av SAND/SEL CR2..............47 F5
Clyde Rd CROY/NA CRO...............3 J2
SUT SM1.............................32 C1
WLGTN SM6..........................34 C1
Cobblestone Pl CROY/NA CRO.........2 C3
Cobden Ms SYD SE26.................9 F2
Cobden Rd SNWD SE25...............17 E5
Cobham Cl WLGTN SM6...............35 E1
Cochrane Rd WIM/MER SW19...........4 A4
Cody Cl WLGTN SM6..................35 E5
Cogan Av WALTH E17.................17 E5
Colborne Wy WPK KT4...............21 H1
Colburn Av PUR/KEN CR8.............54 D5
Colburn Wy SUT SM1................23 F4
Colby Rd NRWD SE19................8 B3
Colcokes Rd BNSTD SM7.............51 G1
Coldharbour La PUR/KEN CR8.........55 E2
Coldharbour Rd CROY/NA CRO.........35 G1
Coldharbour Wy CROY/NA CRO.........35 G1

Coldstream Rd CTHM CR3.............59 E2
Colebrook Ri HAYES BR2.............19 G1
Colebrook Rd STRHM/NOR SW16 ....7 E5
Coleman Cl SNWD SE25...............17 E1
Coleridge Av SUT SM1...............23 G5
Coleridge Rd CROY/NA CRO...........26 D1
Colesburg Rd BECK BR3..............18 B2
Colescroft Hi PUR/KEN CR8..........45 G5
Colin Cl CROY/NA CRO...............28 B4
WWKM BR4............................29 H4
Colin Rd CTHM CR3..................60 A3
College Av EW KT17.................40 D4
College Gn NRWD SE19...............8 C4
College Rd CROY/NA CRO.............2 E3
EW KT17.............................40 D4
NRWD SE19...........................8 D2
WIM/MER SW19.......................5 F1
The College EW KT17 * 41 E5
Colliers CTHM CR3..................60 A5
Colliers Water La THHTH CR7........15 G4
Collingtree Rd SYD SE26............9 G1
Collingwood Av BRYLDS KT5..........20 A2
Colling Wood Cl PGE/AN SE20........9 F5
Collingwood Rd MTCM CR4............13 G1
SUT SM1.............................23 E5
Collyer Av CROY/NA CRO.............25 E5
Collyer Rd CROY/NA CRO.............25 E5
Colman Cl EPSOM KT18...............50 C2
Colmer Rd STRHM/NOR SW16 * 7 E4
Colne Ct HOR/WEW KT19.............20 A5
Colson Rd CROY/NA CRO..............3 G2
Colson Wy STRHM/NOR SW16...........6 C1
Colston Av CAR SM5.................23 G5
Columbia Av WPK KT4................20 D1
Columbine Av SAND/SEL CR2..........35 H3
Colvin Cl SYD SE26.................9 G2
Colvin Rd THHTH CR7................15 G4
Colwood Gdns WIM/MER SW19..........5 H3
Colworth Rd CROY/NA CRO............27 E2
Colwyn Cl STRHM/NOR SW16...........6 C2
Colyton La STRHM/NOR SW16..........7 G2
Combermere Rd MRDN SM4............12 D5
Commerce Wy CROY/NA CRO............25 F4
Commodore Pde
STRHM/NOR SW16 * 7 F4
Commonfield Rd BNSTD SM7...........42 C4
Commonside Cl BELMT SM2............42 D1
COUL/CHIP CR5 ....54 D5
Commonside East MTCM CR4...........14 A2
Commonside West MTCM CR4...........14 A2
Commonwealth Rd CTHM CR3...........60 A3
Comport Gn CROY/NA CRO.............49 G2
Compton Rd CROY/NA CRO.............27 F2
WIM/MER SW19.......................4 B5
Conaways Cl EW KT17................31 E5
Conduit La SAND/SEL CR2............37 E1
Coneybury Cl WARL CR6..............56 B4
Coney Hall Pde WWKM BR4 * 29 G4
Coney Hill Rd WWKM BR4.............29 G3
Conifer Gdns SUT SM1...............22 D3
Conifer Pk EW KT17.................40 C5
Coningsby Rd SAND/SEL CR2..........36 A4
Coniston Gdns BELMT SM2 * 33 F2
Coniston Rd BMLY BR1...............11 G3
COUL/CHIP CR5 ....53 G1
CROY/NA CRO.........................27 G1
Connaught Cl SUT SM1...............23 F5
Connaught Gdns MRDN SM4............13 E4
Connaught Rd SUT SM1..............23 F5
Conrad Dr WPK KT4..................21 G2
Constance Crs HAYES BR2............29 H2
Constance Rd CROY/NA CRO...........25 H1
SUT SM1.............................23 E5
Convent Cl BECK BR3...............11 E4
Convent Hi NRWD SE19...............8 A3
Conway Dr BELMT SM2...............32 D2
Conway Gdns MTCM CR4..............14 D3
Conyer's Rd STRHM/NOR SW16.........6 D1
Cookes La CHEAM SM3................32 A2
Coombe Av CROY/NA CRO..............3 H7
Coombe La CROY/NA CRO..............37 F1
Coombe Rd CROY/NA CRO.............3 E6
SAND/SEL CR2.......................36 C4
SYD SE26............................9 H1
Coomber Wy CROY/NA CRO.............25 E3
Coombe Wood Hi PUR/KEN CR8.........46 A2
Cooper Crs CAR SM5.................23 H4
Cooper Rd CROY/NA CRO..............2 A7
Coopers Ms BECK BR3...............18 C1
Cooper's Yd NRWD SE19 * 8 C3
Copers Cope Rd BECK BR3............10 C5
Copgate Pth STRHM/NOR SW16 ....7 F2
Copleigh Dr
KWD/TDW/WH KT20....................51 E5
Copley Pk STRHM/NOR SW16...........7 E2
Copley Wy KWD/TDW/WH KT20..........50 D5
Coppard Gdns CHEAM SM3 * 31 G2
Copperfield Cl PUR/KEN CR8.........46 A1
Copper Mill La TOOT SW17............5 E1
Coppice Cl BECK BR3................18 D3
Copping Cl CROY/NA CRO.............3 H6
The Coppins CROY/NA CRO............38 D2
Copse Av WWKM BR4..................38 D1
Copse Edge Av EW KT17.............40 D5
Copse Hi BELMT SM2.................32 D3
PUR/KEN CR8.........................55 G1
Copse Vw SAND/SEL CR2 * 37 H5
Copt Hill La KWD/TDW/WH KT20.......51 E5
Copthorne Ri PUR/KEN CR8...........46 B5
Corbet Cl WLGTN SM6...............24 A2
Corbet Rd EW KT17..................30 C5
Corbett Cl CROY/NA CRO.............49 F2
Cordrey Gdns COUL/CHIP CR5.........45 E5
Corkscrew Hi WWKM BR4..............29 E3
Cornflower La CROY/NA CRO..........27 H2
Cornish Gv PGE/AN SE20..............9 G4
Cornwall Gdns SNWD SE25 *..........17 E3
Cornwallis Cl CTHM CR3.............60 A3
Cornwall Rd BELMT SM2..............32 C3
CROY/NA CRO.........................2 B4
Corrib Dr SUT SM1..................34 A1
Corrigan Av COUL/CHIP CR5
Corsehill St STRHM/NOR SW16

Cosdach Av WLGTN SM6 ....34 D3
Cosedge Crs CROY/NA CRO 35 G1
Coteford St TOOT SW17 ....5 H1
Cotelands CROY/NA CRO 3 G4
Cotford Rd THHTH CR7 ....16 A3
Cotherstone HOR/WEW KT19 ..30 B4
Cotswold Rd BELMT SM2 ....22 C7
Cotswold St WNWD SE27 ....7 H1
Cotswold Wy WPK KT4 ....21 G3
Cottage Rd HOR/WEW KT19 ..30 B5
Cottingham Rd PGE/AN SE20 ..9 H4
Cottongrass Cl CROY/NA CRO ..27 H2
Cotton Hi BMLY BR1 ....11 F1
Coulsdon Court Rd
   COUL/CHIP CR5 ....54 B1
Coulsdon La COUL/CHIP CR5 ..53 E4
Coulsdon Pl CTHM CR3 ....59 F2
Coulsdon Ri COUL/CHIP CR5 ..54 A2
Coulsdon Rd COUL/CHIP CR5 ..54 A2
   CTHM CR3 ....59 E1
County Rd THHTH CR7 ....15 H1
Court Av COUL/CHIP CR5 ....54 C5
Court Bushes Rd CTHM CR3 ..56 A4
Court Downs Rd BECK BR3 ..18 D1
Court Dr CROY/NA CRO 2 A6
   SUT SM1 ....23 G5
Courtenay Av BELMT SM2 ....32 A4
Courtenay Dr BECK BR3 ....19 F1
Courtenay Rd PGE/AN SE20 ..10 A4
   WPK KT4 ....21 G4
Court Farm Av HOR/WEW KT19 ..30 B1
Court Farm Gdns
   HOR/WEW KT19 * 40 B1
Court Farm Pk WARL CR6 * ..56 A1
Court Farm Rd WARL CR6 ....56 A3
Courtfield Ri WWKM BR4 ....29 F1
Court Haw BNSTD SM7 ....43 G5
Court Hi SAND/SEL CR2 ....46 C2
Courthope Rd WIM/MER SW19 ..4 A2
Courthope Vls WIM/MER SW19 ..4 A4
Courtland Av STRHM/NOR SW16 ..7 F4
Courtlands Av HAYES BR2 ....28 C7
Courtlands Cl SAND/SEL CR2 ..36 D5
Courtlands Crs BNSTD SM7 ....51 G1
Courtlands Dr HOR/WEW KT19 ..30 C2
Court La HOR/WEW KT19 ....40 A3
Courtney Cl NRWD SE19 * 8 C3
Courtney Crs CAR SM5 ....33 H3
Courtney Rd CROY/NA CRO ..25 G4
   WIM/MER SW19 ....5 J3
Court Rd BNSTD SM7 ....42 C5
   CTHM CR3 ....59 F3
   SNWD SE25 ....25 E2
The Courts STRHM/NOR SW16,..7 E4
The Court WARL CR6 ....57 E5
Court Wood La CROY/NA CRO ..38 B5
Coventry Rd SNWD SE25 ....17 E3
Coverack Cl CROY/NA CRO 28 A1
Coverdale Gdns CROY/NA CRO ..3 J4
Coverton Rd TOOT SW17 * 5 G1
The Covert NRWD SE19 * 8 C2
Covey Cl WIM/MER SW19 ....12 D1
Covington Gdns
   STRHM/NOR SW16 ....7 H3
Covington Wy
   STRHM/NOR SW16 ....7 H2
Cowden St CAT SE6 ....10 C1
Cowdrey Rd WIM/MER SW19 ..4 D3
Cowick Rd TOOT SW17 ....5 H1
Cowley Cl SAND/SEL CR2 ....37 G4
Cowper Gdns WLGTN SM6 ....34 C2
Cowper Rd WIM/MER SW19 ....5 F3
Coxbean EPSOM KT18 ....50 C4
Cox La HOR/WEW KT19 ....30 A1
Coxley Ri PUR/KEN CR8 ....46 A3
Coxs Cots WARL CR6 * 49 G4
Coxwell Rd NRWD SE19 ....8 B5
Crab Hi BECK BR3 ....11 F4
Craigen Av CROY/NA CRO 26 B2
Craignish Av STRHM/NOR SW16 ..15 F1
Crampton Rd PGE/AN SE20 ....9 J3
Cranbourne Cl
   STRHM/NOR SW16 ....16 A1
   WIM/MER SW19 ....4 A4
Cranbrook Rd THHTH CR7 ....16 C2
Cranfield East CAR SM5 ....34 A4
Cranfield West CAR SM5 * 33 J4
Cranford Cl PUR/KEN CR8 ....46 B4
Cranleigh Cl PGE/AN SE20 ....17 F1
   SNWD SE25 ....16 C2
Cranleigh Gdns SAND/SEL CR2 ..47 F2
   SNWD SE25 ....16 C2
Cranleigh Rd WIM/MER SW19 ..12 C2
Cranley Gdns WLGTN SM6 ....34 C3
Cranmer Cl WARL CR6 ....57 F3
Cranmer Farm Cl MTCM CR4 ..13 H3
Cranmer Gdns WARL CR6 ....57 E2
Cranmer Rd CROY/NA CRO 2 A5
   MTCM CR4 ....13 H3
Cranmer Ter TOOT SW17 ....5 F2
Craven Av HAYES BR2 ....29 H1
Craven Rd CROY/NA CRO 27 F2
Credenhill St STRHM/NOR SW16 ..6 C3
Cremorne Gdns HOR/WEW KT19 ..30 B4
Crescent Gv MTCM CR4 ....13 G3
Crescent Rd BECK BR3 ....18 D1
   CTHM CR3 ....61 G3
The Crescent BECK BR3 ....10 C5
   BELMT SM2 ....32 C5
   CTHM CR3 ....61 G3
   SNWD SE25 ....16 D5
   SUT SM1 ....33 F1
   WWKM BR4 ....19 H5
Crescent Wy STRHM/NOR SW16 ..7 H2
Cressingham Gv SUT SM1 ....23 E5
Cresswell Rd SNWD SE25 ....17 E3
Creston Wy WPK KT4 ....21 H2
Crest Rd HAYES BR2 ....29 H1
...swell Dr BECK BR3 ....18 D4
...'s Av WARL CR6 ....56 C1
... Cl WARL CR6 ....56 C1

Crewe's La WARL CR6 ....56 D1
Crichton Av WLGTN SM6 ....34 D1
Crichton Rd CAR SM5 ....33 H3
Cricketers Wk SYD SE26 ....9 G2
Cricket Gn MTCM CR4 ....13 H5
Cricket La BECK BR3 ....10 A3
Crispin Crs CROY/NA CRO 24 D4
Crocus Cl CROY/NA CRO 27 H2
Croft Av WWKM BR4 ....29 E2
Croft Ct SUT SM1 * 23 F3
Crofters Md CROY/NA CRO 38 B4
Croftleigh Av PUR/KEN CR8 ..54 C1
Croft Rd CTHM CR3 ....61 F2
   STRHM/NOR SW16 ....16 A1
   SUT SM1 ....33 H1
   WIM/MER SW19 ....5 E4
Croham Cl SAND/SEL CR2 ....36 C3
Croham Manor Rd
   SAND/SEL CR2 ....36 C3
Croham Mt SAND/SEL CR2 ....36 C4
Croham Park Av SAND/SEL CR2 ..36 D1
Croham Rd SAND/SEL CR2 ....36 C1
Croham Valley Rd
   SAND/SEL CR2 ....37 E2
Croindene Rd STRHM/NOR SW16 ..7 F3
Cromer Hyde MRDN SM4 * 12 D4
Cromer Rd SNWD SE25 ....17 F2
   TOOT SW17 ....6 A3
Cromwell Gv MTCM CR4 ....13 H2
Cromwell Rd BECK BR3 ....18 A1
   CROY/NA CRO 26 B1
   SUT SM1 ....23 F1
   WIM/MER SW19 ....5 F1
   WPK KT4 ....20 B4
Crossland Rd THHTH CR7 ....15 H5
Crosslands Rd HOR/WEW KT19 ..30 B2
Cross Rd BELMT SM2 ....32 C5
   CROY/NA CRO 26 B2
   SUT SM1 ....23 H5
   WIM/MER SW19 ....5 F1
Crossways BELMT SM2 ....32 D5
   SAND/SEL CR2 ....38 B3
Crossways Rd BECK BR3 ....18 C3
   MTCM CR4 ....14 B2
The Crossways WIM/MER SW19,..13 F6
Crouch Cl BECK BR3 ....10 C5
Crowborough Cl WARL CR6 ..57 G3
Crowborough Dr WARL CR6 ..57 F3
Crowborough Rd TOOT SW17 ..6 A2
Crowland Rd THHTH CR7 ....16 B3
Crowland Wk MRDN SM4 ....12 D5
Crowley Crs CROY/NA CRO ..35 G1
Crownbourne Ct SUT SM1 * ..23 F3
Crown Dl NRWD SE19 ....8 A3
Crown Hi CROY/NA CRO 2 D3
Crown La MRDN SM4 ....12 C2
   STRHM/NOR SW16 ....7 G2
Crown Lane Gdns WNWD SE27 * ..7 G2
Crown Pde MRDN SM4 * 12 C1
Crown Rd SUT SM1 ....22 D5
   WIM/MER SW19 ....12 C5
Crowther Rd SNWD SE25 ....17 E3
Croxden Wk MRDN SM4 ....13 E5
The Croydon F/O CROY/NA CRO ..2 C4
Croydon Gv CROY/NA CRO 2 A1
Croydon La BNSTD SM7 ....43 F3
Croydon La South BNSTD SM7 ..42 D4
Croydon Rd BECK BR3 ....18 A2
   CROY/NA CRO 17 H4
   CTHM CR3 ....60 A2
   PGE/AN SE20 ....17 F1
   WLGTN SM6 ....24 B5
   WWKM BR4 ....29 G4
Crozier Dr SAND/SEL CR2 ....37 F5
Crunden Rd SAND/SEL CR2 ....36 B3
Crusader Gdns CROY/NA CRO ..3 H5
Cruse Rd MTCM CR4 ....14 B5
Crystal Palace Pde NRWD SE19 * ..9 E4
Crystal Palace Pde NRWD SE19 ..8 D4
Crystal Palace Park Rd SYD SE26 ..9 E2
Crystal Ter NRWD SE19 ....8 C3
Cubitt St CROY/NA CRO 35 F1
Cuda's Cl HOR/WEW KT19 ....20 D5
Cuddington Av WPK KT4 ....20 D4
Cuddington Cl
   KWD/TDW/WH KT20 ....50 C5
Cuddington Park Cl BNSTD SM7 ..42 B3
Cudham Cl BELMT SM2 ....41 H2
Cudham Cl BELMT SM2 ....32 C6
Cudham Dr CROY/NA CRO 38 D5
Cullerne Cl EW KT17 ....30 D5
Cullesden Rd PUR/KEN CR8 ....45 H5
Culmington Rd SAND/SEL CR2 ..36 A3
Culverhouse Gdns
   STRHM/NOR SW16 ....7 F1
Culvers Av CAR SM5 ....23 H3
Culvers Retreat CAR SM5 ....23 H2
Culverstone Cl HAYES BR2 ....19 H5
Culvers Wy CAR SM5 ....23 H3
Cumberland Cl HOR/WEW KT19 ..30 C1
Cumberland Rd HAYES BR2 ....19 G5
   SNWD SE25 ....17 F5
Cumberlands PUR/KEN CR8 ....46 B5
Cumberland Ter PGE/AN SE20 * ..9 F4
Cumnor Gdns EW KT17 ....31 E2
Cumnor Ri PUR/KEN CR8 ....54 C2
Cumnor Rd BELMT SM2 ....33 E2
Cunliffe Rd HOR/WEW KT19 ..20 D5
Cunliffe St STRHM/NOR SW16 ..6 C3
Cunningham Cl WWKM BR4 ....28 D3
Cunningham Rd BNSTD SM7 ....43 F5
Curlew Cl SAND/SEL CR2 ....47 H1
Curling Cl COUL/CHIP CR5 ....55 F5
Curnick's La WNWD SE27 ....8 A1
Curran Av WLGTN SM6 ....24 A4
Currie Hill Cl WIM/MER SW19 ..4 B1
Curtis Field Rd
   STRHM/NOR SW16 ....7 F1
Curtis Rd HOR/WEW KT19 ....20 A5
Curvan Cl EW KT17 ....30 D5
Curzon Rd THHTH CR7 ....15 G5

Cuthbert Gdns SNWD SE25 ....16 C2
Cuthbert Rd CROY/NA CRO 2 B3
Cyclamen Wy HOR/WEW KT19 ..30 A1
Cypress Rd SNWD SE25 ....16 C1
Cypress Wy EW KT17 ....41 H4

D

Dacre Rd CROY/NA CRO 25 E3
Daffodil Cl CROY/NA CRO 27 H2
Dagmar Rd SNWD SE25 ....16 C3
Dagnall Pk SNWD SE25 ....16 C4
Dagnall Rd SNWD SE25 ....16 C4
Dahlia Gdns MTCM CR4 ....14 D3
Dahomey Rd STRHM/NOR SW16 ..6 C3
Daimler Wy WLGTN SM6 ....35 E3
Dainford Cl BMLY BR1 ....11 F2
Dairy Cl THHTH CR7 ....16 A1
Dairy Cl CROY/NA CRO 27 H2
Dakota Cl CROY/NA CRO 35 E1
Dalegarth Gdns PUR/KEN CR8 ..46 B3
Dale Park Av CAR SM5 ....23 H3
Dale Park Rd NRWD SE19 ....16 A1
Dale Rd PUR/KEN CR8 ....45 G2
   SUT SM1 ....22 B5
Daleside Rd HOR/WEW KT19 ..30 B2
   STRHM/NOR SW16 ....6 B6
Dalewood Gdns WPK KT4 ....21 F3
Dallas Rd CHEAM SM3 ....32 A2
   SYD SE26 ....9 F1
Dalmally Rd CROY/NA CRO 26 D1
Dalmeny Av STRHM/NOR SW16 ..15 J1
Dalmeny Rd CAR SM5 ....34 A3
   WPK KT4 ....21 G2
Dalton Av MTCM CR4 ....13 G1
Danbrook Rd STRHM/NOR SW16 ..7 F3
Danbury Ms CAR SM5 ....24 B5
Danebury CROY/NA CRO 38 D2
Danecourt Gdns CROY/NA CRO ..3 K4
Dane Rd WARL CR6 ....56 D2
   WIM/MER SW19 ....5 E5
Danecourt Crs SUT SM1 ....23 F3
Danetree Cl HOR/WEW KT19 ..30 A3
Danetree Rd HOR/WEW KT19 ..30 A3
Daniel Cl WIM/MER SW19 ....5 G3
Daniell Wy CROY/NA CRO 25 E6
Daniels La WARL CR6 ....57 F1
Daniel Wy BNSTD SM7 ....42 D4
Danvers Wy CTHM CR3 ....59 E3
Darcy Cl CTHM CR3 ....59 E2
Darcy Av WLGTN SM6 ....24 C5
D'arcy Rd CHEAM SM3 ....31 H5
   STRHM/NOR SW16 ....15 E1
Darley Cl CROY/NA CRO 17 H5
Darley Gdns MRDN SM4 ....12 D5
Darlington Rd WNWD SE27 ....7 G3
Darmaine Cl SAND/SEL CR2 ....36 A3
Dartnell Rd CROY/NA CRO 26 D1
Dassett Rd WNWD SE27 ....7 H2
Davidson Rd CROY/NA CRO 26 C1
Davies Cl SNWD SE25 ....16 D5
Daybrook Rd WIM/MER SW19 ..12 D1
Day's Acre SAND/SEL CR2 ....36 D5
Deacon Cl CTHM CR3 ....59 E3
   PUR/KEN CR8 ....45 E5
Deal Rd TOOT SW17 ....6 A2
Deanfield Gdns CROY/NA CRO * ..2 E7
Dean La CTHM CR3 ....58 A4
Dean Rd CROY/NA CRO 2 E7
Deans Cl CROY/NA CRO 28 A3
Deansfield CTHM CR3 ....59 H5
Deans Rd SUT SM1 ....22 D4
Deans Wk COUL/CHIP CR5 ....55 F5
De'arn Gdns MTCM CR4 ....13 G2
De Burgh Gdns
   KWD/TDW/WH KT20 ....50 D4
De Burgh Pk BNSTD SM7 ....51 H5
Deburgh Rd WIM/MER SW19 ....5 G4
Decimus Cl SNWD SE25 * 16 B3
Deepdale Av HAYES BR2 ....19 H3
Deepdene Av CROY/NA CRO 3 K5
Deepfield Wy COUL/CHIP CR5 ..54 A1
Deerhurst Rd STRHM/NOR SW16 ..7 F2
Deer Park Gdns MTCM CR4 * ..13 F5
Deer Park Rd WIM/MER SW19 ..12 D1
Deer Park Wy WWKM BR4 ....29 H1
Deerswood Cl CTHM CR3 ....60 A4
Dee Wy HOR/WEW KT19 ....30 C5
Defiant Wy WLGTN SM6 ....35 E3
Delamare Crs CROY/NA CRO 17 H5
Delaporte Cl EW KT17 ....40 C2
Delcombe Av WPK KT4 ....21 G2
Dell Cl WLGTN SM6 ....24 C1
Dellmead Cl CROY/NA CRO * ..2 D3
Dell La EW KT17 ....31 E1
Dell Rd EW KT17 ....31 E2
The Dell BECK BR3 * 10 C4
   NRWD SE19 ....8 D5
Delmey Cl CROY/NA CRO 3 K4
Delta Cl WPK KT4 ....20 D4
Delta Rd WPK KT4 ....20 C4
Demesne Rd WLGTN SM6 ....24 D2
Denbigh Cl SUT SM1 ....32 B1
Den Cl BECK BR3 ....19 F2
Dene Cl COUL/CHIP CR5 ....54 C2
   HAYES BR2 ....19 J5
   WPK KT4 ....20 D3
Denefield Dr PUR/KEN CR8 ....46 B5
The Dene BELMT SM2 ....42 B1
   CROY/NA CRO 38 A1
Denewood EW KT17 * 40 C3
Denham Crs MTCM CR4 ....13 H3
Denham Rd EW KT17 ....40 D2
Denison Rd WIM/MER SW19 ....5 F3
Denmark Av WIM/MER SW19 ....4 A4

Denmark Ct MRDN SM4 ....12 C4
Denmark Gdns CAR SM5 ....23 H4
Denmark Rd CAR SM5 ....23 H4
   SNWD SE25 ....17 E4
Denmead Rd CROY/NA CRO 25 H2
Dennett Rd CROY/NA CRO 25 G1
Denning Av CROY/NA CRO 35 G1
The Denningtons WPK KT4 ....20 C3
Dennis Park Crs RYNPK SW20 ..4 A5
Dennis Reeve Cl MTCM CR4 ....5 H5
Den Rd HAYES BR2 ....19 F2
Densham Dr PUR/KEN CR8 ....54 A4
Densole Cl BECK BR3 * 10 A5
Denvale Trade Pk MTCM CR4 ..13 F3
Depot Rd EW KT17 ....40 C3
Derby Cl EPSOM KT18 ....50 B4
Derby Rd CROY/NA CRO 25 G1
   SUT SM1 ....32 B2
   WIM/MER SW19 ....4 C4
Derek Av WLGTN SM6 ....24 B4
Dering Pl CROY/NA CRO 2 C7
Dering Rd CROY/NA CRO 2 D7
Derinton Rd TOOT SW17 ....6 A1
Deroy Cl CAR SM5 ....33 H2
Derrick Av SAND/SEL CR2 ....36 A5
Derrick Rd BECK BR3 ....18 B2
Derry Rd CROY/NA CRO 25 E4
Derwent Dr PUR/KEN CR8 ....46 B4
Derwent Rd PGE/AN SE20 ....17 F1
   WIM/MER SW19 ....12 B4
Devana End CAR SM5 ....23 H4
Devereux Ct SAND/SEL CR2 ....19 E4
De Vere Cl WLGTN SM6 ....35 E3
Devon Cl PUR/KEN CR8 ....55 G1
Devon Rd BELMT SM2 ....32 A4
Devonshire Av BELMT SM2 ....33 E3
Devonshire Rd CROY/NA CRO ..16 D7
   CAR SM5 ....24 A5
   CROY/NA CRO 26 B1
   SUT SM1 ....32 D3
Devonshire Wy CROY/NA CRO ..28 B5
Dewey St TOOT SW17 * 5 J2
Dewsbury Gdns WPK KT4 ....21 E4
Dibdin Cl SUT SM1 ....22 C4
Dibdin Rd SUT SM1 ....22 C4
Diceland Rd BNSTD SM7 ....51 F1
Dickenson's La SNWD SE25 ....17 E5
Dickenson's Pl SNWD SE25 ....17 E5
Digby Pl CROY/NA CRO 3 K6
Digdens Ri EPSOM KT18 ....40 A5
Dillwyn Cl SYD SE26 ....10 A1
Dingwall Av CROY/NA CRO 2 D4
Dingwall Rd CAR SM5 ....33 H4
   CROY/NA CRO 3 F3
Dinsdale Gdns SNWD SE25 ....16 C3
Dinton Rd WIM/MER SW19 ....5 H3
Dirdene Cl EW KT17 ....40 D1
Dirdene Gdns EW KT17 ....40 D1
Dirdene Gv EW KT17 ....40 C2
Ditches La COUL/CHIP CR5 ....58 C5
Dittoncroft Cl SAND/SEL CR2 ..36 C4
Ditton Pl PGE/AN SE20 * 9 F5
Dixon Pl WWKM BR4 ....28 D2
Dixon Rd SNWD SE25 ....16 C2
Doctors Cl SYD SE26 ....9 J2
Doctors La CTHM CR3 ....58 C4
Doel Cl WIM/MER SW19 ....5 H4
Doghurst La COUL/CHIP CR5 ..52 D5
Dome Hill Pk SYD SE26 ....9 E4
Dominion Rd CROY/NA CRO 26 D1
Donald Rd CROY/NA CRO 15 F5
Dome M MTCM CR4 ....14 B3
Donnington Rd WPK KT4 ....21 E3
Donnybrook Rd
   STRHM/NOR SW16 ....6 D4
Donovan Cl HOR/WEW KT19 ..30 B5
Doral Wy CAR SM5 ....33 H1
Dorchester Ms WIM/MER SW19 ..4 C2
Dorchester Rd MRDN SM4 ....21 H1
   WPK KT4 ....21 G1
Dore Gdns MRDN SM4 ....21 E1
Dorian Ct WARL CR6 * 56 B4
Doric Dr KWD/TDW/WH KT20 ..51 F5
Dorin Ct WARL CR6 * 56 B5
Dorking Cl WPK KT4 ....21 G1
Dorking Rd EPSOM KT18 ....40 A5
Dorling Dr EW KT17 ....40 D1
Dornden Gdns CROY/NA CRO * ..2 E2
Dornton Rd SAND/SEL CR2 ....36 C1
Dorrington Wy BECK BR3 ....19 E4
Dorset Gdns STRHM/NOR SW16 ..15 F7
Dorset Rd BECK BR3 ....17 H2
   BELMT SM2 ....32 C5
   MTCM CR4 ....13 G1
   WIM/MER SW19 ....4 C5
Douglas Av WPK KT4 ....21 E1
Douglas Cl CTHM CR3 ....55 E2
Douglas Gv CROY/NA CRO 28 C4
Douglas Ms BNSTD SM7 ....51 H5
Dove Cl CROY/NA CRO 35 F3
   SAND/SEL CR2 ....47 H1
Dovedale Ri MTCM CR4 ....5 H4
Dovercourt Av THHTH CR7 ....15 G3
Dovercourt La SUT SM1 ....23 H4
Dover Gdns CAR SM5 ....23 J3
Dover Rd SNWD SE25 ....8 B5
Doveton Rd SAND/SEL CR2 ....36 B1
Dower Av WLGTN SM6 ....34 B4
Dowman Cl WIM/MER SW19 * ..5 E3
Downe Rd MTCM CR4 ....13 H1
Downfield WPK KT4 ....21 E1
Downland Cl COUL/CHIP CR5 ..44 C7
   EPSOM KT18 ....50 B5
Downland Gdns EPSOM KT18 ..50 B5
Downlands Rd PUR/KEN CR8 ..45 E5
Downland Wy EPSOM KT18 ....50 B5
Downs Av CTHM CR3 ....59 H3
Downs Bridge Rd BECK BR3 ....11 F5
Downs Court Rd PUR/KEN CR8 ..45 H3
Downside BECK BR3 * 10 C5
   EPSOM KT18 ....40 C5

Downside Cl WIM/MER SW19 ..5 H4
Downside Rd BELMT SM2 ....33 F3
Downs Lodge Ct EPSOM KT18 * ..50 C5
Downs Rd BECK BR3 ....18 D1
   BELMT SM2 ....33 E5
   COUL/CHIP CR5 ....54 C3
   EPSOM KT18 ....50 C6
   PUR/KEN CR8 ....45 H3
   THHTH CR7 ....16 A4
Downs Side BELMT SM2 ....32 C6
Downsview Gdns NRWD SE19 ..8 A4
Downsview Rd NRWD SE19 ....8 A4
Downsway CTHM CR3 ....59 H4
   SAND/SEL CR2 ....36 D5
The Downsway BELMT SM2 ....33 F5
Downs Wd EPSOM KT18 ....50 D5
Doyle Rd SNWD SE25 ....17 E3
Drake Av CTHM CR3 ....59 F3
Drake Rd CROY/NA CRO 25 F1
   MTCM CR4 ....13 J4
Drakewood Rd
   STRHM/NOR SW16 ....6 D4
Draven Cl HAYES BR2 ....28 D5
Draxmont WIM/MER SW19 ....4 B2
Drayton Rd CROY/NA CRO 2 B3
Drew Pl CTHM CR3 ....59 F3
The Driftway BNSTD SM7 ....42 A5
   MTCM CR4 ....14 A5
Drive Rd COUL/CHIP CR5 ....58 A5
The Drive BECK BR3 ....18 C1
   BELMT SM2 ....33 E5
   BNSTD SM7 ....42 A2
   COUL/CHIP CR5 ....54 D2
   HOR/WEW KT19 ....30 C5
   MRDN SM4 ....13 F4
   THHTH CR7 ....16 C2
   WLGTN SM6 ....34 D5
   WWKM BR4 ....19 J4
Drovers Rd SAND/SEL CR2 ....36 C2
Druids Wy HAYES BR2 ....27 J1
Drumaline Rdg WPK KT4 ....20 C2
Drummond Rd CROY/NA CRO ..2 C4
Drury Crs CROY/NA CRO 25 E1
Dryden Rd WIM/MER SW19 ....5 H3
Duchess Cl SUT SM1 ....23 F4
Dudley Dr MRDN SM4 ....21 E3
Dudley Gv EPSOM KT18 ....40 A3
Dudley Rd WIM/MER SW19 ....5 E3
Duke of Edinburgh Rd SUT SM1 ..23 F7
Dukes Hi CTHM CR3 ....56 D5
Dukesthorpe Rd SYD SE26 ....9 H2
Duke St SUT SM1 ....23 F4
Dukes Wy WWKM BR4 ....29 G2
Dulverton Rd SAND/SEL CR2 ..37 G4
Dulwich Wood Av NRWD SE19 ..8 D2
Dulwich Wood Pk NRWD SE19 ..8 D1
Dunbar Av BECK BR3 ....17 G4
   STRHM/NOR SW16 ....15 J1
Duncan Rd KWD/TDW/WH KT20 ..51 E6
Dundee Rd SNWD SE25 ....17 F4
Dundela Gdns WPK KT4 ....21 F3
Dundonald Rd WIM/MER SW19 ..4 B3
Dunedin Dr CTHM CR3 ....59 H5
Dunelm Gv WNWD SE27 ....7 H1
Dunfield Rd CAT SE6 ....10 D1
Dunheved Cl THHTH CR7 ....15 H5
Dunheved Rd North
   THHTH CR7 ....15 H5
Dunheved Rd South
   THHTH CR7 ....15 H5
Dunheved Rd West THHTH CR7 ..15 H5
Dunkeld Rd SNWD SE25 ....16 A3
Dunkirk St WNWD SE27 * 7 H1
Dunley Dr CROY/NA CRO 38 C4
Dunmail Dr PUR/KEN CR8 ....55 J2
Dunnymans Rd BNSTD SM7 ....42 A5
Dunsbury Cl BELMT SM2 ....32 D5
Dunsfold Ri COUL/CHIP CR5 ....45 E7
Dunsfold Wy CROY/NA CRO 38 B4
Dunstan Rd COUL/CHIP CR5 ....55 E3
Dunster Av MRDN SM4 ....20 D4
Duppas Av CROY/NA CRO 2 A7
Duppas Hill Rd CROY/NA CRO ..2 A7
Duppas Hill Ter CROY/NA CRO ..2 B7
Duppas Rd CROY/NA CRO 2 A6
Dura Den Cl BECK BR3 ....10 D4
Durban Rd BECK BR3 ....17 H1
   WNWD SE27 ....7 J2
Durham Hill BMLY BR1 ....11 H1
Durham Rd WIM/MER SW19 ....4 C4
Durham Ter PGE/AN SE20 * 9 H5
Durning Rd NRWD SE19 ....8 C3
Durnsford Rd WIM/MER SW19 ..5 E1
Dykes Wy HAYES BR2 ....19 J3

E

Eagle Cl WLGTN SM6 ....35 E2
Eagle Hl NRWD SE19 ....8 C3
Eardley Rd STRHM/NOR SW16 ..6 C6
Earlsthorpe Rd SYD SE26 ....9 H3
Earlswood Av THHTH CR7 ....15 H4
Eastby Crs MRDN SM4 ....21 G1
East Av CROY/NA CRO 2 E5
Eastbourne Rd TOOT SW17 ....6 A2
Eastcroft Rd HOR/WEW KT19 ..30 B4
East Dr CAR SM5 ....23 G2
Eastfields Rd MTCM CR4 ....13 H1
Eastgate BNSTD SM7 ....42 A5
East Hi SAND/SEL CR2 ....36 C3
East India Wy CROY/NA CRO 26 D1
Eastleigh Cl BELMT SM2 ....32 D5
Eastney Rd CROY/NA CRO 25 G1
East Parkside WARL CR6 ....57 F4
East Pl WNWD SE27 ....7 H1
East Rd WIM/MER SW19 ....5 F4
Eastry Av HAYES BR2 ....27 J1

a CTHM CR3 ...57 F4
evel Dr SYD SE26 ...9 E1
imes NRWD SE19 * ...8 C3
d WWKM BR4 ...29 F3
th WIM/MER SW19 ...4 D5
ines WARL CR6 ...56 C5
dge Cl EPSOM KT18 * ...40 C5
standing CTHM CR3 ...59 E5
st BECK BR3 ...10 C5
MT SM2 ...32 D2
STD SM7 ...51 H4
STD SM7 ...42 C5
SM1 ...33 H1
EAM SM3 ...32 A2
OY/NA CR0 ...2 D4
CR3 ...59 C3
OY/NA CR0 ...30 D5
R/WEW KT19 ...9 C4
EAN SE20 ...9 C4
CTHM CR7 ...16 D3
KM BR4 ...29 F2
street Collier's Wd
/MER SW19 ...5 F4
treet Ms WIM/MER SW19 ...4 A2
rees CROY/NA CR0 ...28 A2
rees CTHM CR3 ...59 H2
ghway BELMT SM2 ...33 E4
old COUL/CHIP CR5 ...55 F4
ood Cl PUR/KEN CR8 ...55 C3
oods CTHM CR3 ...59 C5
Av MTCM CR4 ...14 A2
t Rd CHEAM SM5 ...21 H5
ough Cl WIM/MER SW19 * ...4
borough Gdns BMLY BR1 ...11 C5
lea Rd HAYES BR2 ...19 H3
leath Rd
n SAND/SEL CR2 ...45 E5
rough Cl WIM/MER SW19 * ...1
ty Cl WARL CR6 ...56 B3
ry Gdns WARL CR6 ...56 C3
ty Rd WARL CR6 ...56 C3
PUR/KEN CR8 ...46 A2
iew Av STRHM/NOR SW16...7 C4
s WPK KT4 ...33 E5
st Cl BECK BR3 ...18 B5
OM KT18 ...40 D5
SE26 ...
st Rd CTHM CR3 ...55 H2
st Vw BECK BR3 ...55 F4
ft Av PUR/KEN CR8 ...44 C5
ome Rd BELMT SM2 ...33 F2
ss Av MRDN SM4 ...12 A5
e Rd SUT SM1 ...22 B5
ane Rd PUR/KEN CR8 ...45 H3
ts Rd BMLY BR1 ...29 G2
HM/NOR SW16 ...15 C5
STRHM/NOR SW16 ...15 C5
d Av MRDN SM4 ...13 C5
st Pde MRDN SM4 ...13 F1
se Rd STRHM/NOR SW16 ...7 F2
st Gdns CTHM CR3 ...55 C5
Gdns CROY/NA CR0 ...3 H4
s La CROY/NA CR0 ...2 D4
re Gv SYD SE26 ...9 F2
CAR SM5 ...
CM CR4 ...
R/KEN CR8 ...45 F2
SUT SM1 ...32 D1
BNSTD SM7 ...42 A5
e Av PUR/KEN CR8 ...45 H3
e Cl BNSTD SM7 ...51 E1
ON SM4 ...12 A5
e Cots BNSTD SM7 * ...48 A5
e Gdns WLGTN SM6 ...34 C5
e Rd BELMT SM2 ...33 E2
L/CHIP CR5 ...
CR5 ...2 A7
M CR3 ...
t Rd ...56 A3
ES BR2 ...
ead Wy SAND/SEL CR2...47 E5
l CTHM CR3 ...59 H4
o MRDN SM4 ...22 B1
Cots SYD SE26 * ...9 F1
l CTHM CR3 ...55 G2
WK CTHM CR3 ...57 F5
e CTHM CR3 ...55 H2
w Cl PUR/KEN CR8 ...45 H1
w Rd SUT SM1 ...
th BECK BR3 ...18 D1
Wy SAND/SEL CR2 ...47 E5
t TOOT SW17 ...5 G2
ead Wy WLGTN SM6 ...35 E4
Rd WLGTN SM6 ...34 C2
wood Dr SUT SE21 ...
e Gdns THHTH CR7 ...16 B2
e WPK KT4 ...21 H4
Rd WNWD SE27 ...8 A1
ts CROY/NA CR0 ...28 A1
ill Wy HOR/WEW KT19 ...30 A1
n Wy MTCM CR4 ...13 H2
ness Wy WNWD SE27 ...
Av BELMT SM2 ...32 C3
l Cl HAYES BR2 ...29 H2
Rd SNWD SE25 ...17 E4
llands WPK KT4 ...20 D2
1 Wy HAYES ...29 H5
Cl STRHM/NOR SW16 ...7 H3
sworth Rd
D/SEL CR2 ...37 F2
n Gdns
/NOR SW16 ...7 H3

Hollybush Ter NRWD SE19 * ...8 C3
Holly Cl BECK BR3 ...19 E3
Holly Crs BECK BR3 ...18 B4
Hollycroft Cl SAND/SEL CR2 ...36 C1
Holly Hill Dr BNSTD SM7 ...51 G2
Holly La BNSTD SM7 ...52 B5
Holly La East BNSTD SM7 ...51 H1
Holly La West BNSTD SM7 ...51 H2
Hollymead CAR SM5 ...23 H4
Hollymead Rd COUL/CHIP CR5 ...53 E5
Hollymoor La HOR/WEW KT19 ...30 B5
Holly Tree Rd CTHM CR3 * ...59 G3
Holly Wy MTCM CR4 ...14 D3
Hollywoods CROY/NA CR0 ...38 B5
Holman Ct EW KT17 * ...31 E4
Holman Rd HOR/WEW KT19 ...30 A1
Holmbury Ct WIM/MER SW19 ...5 C4
Holmbury Gv CROY/NA CR0 ...38 B5
Holmdene Cl BECK BR3 ...19 E1
Holmesdale Cl SNWD SE25 ...16 D2
Holmesdale Rd CROY/NA CR0 ...16 B4
Holmes Rd WIM/MER SW19 ...5 C4
Holmewood Rd SNWD SE25 ...16 C2
Holmshaw Cl SYD SE26 ...10 A1
Holmwood Av SAND/SEL CR2 ...46 D3
Holmwood Cl BELMT SM2 ...31 H4
Holmwood Gdns WLGTN SM6 ...34 B2
Holmwood Rd BELMT SM2 ...31 G4
Holne Cha MRDN SM4 ...12 C5
The Holt MRDN SM4 * ...24 C5
Home Cl CAR SM5 ...23 H3
Homecroft Rd SYD SE26 ...9 G2
Home Farm Cl EPSOM KT18 ...50 D2
Homefield Gdns
  KWD/TDW/WH KT20 ...50 C5
  WIM/MER SW19 ...13 E1
Homefield Ms BECK BR3 * ...10 C5
Homefield Pk SUT SM1 ...32 D2
Homefield Rd CTHM CR3 ...54 D5
  WARL CR6 ...56 C4
  WIM/MER SW19 ...4 C5
The Homefield MRDN SM4 * ...12 C5
Homeland Dr BELMT SM2 ...32 D4
Homelands Dr NRWD SE19 ...8 C4
Home Meadow BNSTD SM7 ...51 G1
Homemead Rd CROY/NA CR0 ...14 C5
Home Park Rd WIM/MER SW19 ...5 E3
Homer Rd CROY/NA CR0 ...17 H5
Homesdale Rd CTHM CR3 ...59 F3
Homestead Rd CTHM CR3 ...59 F3
Homestead Wy CROY/NA CR0 ...49 E1
Homewood Gdns SNWD SE25 * ...16 C4
Honeysuckle Gdns
  CROY/NA CR0 ...27 H1
Honeywood Wk CAR SM5 ...23 H5
Honister Hts PUR/KEN CR8 ...46 B4
Hood Cl CROY/NA CR0 ...2 B1
Hookfield HOR/WEW KT19 ...40 A5
Hook Hi SAND/SEL CR2 ...46 C5
Hook Rd HOR/WEW KT19 ...30 A5
Hope Cl SUT SM1 ...33 E1
Hope Pk BMLY BR1 ...11 H1
Hopton Pde STRHM/NOR SW16 * ...7 F2
Hopton Rd STRHM/NOR SW16 ...7 F2
Horatius Wy CROY/NA CR0 ...35 H2
Hornchurch Hl CTHM CR3 ...55 H2
Horner La MTCM CR4 ...13 F1
Horsecroft BNSTD SM7 ...51 F2
Horscroft Mdw PUR/KEN CR8 * ...51 G1
The Horseshoe BNSTD SM7 ...42 B5
Horsley Cl HOR/WEW KT19 ...40 B5
Horsley Dr CROY/NA CR0 ...39 E5
Horton Gdns HOR/WEW KT19 ...40 A1
Horton Hl HOR/WEW KT19 ...40 A1
Horton Wy CROY/NA CR0 ...17 H4
Hotham Rd WIM/MER SW19 ...5 H4
Houlder Crs CROY/NA CR0 ...35 H2
Hove Gdns SUT SM1 ...22 D2
Howard Cl HOR/WEW KT19 ...31 E5
Howard Rd COUL/CHIP CR5 ...44 C5
  PGE/AN SE20 ...9 G5
  SNWD SE25 ...17 E4
Howards Crest Cl BECK BR3 ...19 F1
Howberry Rd THHTH CR7 ...8 B5
Howden Rd SNWD SE25 ...16 D1
Howe Dr CTHM CR3 ...59 F2
Howell Hl HOR/WEW KT19 * ...31 G5
Howell Hill Cl EW KT17 ...41 G1
Howell Hill Gv EW KT17 ...41 G1
How La COUL/CHIP CR5 ...53 E5
Howley Rd CROY/NA CR0 ...2 B4
Hoylake Gdns MTCM CR4 ...14 C2
Hoyle Rd TOOT SW17 ...5 C2
Hubbard Rd WNWD SE27 ...8 A1
Hubert Cl WIM/MER SW19 * ...5 F5
Hughenden Rd WPK KT4 ...21 E1
Hughes Wk CROY/NA CR0 ...26 A1
Hulverston Cl BELMT SM2 ...32 D5
Hunston Rd MRDN SM4 ...22 D2
Hunter Cl WLGTN SM6 ...35 E5
Hunter Rd THHTH CR7 ...16 B2
Hunters Cl HOR/WEW KT19 ...40 A3
Hunters Meadow NRWD SE19 ...8 C1
Hunters Wy CROY/NA CR0 ...3 H6
Huntingdon Cl MTCM CR4 ...15 E4
Huntingdon Gdns WPK KT4 ...21 C4
Huntingfield CROY/NA CR0 ...38 B5
Huntly Rd SNWD SE25 ...16 C3
Huntsmans Cl WARL CR6 ...56 C5
Huntsmoor Rd HOR/WEW KT19 ...30 D1
Hurlstone Rd SNWD SE25 ...16 B4
Hurnford Cl SAND/SEL CR2 ...36 C5
Huron Rd TOOT SW17 ...5 E1
Hurst Av WLGTN SM6 ...15 H5
Hurst Cl HAYES BR2 ...29 H2
Hurstcourt Rd SUT SM1 ...22 D2
Hurstdene Av HAYES BR2 ...29 H2
Hurst Cl CROY/NA CR0 ...36 B1
Hurst La EW KT17 * ...40 B1
Hurst View Rd SAND/SEL CR2 ...37 F4
Hurst Wy SAND/SEL CR2 ...36 C2
Hutchinson's Rd CROY/NA CR0 ...49 E1
Hyde Rd SAND/SEL CR2 ...46 C3

Hyde Wk MRDN SM4 ...22 C1
Hylands Ms EPSOM KT18 ...40 A5
Hylands Rd EPSOM KT18 ...40 A5
Hyperion Pl HOR/WEW KT19 ...30 B4
Hythe Rd THHTH CR7 ...16 B1

Iberian Av WLGTN SM6 ...24 D5
Iden Cl HAYES BR2 ...19 G2
Idlecombe Rd TOOT SW17 ...6 A3
Idmiston Rd WPK KT4 ...20 D1
Idmiston Sq WPK KT4 ...20 D1
Ilex Wy STRHM/NOR SW16 ...7 G2
Ilkley Rd NRWD SE19 * ...8 B5
Illingworth Cl MTCM CR4 ...13 F2
Imperial Gdns MTCM CR4 ...14 B2
Imperial Wy CROY/NA CR0 ...35 E2
Inchwood CROY/NA CR0 ...28 D5
Ingatestone Rd SNWD SE25 ...17 F4
Ingham Cl SAND/SEL CR2 ...37 H4
Ingham Rd SAND/SEL CR2 ...37 G4
Ingleboro Dr PUR/KEN CR8 ...46 B5
Ingleby Wy WLGTN SM6 ...34 D4
Inglemere Rd TOOT SW17 ...5 H4
Ingleside Cl BECK BR3 ...10 C4
Ingleton Rd CAR SM5 ...33 G4
Inglewood CROY/NA CR0 ...38 A4
Inglis Rd CROY/NA CR0 ...26 D2
Ingram Rd THHTH CR7 ...8 A5
Innes Cl RYNPK SW20 ...12 A1
Innes Yd CROY/NA CR0 ...2 D5
Inveresk Gdns WPK KT4 ...20 D4
Inverness Rd WPK KT4 ...21 H2
Inwood Av COUL/CHIP CR5 ...53 H5
Inwood Cl CROY/NA CR0 ...28 A3
Iona Cl MRDN SM4 ...22 C2
Ipswich Rd TOOT SW17 ...6 A1
Iris Cl CROY/NA CR0 ...27 H1
Isham Rd STRHM/NOR SW16 ...15 E1
Island Rd MTCM CR4 ...5 H5
Ivers Wy CROY/NA CR0 ...38 D3
ivychurch Cl PGE/AN SE20 ...9 G4
ivydale Rd CAR SM5 ...23 H5
ivydene Cl SUT SM1 ...23 E5
Ivy Gdns MTCM CR4 ...14 D2
Ivy Rd TOOT SW17 ...5 G1

Jackson Cl EPSOM KT18 ...40 B4
Jackson's Pl CROY/NA CR0 ...3 F1
Jackson's Wy CROY/NA CR0 ...28 D1
Jamaica Rd THHTH CR7 ...15 H5
Jarrow Cl MRDN SM4 ...12 D4
Jarvis Rd SAND/SEL CR2 ...36 B2
Jasmine Gdns CROY/NA CR0 ...28 D1
Jasmine Gv PGE/AN SE20 ...9 F5
Jasper Rd NRWD SE19 ...8 D3
Jean Batten Cl CROY/NA CR0 ...35 F3
Jeffs Rd SUT SM1 ...22 B5
Jengar Cl SUT SM1 ...32 D1
Jennett Rd CROY/NA CR0 ...25 C4
Jenson Wy NRWD SE19 ...8 D4
Jeppo's La MTCM CR4 ...13 H5
Jersey Rd TOOT SW17 ...5 H5
Jerviston Gdns
  STRHM/NOR SW16 ...7 G3
Jesmond Cl MTCM CR4 ...14 B1
Jesmond Rd CROY/NA CR0 ...26 D1
Jessops Wy MTCM CR4 ...14 D5
Jews Wk SYD SE26 ...9 F1
Johns La MRDN SM4 ...13 E4
Johnson Cl CROY/NA CR0 ...26 B1
Johnson's Cl CAR SM5 ...23 H4
John's Ter CROY/NA CR0 ...3 F1
John St SNWD SE25 ...17 E3
Johns Wk CTHM CR3 ...56 A4
Jonson Cl MTCM CR4 ...14 B3
Jordan Cl SAND/SEL CR2 ...47 E5
Josephine Av KWD/TDW/WH KT20 ...50 D5
Jubilee Rd CHEAM SM3 ...31 H5
Jubilee Wy WIM/MER SW19 ...4 D5
Julien Rd COUL/CHIP CR5 ...44 C5
Junction Rd SAND/SEL CR2 ...36 B2
June Cl COUL/CHIP CR5 ...44 C4
Juniper Gdns MTCM CR4 ...6 C5

Kangley Bridge Rd SYD SE26 ...10 B2
Karen Ct BMLY BR1 ...11 H1
Katharine St CROY/NA CR0 ...2 D4
Kayemoor Rd BELMT SM2 ...33 G3
Kearton Cl PUR/KEN CR8 ...54 D2
Keats Cl WIM/MER SW19 ...5 F3
Keats Wy CROY/NA CR0 ...17 G5
Keble Cl WPK KT4 ...20 D2
Keble St TOOT SW17 ...5 E1
Keedonwood Rd BMLY BR1 ...11 H1
Keeley Rd CROY/NA CR0 ...2 C3
Keens Rd STRHM/NOR SW16 ...6 D1
Keen's Rd CROY/NA CR0 ...2 D6
Kelling Gdns CROY/NA CR0 ...25 H1
Kellino St TOOT SW17 ...5 H1
Kelsey La BECK BR3 ...18 D2
Kelsey Park Av BECK BR3 ...18 D2
Kelsey Park Rd BECK BR3 ...18 C1
Kelsey Sq BECK BR3 ...18 C1

Kelsey Wy BECK BR3 ...18 C2
Kelso Rd CAR SM5 ...23 E1
Kelvin Gdns CROY/NA CR0 ...25 E1
Kelvington Cl CROY/NA CR0 ...28 A1
Kemble Rd CROY/NA CR0 ...2 A4
Kemerton Rd BECK BR3 ...18 D1
  CROY/NA CR0 ...26 D1
Kemp Gdns CROY/NA CR0 ...16 A5
Kempshott Rd
  STRHM/NOR SW16 ...7 E4
Kempton Wk CROY/NA CR0 ...18 A1
Kemsing Cl THHTH CR7 * ...16 A3
Kendal Av BMLY BR1 ...11 G2
Kendall Av BECK BR3 ...18 A1
Kendall Av South
  SAND/SEL CR2 ...36 B4
Kendal Gdns SUT SM1 ...23 E3
Kendall Av BECK BR3 ...18 A1
  SAND/SEL CR2 ...36 B4
Kendal Rd South
  SAND/SEL CR2 ...36 A5
Kendal Rd BECK BR3 ...18 A1
Kendra Hall Rd SAND/SEL CR2 ...35 H5
Kenilworth Av WIM/MER SW19 ...4 C2
Kenilworth Cl BNSTD SM7 ...51 H1
Kenilworth Rd EW KT17 ...31 G2
  PGE/AN SE20 ...10 A5
Kenilworth Ter BELMT SM2 ...32 C3
Kenley Cl CTHM CR3 ...55 H4
Kenley Gdns THHTH CR7 ...15 H3
Kenley La PUR/KEN CR8 ...46 A5
Kenley Rd WIM/MER SW19 ...12 C2
Kenley Wk CHEAM SM3 ...21 H5
Kenlor Rd TOOT SW17 ...5 E2
Kenmara Cl ...5 H4
Kenmare Dr MTCM CR4 ...5 H4
Kenmare Rd THHTH CR7 ...15 H5
Kennedy Cl MTCM CR4 ...14 A1
Kennel Wood Crs CROY/NA CR0 ...49 F1
Kenneth Rd BNSTD SM7 ...51 G1
Kenny Dr CAR SM5 ...34 A4
Kensington Av THHTH CR7 ...7 G5
Kensington Ter SAND/SEL CR2 ...36 B5
Kent Cl STRHM/NOR SW16 ...15 E3
Kent Gate Wy CROY/NA CR0 ...38 B2
Kent House La BECK BR3 ...10 A3
Kent House Rd BECK BR3 ...9 H4
Kent Rd WWKM BR4 ...28 D2
Kenwood Dr BECK BR3 ...19 F2
Kenwood Rdg PUR/KEN CR8 ...54 D2
Kerrill Av COUL/CHIP CR5 ...54 C4
Kersey Dr SAND/SEL CR2 ...47 E5
Keston Av COUL/CHIP CR5 ...53 H5
Keston Rd THHTH CR7 ...15 H5
Kestrel Wy CROY/NA CR0 ...39 F4
Keswick Av WIM/MER SW19 ...12 C1
Keswick Cl SUT SM1 ...23 E5
Keswick Rd WWKM BR4 ...29 G3
Kettering St STRHM/NOR SW16 ...6 D3
Kew Crs CHEAM SM3 ...22 B4
Keynsham Rd MRDN SM4 ...22 D2
Khama Rd TOOT SW17 ...5 G1
Khartoum Rd TOOT SW17 ...5 E1
Kidderminster Pl CROY/NA CR0 ...25 H2
Kidderminster Rd CROY/NA CR0 ...25 H2
Kilcorral Cl EW KT17 ...41 G3
Kilburns Mill Cl WLGTN SM6 ...24 B4
Killester Gdns EW KT17 ...21 F5
Kilmartin Av STRHM/NOR SW16 ...15 F4
Kiln La EW KT17 ...40 D2
Kiln Ms TOOT SW17 ...5 E2
Kimberley Pl PUR/KEN CR8 ...45 G1
Kimberley Rd BECK BR3 ...17 H1
  CROY/NA CR0 ...15 H5
Kimble Rd WIM/MER SW19 ...5 H3
Kimpton Rd CHEAM SM3 ...22 A3
King Alfred Av CAT SE6 ...10 C1
Kingcup Cl CROY/NA CR0 ...27 H1
Kingfisher Gdns SAND/SEL CR2 ...37 H5
Kingfisher Wy CROY/NA CR0 ...35 H1
King George VI Av MTCM CR4 ...13 H3
King Henry's Dr CROY/NA CR0 ...39 E5
Kings Av CAR SM5 ...33 G3
Kingsbridge Rd MRDN SM4 ...22 C1
Kingscote Rd CROY/NA CR0 ...27 F1
Kingscroft Rd BNSTD SM7 ...43 F5
Kingsdale Rd PGE/AN SE20 ...10 A5
Kingsdown Av SAND/SEL CR2 ...46 B1
Kingsdown Rd CHEAM SM3 ...32 A1
  EW KT17 ...41 E5
Kings Hall Rd BECK BR3 ...9 H4
Kings Keep HAYES BR2 * ...29 H5
King's La SUT SM1 ...33 F1
Kingsleigh Pl MTCM CR4 ...13 H2
Kingsleigh Wk HAYES BR2 ...19 H5
Kingsley Av BNSTD SM7 ...42 C5
  SUT SM1 ...23 F5
Kingsley Rd WPK KT4 ...20 D2
  WIM/MER SW19 ...4 D2
Kingslyn Crs NRWD SE19 ...8 C5
Kingsmead Av MTCM CR4 ...14 C2
  WPK KT4 ...21 F2
Kingsmead Cl HOR/WEW KT19 ...30 B3
Kings Pde CAR SM5 * ...23 C4
Kings Rd BELMT SM2 ...32 C5
  MTCM CR4 ...5 H1
  SNWD SE25 ...17 E2
Kings Shade Wk
  HOR/WEW KT19 * ...40 B3
Kingsthorpe Rd SYD SE26 ...9 H1
Kingston Av CHEAM SM3 ...22 A4
Kingston Crs BECK BR3 ...10 B5
Kingston Gdns CROY/NA CR0 ...25 E3
Kingston Rd WIM/MER SW19 ...13 E1
  RYNPK SW20 ...12 A1
  WIM/MER SW19 ...12 A1
Kingston Sq NRWD SE19 ...8 C3
Kings Wk SAND/SEL CR2 ...47 F4
Kingsway CROY/NA CR0 ...35 F1
Kingsway WWKM BR4 ...29 H4
Kingsway Av SAND/SEL CR2 ...37 E5
Kingsway Rd CHEAM SM3 ...31 H1
The Kingsway EW KT17 ...30 D5

Kingswood Av HAYES BR2 ...19 G5
  SAND/SEL CR2 ...47 F5
  THHTH CR7 ...15 G4
Kingswood Dr BELMT SM2 ...32 D4
  CAR SM5 ...23 H2
  NRWD SE19 ...8 D3
Kingswood La WARL CR6 ...47 G5
  PGE/AN SE20 ...9 G3
Kingswood Wy SAND/SEL CR2 ...47 H2
  WLGTN SM6 ...35 E5
Kingsworth Cl BECK BR3 ...18 A4
Kinloss Rd CAR SM5 ...23 E1
Kinnaird Av BMLY BR1 ...11 H3
Kinnaird Cl BMLY BR1 ...11 H3
Kinross Av WPK KT4 ...21 E5
Kintyre Cl STRHM/NOR SW16 ...15 F3
Kinver Rd SYD SE26 ...9 G1
Kipling Dr WIM/MER SW19 ...5 F3
Kirby Cl HOR/WEW KT19 ...30 D1
Kirkdale SYD SE26 ...9 F1
Kirkdale Cnr SYD SE26 * ...9 F2
Kirkland Ter BECK BR3 ...17 H4
Kirklees Rd THHTH CR7 ...15 G4
Kirkley Rd WIM/MER SW19 ...4 C5
Kirkly Cl SAND/SEL CR2 ...36 C4
Kirksted Rd MRDN SM4 ...22 D2
Kirkstone Wy BMLY BR1 ...11 G1
Kirkville Rd SYD SE26 ...10 B1
Kitchener Rd THHTH CR7 ...16 B1
Kitley Gdns NRWD SE19 ...8 D5
Kittiwake Cl SAND/SEL CR2 ...38 A5
Knapton Ms TOOT SW17 ...5 H2
Kneller Rd NWMAL KT3 ...20 C1
Knighton Cl SAND/SEL CR2 ...35 H4
Knighton Park Rd SYD SE26 ...9 H2
Knight's Hl WNWD SE27 ...7 H2
Knight's Hill Sq WNWD SE27 * ...7 H1
Knole Cl CROY/NA CR0 ...17 G5
Knollmead BRYLDS KT5 ...20 A2
Knolls Cl WPK KT4 ...21 G2
The Knolls EW KT17 ...50 C1
The Knoll BECK BR3 ...10 D5
Knowlton Gn HAYES BR2 ...19 H4
Kohat Rd WIM/MER SW19 ...4 D2
Kooringa WARL CR6 ...56 B4
Kuala Gdns STRHM/NOR SW16 ...15 H1
Kynaston Av THHTH CR7 ...16 A4
Kynaston Cl CTHM CR3 ...59 C5
Kynaston Crs THHTH CR7 ...16 A4
Kynaston Rd THHTH CR7 ...16 A4
Kynersley Cl CAR SM5 ...23 H4

Laburnum Av SUT SM1 ...23 G4
Laburnum Gdns CROY/NA CR0 ...27 H1
Laburnum Rd EPSOM KT18 ...40 C3
  MTCM CR4 ...14 A1
  WIM/MER SW19 ...5 H5
Lacey Av COUL/CHIP CR5 ...54 C5
Lacey Dr COUL/CHIP CR5 ...54 C5
Lackford Rd COUL/CHIP CR5 ...52 D3
Lacock Cl WIM/MER SW19 ...5 H3
Lacrosse Wy STRHM/NOR SW16 ...6 D5
Ladas Rd WNWD SE27 ...8 A2
Ladbroke Rd EPSOM KT18 ...40 B4
Ladbrook Rd SNWD SE25 ...16 B2
Ladygrove CROY/NA CR0 ...38 A4
Lady Hay WPK KT4 ...20 D3
Ladymount WLGTN SM6 ...24 D5
Laings Av MTCM CR4 ...13 H1
Lake Gdns WLGTN SM6 ...24 B4
Lakehall Gdns THHTH CR7 ...15 H4
Lakehall Rd THHTH CR7 ...15 H4
Lakehurst Rd HOR/WEW KT19 ...30 C1
Lake Rd CROY/NA CR0 ...28 A3
  WIM/MER SW19 ...4 B2
Lakers Ri BNSTD SM7 ...52 C1
Lakeside BECK BR3 ...19 E1
  HOR/WEW KT19 ...30 C2
  WLGTN SM6 ...24 B5
Lakeside Cl SNWD SE25 ...17 E1
Lakeview Rd WNWD SE27 ...7 G2
Laleham Cl SUT SM1 * ...33 E1
Lamberhurst Rd WNWD SE27 ...7 G1
Lambert Rd BNSTD SM7 ...42 C4
Lambert's Pl CROY/NA CR0 ...26 D2
Lambeth Rd CROY/NA CR0 ...25 G2
Lambourne Av WIM/MER SW19 ...4 D3
Lamerock Rd BMLY BR1 ...11 H1
Lammas Av MTCM CR4 ...14 A1
Lancaster Av MTCM CR4 ...15 E4
Lancaster Cl PUR/KEN CR8 ...45 H3
Lancaster Gdns WIM/MER SW19 ...4 A2
Lancaster Rd SNWD SE25 ...16 D1
Lancaster Wy WPK KT4 ...21 C1
Lancastrian Rd WLGTN SM6 ...35 E3
Lancing Rd CROY/NA CR0 ...15 F5
Landgrove Rd WIM/MER SW19 ...4 C2
Landscape Rd WARL CR6 ...56 B4
Landseer Rd CHEAM SM3 ...31 H3
  NWMAL KT3 ...20 B1
  SUT SM1 ...32 C2
Langcroft Cl CAR SM5 ...23 H4
Langdale Av MTCM CR4 ...13 H3
Langdale Pde MTCM CR4 * ...13 H2
Langdale Rd THHTH CR7 ...15 H4
Langdon Rd MRDN SM4 ...13 E4
Langdon Wk MRDN SM4 ...13 E4
Langham Dene PUR/KEN CR8 ...45 H5
Langham Park Pl HAYES BR2 ...19 H3
Langland Gdns CROY/NA CR0 ...28 B5
Langlands Ri HOR/WEW KT19 ...40 A3
Langley Av WPK KT4 ...21 H1
Langley Ct BECK BR3 * ...18 D3
Langley Oaks Av SAND/SEL CR2 ...37 E5

Langley Park Rd BELMT SM2 ...33 E2
Langley Rd BECK BR3 ...17 H3
  SAND/SEL CR2 ...37 H4
  WIM/MER SW19 ...4 B5
Langley Wy WWKM BR4 ...29 F2
Langley Wd BECK BR3 * ...19 G4
Langmead St WNWD SE27 ...19 F4
Langton Av EW KT17 ...40 D1
Langton Wy CROY/NA CRO ...3 H6
Lankton Cl BECK BR3 ...11 E5
Lansdell Rd MTCM CR4 ...14 A1
Lansdowne Copse WPK KT4 * ...21 E3
Lansdowne Ct WPK KT4 ...21 E3
Lansdowne Pl NRWD SE19 ...8 D4
Lansdowne Rd CROY/NA CRO ...2 D2
  HOR/WEW KT19 ...30 A3
  PUR/KEN CR8 ...45 G2
Lapwing Cl CROY/NA CRO ...58 A5
Larbert Rd STRHM/NOR SW16 ...15 F5
Larby Pl EW KT17 ...30 D5
Larch Cl WARL CR6 ...57 E4
Larch Tree Wy CROY/NA CRO ...4 A1
Larchwood Cl BNSTD SM7 ...51 E3
Larcombe Cl CROY/NA CRO ...3 J7
Lardkbere Rd SYD SE26 ...10 A1
Larkin Cl COUL/CHIP CR5 ...54 B2
Larkspur Wy HOR/WEW KT19 ...30 A4
Lark Wy CAR SM5 ...23 G1
Latham's Wy CROY/NA CRO ...25 F2
Latimer Cl WPK KT4 ...21 G1
Latimer Rd CROY/NA CRO ...2 B4
  WIM/MER SW19 ...4 D3
Laud St CROY/NA CRO ...2 C5
Laurel Cl TOOT SW17 ...5 H2
Laurel Crs CROY/NA CRO ...28 C4
Laurel Gv SYD SE26 ...10 A2
The Laurels BNSTD SM7 ...51 F2
Laurier Rd CROY/NA CRO ...26 D1
Lavender Av MTCM CR4 ...5 H5
  WPK KT4 ...21 G4
Lavender Cl CAR SM5 ...24 A5
  COUL/CHIP CR5 * ...54 D5
  CTHM CR3 ...59 E5
Lavender Gv MTCM CR4 ...5 H5
Lavender Rd CAR SM5 ...24 A5
  CROY/NA CRO ...15 F5
  SUT SM1 ...23 F5
Lavender V WLGTN SM6 ...23 G5
Lavender Wy CROY/NA CRO ...17 H5
Lavington Rd CROY/NA CRO ...2 B4
Lawdon Gdns CROY/NA CRO ...2 B6
Lawford Gdns PUR/KEN CR8 ...55 E1
Lawn Rd BECK BR3 ...10 C4
The Lawns BELMT SM2 ...32 A3
  NRWD SE19 ...8 C4
Lawrence Av NWMAL KT3 ...20 C1
Lawrence Rd SNWD SE25 ...16 D3
Lawrie Park Av SYD SE26 ...9 F2
Lawrie Park Crs SYD SE26 ...9 F2
Lawrie Park Gdns SYD SE26 ...9 F2
Lawrie Park Rd SYD SE26 ...9 F3
Laws Cl THHTH CR7 ...16 B5
Lawson Wk CAR SM5 ...33 H5
Layard Rd THHTH CR7 ...16 B1
Layhams Rd WWKM BR4 ...29 G5
Layton Crs CROY/NA CRO ...2 B7
Lea Cots MTCM CR4 ...14 A1
Leacroft Cl PUR/KEN CR8 ...55 E1
Leaf Gv STRHM/NOR SW16 ...7 C2
Leafield Cl STRHM/NOR SW16 ...7 H3
Leafield Rd RYNPK SW20 ...12 B2
  SUT SM1 ...22 C3
Leafy Wy CROY/NA CRO ...3 K3
Leamington Av MRDN SM4 ...12 B3
Leander Rd THHTH CR7 ...15 F3
Lea Rd BECK BR3 ...18 C1
Leas La WARL CR6 ...56 D5
Leas Rd WARL CR6 ...56 D5
Leather Cl MTCM CR4 ...6 A1
Leather Ct MTCM CR4 * ...6 A1
Leaveland Cl BECK BR3 ...18 C5
Leazes Av CTHM CR3 ...58 C3
Lebanon Rd CROY/NA CRO ...3 H1
Ledbury Rd CROY/NA CRO ...2 E7
Ledgers Rd WARL CR6 ...57 G1
Ledrington Rd NRWD SE19 ...9 E3
Leechcroft Rd WLGTN SM6 ...24 A4
Lee Rd WIM/MER SW19 ...4 D5
The Lees CROY/NA CRO ...28 B5
Leeward Gdns RYNPK SW20 ...12 D1
The Leeways CHEAM SM3 * ...32 A2
Leicester Av MTCM CR4 ...15 E3
Leicester Cl WPK KT4 ...21 G5
Leicester Rd CROY/NA CRO ...26 C1
Leigh Crs CROY/NA CRO ...38 D5
Leighton Gdns SAND/SEL CR2 ...47 F3
Leighton St CROY/NA CRO ...2 A1
Leighton Wy EPSOM KT18 ...40 B4
Leithcote Gdns
  STRHM/NOR SW16 ...7 F1
Leith Rd EW KT17 ...40 C2
Leith Towers BELMT SM2 * ...32 A4
Lenham Rd SUT SM1 ...22 D5
  THHTH CR7 ...16 C1
Lennard Av WWKM BR4 ...29 H4
Lennard Cl WWKM BR4 ...29 G3
Lennard Rd CROY/NA CRO ...26 A2
  PGE/AN SE20 ...9 H3
Lennard Ter SYD SE26 * ...9 H3
Lennox Gdns CROY/NA CRO ...2 B6
Leof Crs CAT SE6 ...10 D2
Leominster Rd MRDN SM4 ...13 E5
Leominster Wk MRDN SM4 ...13 E5
Leonard Av MRDN SM4 ...13 E4
Leonard Rd MTCM CR4 ...6 C5
Leopold Av WIM/MER SW19 ...4 B2
Leopold Rd WIM/MER SW19 ...4 B2
Le Personne Rd CTHM CR3 ...59 F2
Leslie Gdns BELMT SM2 ...32 C3
Leslie Grove Cl CROY/NA CRO ...26 C2
Leslie Grove Pl CROY/NA CRO ...3 H1
Leslie Park Rd CROY/NA CRO ...3 H1
Lessingham Av TOOT SW17 ...5 H1
Lessness Rd MRDN SM4 ...13 E5
Lestock Cl SNWD SE25 ...17 E2

Letchworth St TOOT SW17 ...5 H1
Leveret Cl CROY/NA CRO ...49 F1
Leverson St STRHM/NOR SW16 ...6 C3
Lewin Rd STRHM/NOR SW16 ...6 D3
Lewis Rd MTCM CR4 ...13 G1
  SUT SM1 ...22 D5
Lewiston Cl WPK KT4 ...21 F1
Lexden Rd MTCM CR4 ...14 D3
Lexington Ct PUR/KEN CR8 ...36 A5
Leyburn Gdns CROY/NA CRO ...3 H3
Leyfield WPK KT4 ...20 C3
Leyton Rd WIM/MER SW19 ...5 E4
Liberty Av WIM/MER SW19 ...5 F5
Lichfield Wy SAND/SEL CR2 ...37 H5
Lilac Gdns CROY/NA CRO ...28 C4
Lilah Ms HAYES BR2 ...19 H1
Lilian Rd MTCM CR4 ...6 C5
Lilleshall Rd MRDN SM4 ...13 F5
Limecroft Cl HOR/WEW KT19 ...30 B5
Lime Gv WARL CR6 ...57 E4
Lime Meadow Av
  SAND/SEL CR2 ...47 E3
Limes Av CAR SM5 ...23 H2
  CROY/NA CRO ...25 F4
  PGE/AN SE20 ...9 G4
Limes Cl CAR SM5 ...23 H1
Limes Rd BECK BR3 ...18 D1
  CROY/NA CRO ...16 B5
Lime Tree Gv CROY/NA CRO ...28 B4
Limetree Pl MTCM CR4 ...6 B1
Lime Tree Wk WWKM BR4 ...29 H5
Limewood Cl BECK BR3 ...19 E4
Limpsfield Av THHTH CR7 ...15 F4
Limpsfield Rd SAND/SEL CR2 ...47 E2
Lincoln Rd MTCM CR4 ...15 E4
  SNWD SE25 ...17 G3
  WPK KT4 ...21 F2
Lincoln Ter BELMT SM2 * ...32 C3
Linden Av COUL/CHIP CR5 ...53 F1
  THHTH CR7 ...15 H3
Linden Cl KWD/TDW/WH KT20 ...50 D5
Linden Cots WIM/MER SW19 * ...4 A5
Linden Gr CTHM CR3 ...59 E4
Linden Gv SYD SE26 ...9 H4
  WARL CR6 ...57 E3
Linden Leas WWKM BR4 ...29 F3
Linden Pl EW KT17 ...40 C2
The Lindens CROY/NA CRO ...13 G5
Linden Wy WLGTN SM6 ...34 C5
Lindfield Rd CROY/NA CRO ...16 D5
Lindores Rd CAR SM5 ...23 E1
Lind Rd SUT SM1 ...33 E1
Lindsay Dr HOR/WEW KT19 ...40 A3
Lindsay Rd WPK KT4 ...21 G1
Lindsey Cl MTCM CR4 ...15 E3
Lindway WNWD SE27 ...7 H2
Lingfield Gdns COUL/CHIP CR5 ...54 D4
Lingfield Rd WPK KT4 ...21 G2
Link La WLGTN SM6 ...34 D2
Link Rd WLGTN SM6 ...23 G2
Links Av MRDN SM4 ...12 C3
Links Gdns STRHM/NOR SW16 ...7 G4
Link's Rd EW KT17 ...41 E3
  TOOT SW17 ...6 A3
  WWKM BR4 ...29 E2
Links View Rd CROY/NA CRO ...28 D2
Links Wy BECK BR3 ...18 C5
The Linkway BELMT SM2 ...33 E4
Linnet Cl SAND/SEL CR2 ...37 H5
Linton Cl MTCM CR4 ...14 A5
Linton Gv CROY/NA CRO ...38 A5
Linton Gv WNWD SE27 ...7 H3
Linton's La EW KT17 ...40 C2
Lion Green Rd COUL/CHIP CR5 ...44 D5
Lion Rd CROY/NA CRO ...16 A4
Lipsham Cl BNSTD SM7 ...43 F3
Lisle Cl TOOT SW17 ...6 B1
Lismore Cl WIM/MER SW19 * ...3 J3
Lismore Rd SAND/SEL CR2 ...36 C2
Lissoms Rd COUL/CHIP CR5 ...53 E3
Lister Cl WIM/MER SW19 ...5 G5
Litchfield Av MRDN SM4 ...22 B1
Litchfield Rd SUT SM1 ...33 E1
Little Acre BECK BR3 ...18 C2
Little Bornes DUL SE21 ...8 C1
Littlebrook Cl CROY/NA CRO ...17 H5
Little Ct WWKM BR4 ...29 G3
Littleheath Rd SAND/SEL CR2 ...37 F4
Little Orchards EPSOM KT18 ...40 C4
Little Roke Av PUR/KEN CR8 ...45 H4
Little Roke Rd PUR/KEN CR8 ...45 H4
Littlers Cl WIM/MER SW19 ...5 F5
Littlestone Cl BECK BR3 ...10 C3
Little Woodcote Est
  WLGTN SM6 ...34 B5
Little Woodcote La CAR SM5 ...34 B2
Liverpool Rd THHTH CR7 ...16 A2
Livingstone Rd CTHM CR3 ...59 F2
  THHTH CR7 ...16 B1
Llanthony Rd MRDN SM4 ...13 F5
Lloyd Av COUL/CHIP CR5 ...44 A4
  STRHM/NOR SW16 ...15 H1
Lloyd Park Av CROY/NA CRO ...3 J7
Lloyd Rd WPK KT4 ...21 G4
Lloyds Wy BECK BR3 ...18 A4
Lock's La MTCM CR4 ...6 A5
Lockwood Cl SYD SE26 ...9 H1
Lodge Av CROY/NA CRO ...25 F4
Lodge Cl EW KT17 ...31 E5
  WLGTN SM6 ...24 A2
Lodge Gdns BECK BR3 ...18 B4
Lodge Hl PUR/KEN CR8 ...45 G5
Lodge La CROY/NA CRO ...38 D3
Lodge Pl SUT SM1 ...32 D1
Lodge Rd CROY/NA CRO ...16 A4
  SUT SM1 ...32 D1
  WLGTN SM6 ...24 A3
Lodge Wk WARL CR6 ...57 G1
Lomas Cl CROY/NA CRO ...39 E3
Lombard Rd WIM/MER SW19 ...12 D1
Lomond Gdns SAND/SEL CR2 ...48 A5
London La BMLY BR1 ...11 H4
London Loop BNSTD SM7 ...42 B3

  COUL/CHIP CR5 ...54 A4
  CROY/NA CRO ...27 H4
  PUR/KEN CR8 ...55 F5
  WWKM BR4 ...29 F4
London Rd BMLY BR1 ...11 H4
  CROY/NA CRO ...25 H2
  CTHM CR3 ...59 F3
  EW KT17 ...31 F1
  MRDN SM4 ...12 C4
  MTCM CR4 ...24 A1
  STRHM/NOR SW16 ...15 H5
  WLGTN SM6 ...24 B5
Lonesome Wy MTCM CR4 ...14 A5
Longacre Pl CAR SM5 * ...34 A2
Longcroft Av BNSTD SM7 ...43 H3
Longdown La North EW KT17 ...41 E3
Longdown La South EW KT17 ...41 E5
Longdown Rd CAT SE6 ...10 C1
  EW KT17 ...41 E4
Longfellow Rd WPK KT4 ...21 F3
Longfield BMLY BR1 ...11 H5
Longfield Av WLGTN SM6 ...24 A2
Longfield Crs
  KWD/TDW/WH KT20 ...50 C5
Longfield Dr WIM/MER SW19 ...5 C5
Longford Ct HOR/WEW KT19 ...20 A5
Longford Gdns SUT SM1 ...23 E5
Long Grove Rd HOR/WEW KT19 ...30 A5
  PUR/KEN CR8 ...44 D1
Longheath Gdns CROY/NA CRO ...17 G4
Long Hl CTHM CR3 ...61 E1
Longhurst Rd CROY/NA CRO ...17 F5
Longlands Av COUL/CHIP CR5 ...44 B4
Long La CROY/NA CRO ...17 F4
Longley Rd CROY/NA CRO ...25 H1
  TOOT SW17 ...5 G3
Longmead Cl CTHM CR3 ...59 G4
Long Meadow Cl BECK BR3 ...29 E1
Longmead Rd HOR/WEW KT19 ...30 C5
  TOOT SW17 ...5 H2
Longmere Gdns
  KWD/TDW/WH KT20 ...50 C5
Longsdon Wy CTHM CR3 ...60 A4
Longstone Rd
  STRHM/NOR SW16 ...6 B2
Longthornton Rd
  STRHM/NOR SW16 ...14 C1
Longton Av SYD SE26 ...9 E5
Longton Gv SYD SE26 ...9 F5
Long Wk EPSOM KT18 ...50 D4
Longwood Ct WPK KT4 ...21 E3
Longwood Rd PUR/KEN CR8 ...55 F3
Lonsdale Gdns
  STRHM/NOR SW16 ...15 F3
Lonsdale Rd SNWD SE25 ...17 F3
Lordsbury Fld WLGTN SM6 ...34 C5
Lordsgrove Cl
  KWD/TDW/WH KT20 ...50 B5
Lorne Av CROY/NA CRO ...27 H1
Lorne Gdns CROY/NA CRO ...27 H1
Loubet St TOOT SW17 ...5 H5
Love La CHEAM SM3 ...32 A2
  MRDN SM4 ...12 D5
  MTCM CR4 ...13 G2
  SNWD SE25 ...17 F3
Lovelock Cl PUR/KEN CR8 ...55 E2
Lovett Dr CAR SM5 ...23 E1
Lower Addiscombe Rd
  CROY/NA CRO ...3 J1
Lower Barn Rd PUR/KEN CR8 ...46 A2
Lower Church St CROY/NA CRO ...2 B5
Lower Coombe St CROY/NA CRO ...2 C6
Lower Ct HOR/WEW KT19 ...40 B1
Lower Court Rd
  HOR/WEW KT19 ...40 A1
Lower Dunnymans BNSTD SM7 ...42 B4
Lower Green Gdns WPK KT4 ...21 E2
Lower Gn West MTCM CR4 ...13 G2
Lower Morden La MRDN SM4 ...12 A5
Lower Northfield BNSTD SM7 ...42 B4
Lower Park Rd BNSTD SM7 ...52 C3
Lower Pillory Down CAR SM5 ...44 A3
Lower Rd PUR/KEN CR8 ...45 H3
Lower Sawleywood
  BNSTD SM7 * ...42 B4
Lowry Crs MTCM CR4 ...13 G1
Loxford Rd CTHM CR3 ...59 H5
Loxford Wy CTHM CR3 ...59 H5
Loxley Cl SYD SE26 ...9 H3
Lucas Rd PGE/AN SE20 ...9 G3
Lucerne Rd THHTH CR7 ...15 H4
Lucien Rd TOOT SW17 ...6 A1
Ludford Cl CROY/NA CRO ...2 A5
Lullington Garth BMLY BR1 * ...11 G4
Lullington Rd PGE/AN SE20 ...9 E4
Lulworth Crs MTCM CR4 ...13 G1
Lumley Gdns CHEAM SM3 ...32 A1
Lumley Rd CHEAM SM3 ...32 A2
Luna Rd THHTH CR7 ...16 A2
Lunghurst Rd CTHM CR3 ...61 G1
Lunham Rd NRWD SE19 ...8 D3
Lupin Cl CROY/NA CRO ...28 A5
Lushington Rd CAT SE6 ...10 D2
Lyall Av DUL SE21 ...8 C1
Lyconby Gdns CROY/NA CRO ...28 A1
Lyle Cl MTCM CR4 ...14 A5
Lymbourne Cl BELMT SM2 ...32 C5
Lymer Av NRWD SE19 ...8 D2
Lyme Regis Rd BNSTD SM7 ...51 F2
Lymescote Gdns SUT SM1 ...22 C3
Lymington Cl
  STRHM/NOR SW16 ...14 D1
Lymington Gdns
  HOR/WEW KT19 ...30 D4
Lyncroft Gdns EW KT17 ...30 D4
Lyndhurst Av
  STRHM/NOR SW16 ...14 D1
Lyndhurst Cl CROY/NA CRO ...3 J5
Lyndhurst Ct BELMT SM2 * ...32 C5
Lyndhurst Leys HAYES BR2 * ...19 F1
Lyndhurst Prior SNWD SE25 * ...16 C2
Lyndhurst Rd COUL/CHIP CR5 ...53 E1
  THHTH CR7 ...15 G3

Lyndhurst Wy BELMT SM2 ...32 C4
Lyndon Av WLGTN SM6 ...24 A4
Lyndon Yd TOOT SW17 ...5 F1
Lynmouth Av MRDN SM4 ...21 H1
Lynne Cl SAND/SEL CR2 ...47 G1
Lynscott Wy SAND/SEL CR2 ...35 H4
Lynsted Ct BECK BR3 * ...17 H1
Lynton Rd CROY/NA CRO ...16 B4
Lynwood Av COUL/CHIP CR5 ...44 B5
  EW KT17 ...40 D4
Lynwood Dr WPK KT4 ...21 E3
Lynwood Gdns CROY/NA CRO ...25 F3
Lynwood Rd EW KT17 ...40 D4
Lynwood Ter WIM/MER SW19 * ...4 B5
Lyon Rd WIM/MER SW19 ...5 E5
Lyric Ms SYD SE26 ...9 G1
Lysander Rd CROY/NA CRO ...35 F2
Lytchgate Cl SAND/SEL CR2 ...36 C5
Lytton Gdns WLGTN SM6 ...24 C4
Lyveden Rd WIM/MER SW19 ...5 G3

M

Maberley Crs NRWD SE19 ...9 E4
Maberley Rd BECK BR3 ...17 H2
  NRWD SE19 ...8 D5
Macaulay Rd CTHM CR3 ...59 G2
Macclesfield Rd SNWD SE25 ...17 F4
Mackenzie Rd BECK BR3 ...10 A5
Macmillan Wy TOOT SW17 ...6 B1
Madeira Av BMLY BR1 ...11 G5
Madeira Rd MTCM CR4 ...13 H5
  STRHM/NOR SW16 ...7 E2
Madeira Wk EW KT17 ...40 B4
Madeline Rd PGE/AN SE20 ...9 E4
Magazine Rd CTHM CR3 ...58 D2
Magdala Rd SAND/SEL CR2 ...36 B3
Magnolia Wy HOR/WEW KT19 ...30 A4
Magpie Cl COUL/CHIP CR5 ...53 G3
Maidenshaw Rd
  HOR/WEW KT19 ...40 B2
The Maisonettes SUT SM1 * ...32 B1
Malcolm Cl PGE/AN SE20 * ...9 G4
Malcolm Rd COUL/CHIP CR5 ...44 D5
  PGE/AN SE20 ...9 G4
  SNWD SE25 ...17 E5
Malden Av SNWD SE25 ...17 F3
Malden Green Av WPK KT4 ...21 E2
Malden Rd CHEAM SM3 ...31 G2
  NWMAL KT3 ...20 D1
Maldon Rd WLGTN SM6 ...34 B1
Mallard Rd SAND/SEL CR2 ...37 H5
Mallard Wk CROY/NA CRO ...17 H4
Mallard Wy WLGTN SM6 ...34 C4
Malling Cl CROY/NA CRO * ...17 H4
Malling Gdns MRDN SM4 ...13 E5
Mallinson Rd CROY/NA CRO ...24 D4
Mallory Cl BECK BR3 ...18 A4
Mallow Cl CROY/NA CRO ...27 H2
  KWD/TDW/WH KT20 ...50 B4
Malmains Cl BECK BR3 ...19 F4
Malmains Wy BECK BR3 ...19 E4
Malmesbury Rd MRDN SM4 ...23 E1
The Maltings SNWD SE25 * ...14 C2
Malvern Cl MTCM CR4 ...14 C2
Malvern Rd THHTH CR7 ...15 H2
Manchester Rd THHTH CR7 ...16 A2
Mandeville Cl WIM/MER SW19 ...4 A4
Mann Cl CROY/NA CRO ...2 C6
Manor Av CTHM CR3 ...59 G4
Manor Cl WPK KT4 ...20 C2
Manor Dr HOR/WEW KT19 ...30 C2
Manor Dr North NWMAL KT3 ...20 C2
The Manor Dr WPK KT4 ...20 C2
Manor Farm Rd
  STRHM/NOR SW16 ...15 H2
Manor Gdns RYNPK SW20 ...12 B1
  SAND/SEL CR2 ...36 D2
Manor Green Rd
  HOR/WEW KT19 ...40 A2
Manor Gv BECK BR3 ...18 D1
Manor Hl BNSTD SM7 ...52 B2
Manor House Ct EPSOM KT18 * ...40 A2
Manor La SUT SM1 ...33 E1
Manor Park Cl WWKM BR4 ...28 D1
Manor Park Rd SUT SM1 ...32 D1
  WWKM BR4 ...28 D5
Manor Pl MTCM CR4 ...14 C2
  SUT SM1 ...32 D1
Manor Rd BECK BR3 ...18 D1
  BELMT SM2 ...32 B3
  MTCM CR4 ...14 C2
  RYNPK SW20 ...12 B1
  SNWD SE25 ...17 F3
  WLGTN SM6 ...24 B4
  WWKM BR4 ...28 D5
Manor Rd North WLGTN SM6 ...24 B5
Manor Wy BECK BR3 ...18 C1
  BNSTD SM7 ...52 B1
  MTCM CR4 ...14 C2
  PUR/KEN CR8 ...45 G2
  SAND/SEL CR2 ...37 E1
  WPK KT4 ...20 C2
The Manor Wy WLGTN SM6 ...24 A4
Manor Wood Rd PUR/KEN CR8 ...45 E3
Mansard Beeches THHTH CR7 ...16 A2
Mansell Wy CTHM CR3 ...59 E2
Mansel Rd WIM/MER SW19 ...4 A3
Mansfield Rd SAND/SEL CR2 ...36 B2
Manship Rd MTCM CR4 ...6 B4
Manston Cl PGE/AN SE20 ...9 G5
Mantilla Rd TOOT SW17 ...6 A1
Mantlet Cl STRHM/NOR SW16 ...14 C2
Maple Cl CTHM CR3 ...59 H3
  MTCM CR4 ...6 B5

Mapledale Av CROY/NA CRO ...3 K2
Maple Ms STRHM/NOR SW16 ...7 F3
Maple Pl EW KT17 ...40 D1
Maple Rd CTHM CR3 ...59 H3
  PGE/AN SE20 ...9 G5
The Maples BNSTD SM7 ...43 F5
Maplethorpe Rd THHTH CR7 ...15 H3
Marbles Wy
  KWD/TDW/WH KT20 ...50 D2
Marchmont Rd WLGTN SM6 ...34 C2
Marcuse Rd CTHM CR3 ...59 G4
Mardell Rd CROY/NA CRO ...17 H3
Marden Crs CROY/NA CRO ...15 G5
Marden Rd CROY/NA CRO ...15 G5
Maresfield CROY/NA CRO ...3 K4
Marfield Cl WPK KT4 ...21 G2
Marfleet Cl CAR SM5 ...23 F5
Margaret Wy PUR/KEN CR8 ...46 A5
Marham Gdns MRDN SM4 ...13 F5
Marian Rd STRHM/NOR SW16 ...14 C1
Mariette Wy WLGTN SM6 ...34 D4
Marigold Wy CROY/NA CRO ...28 A5
Marion Rd THHTH CR7 ...16 A3
Market Pde EW KT17 * ...40 D2
  SNWD SE25 * ...17 F3
Markfield CROY/NA CRO * ...49 E4
Markfield Rd CTHM CR3 ...60 C5
Markville Gdns CTHM CR3 ...59 H5
Markwell Cl SYD SE26 ...9 H5
Marlborough Cl
  WIM/MER SW19 ...5 H3
Marlborough Rd
  SAND/SEL CR2 ...36 B3
  SUT SM1 ...22 D4
Marlings Cl CTHM CR3 ...59 H1
Marlins Cl SUT SM1 * ...33 E1
Marlow Cl PGE/AN SE20 ...17 F1
Marlow Dr CHEAM SM3 ...21 G5
Marlow Wy CROY/NA CRO ...35 F1
Marlpit Av COUL/CHIP CR5 ...54 D5
Marlpit La COUL/CHIP CR5 ...54 C4
Maroons Wy CAT SE6 ...10 D1
Marryat Pl WIM/MER SW19 ...4 A2
Marshall Cl SAND/SEL CR2 ...47 H3
Marshalls Cl HOR/WEW KT19 ...40 A3
Marshall's Rd SUT SM1 ...22 D5
Marsh Av HOR/WEW KT19 ...30 A5
  MTCM CR4 ...13 H5
Marston HOR/WEW KT19 ...30 A4
Marston Av CHEAM SM3 ...21 G5
Marston Dr WARL CR6 ...57 H1
Marston Wy NRWD SE19 ...8 A4
Martin Cl SAND/SEL CR2 ...48 A5
  WARL CR6 ...57 H1
Martin Crs CROY/NA CRO ...25 G1
Martin Gv WIM/MER SW19 ...13 E1
Martins Cl WWKM BR4 ...29 G5
The Martins SYD SE26 ...9 H5
Martin Wy RYNPK SW20 ...12 C4
Marwell Cl WWKM BR4 ...29 H5
Maryhill Cl PUR/KEN CR8 ...55 G1
Maryland Rd THHTH CR7 ...15 H1
Mason's Av CROY/NA CRO ...2 D3
Masons Ct EW KT17 * ...41 E4
Mason's Pl MTCM CR4 ...13 H4
Massingberd Wy TOOT SW17 ...6 B1
Masters Cl STRHM/NOR SW16 ...14 C1
Mathias Cl EPSOM KT18 ...40 A3
Matilda Cl NRWD SE19 ...8 C4
Matlock Crs CHEAM SM3 ...21 G5
Matlock Gdns CHEAM SM3 ...21 G5
Matlock Pl CHEAM SM3 ...21 G5
Matlock Rd CTHM CR3 ...59 G2
Matthew Ct MTCM CR4 ...15 E3
Matthew's Gdns CROY/NA CRO ...49 F1
Maurice Av CTHM CR3 ...59 F2
Mavis Av HOR/WEW KT19 ...30 B2
Mavis Cl HOR/WEW KT19 ...30 B2
Mawson Cl RYNPK SW20 ...12 D3
Maxwell Cl CROY/NA CRO ...25 E1
Maybourne Cl SYD SE26 ...9 F3
Maybury Cl KWD/TDW/WH KT20 ...50 D3
Maybury St TOOT SW17 ...5 H1
Maycross Av MRDN SM4 ...12 C3
Mayday Rd THHTH CR7 ...15 H3
Mayes Cl WARL CR6 ...57 H1
Mayfair Av WPK KT4 ...21 E1
Mayfair Cl BECK BR3 ...10 D5
Mayfield Cl PGE/AN SE20 * ...9 F5
Mayfield Crs THHTH CR7 ...15 F3
Mayfield Rd BELMT SM2 ...33 E4
  SAND/SEL CR2 ...47 E3
  WIM/MER SW19 ...13 E1
Mayford Cl BECK BR3 ...17 F1
Maynooth Gdns MTCM CR4 ...14 A5
Mayo Rd CROY/NA CRO ...16 C4
Mayow Rd SYD SE26 ...9 H4
May's Hill Rd HAYES BR2 ...19 H2
Maytree Ct MTCM CR4 ...14 A4
Maywater Cl SAND/SEL CR2 ...46 C2
Maywood Cl BECK BR3 * ...10 D5
McIntosh Cl WLGTN SM6 ...34 D4
McRae La MTCM CR4 ...14 A5
Mead Crs SUT SM1 ...23 H5
Mead Dr COUL/CHIP CR5 ...44 C5
Meadfoot Rd STRHM/NOR SW16 ...14 C2
Meadow Av CROY/NA CRO ...18 A5
Meadow Cl CAT SE6 ...10 D1
  PUR/KEN CR8 ...55 H1
Meadow Cl EPSOM KT18 ...40 D5
Meadow Hl COUL/CHIP CR5 ...44 C5
Meadow Ri COUL/CHIP CR5 ...44 C4
Meadow Rd HAYES BR2 ...19 H5
  SUT SM1 ...23 H5
  WIM/MER SW19 ...5 E4
Meadowside Rd BELMT SM2 ...31 H4
The Meadows WARL CR6 ...57 H3
Meadow Stile CROY/NA CRO ...2 C4
Meadow View Rd THHTH CR7 ...15 H3
Meadowview Rd HOR/WEW KT19 ...30 C5

Oslac Rd CAT SE6 ....10 D2
Osmond Gdns WLGTN SM6.....34 C1
Osney Wk MRDN SM4 ....13 F5
Osprey Gdns SAND/SEL CR2...37 H5
Ospringe Cl PGE/AN SE20 ....9 C4
Osterley Gdns THHTH CR7 ......16 A1
Osward CROY/NA CRO................38 B5
Otford Cl PGE/AN SE20 ....9 G5
Otterbourne Rd CROY/NA CRO ..2 C2
Otterburn St TOOT SW17.........5 H2
Otterden St CAT SE6 ....10 C1
Outram Rd CROY/NA CRO 28 A1
Oval Rd CROY/NA CRO 3 G1
The Oval BNSTD SM7................42 C4
Overbrae BECK BR3...................8 A1
Overbury Av BECK BR3.............18 D2
Overbury Crs CROY/NA CRO....39 E5
Overdown Rd CAT SE6 ....10 C1
Overhill WARL CR6.....................6 C5
Overhill Cots MTCM CR4 *.......14 A1
Overhill Rd PUR/KEN CR8.........35 G4
Overstand Cl BECK BR3............19 F4
Overstone Gdns CROY/NA CRO ..28 D1
Overton Rd BELMT SM2 ....32 C3
Overton's Yd CROY/NA CRO 2 C4
Ovett Cl NRWD SE19 ....8 E2
Owen Cl CROY/NA CRO 16 B5
Owen Gdns WLGTN SM6 ....34 E5
Owl Cl SAND/SEL CR2 ....37 H5
Ownstead Gdns SAND/SEL CR2...46 D1
Ownsted Hl CROY/NA CRO 39 F5
Oxford Av RYNPK SW20...........12 A1
Oxford Cl MTCM CR4................14 C2
Oxford Rd CAR SM5...................33 G2
 NRWD SE19 ....8 E3
 WLGTN SM6 * 34 B2
Oxted Cl MTCM CR4 ....13 F2
Oxtoby Wy STRHM/NOR SW16 ...6 D5

P

Paddock Cl SYD SE26 ....9 H1
 WPK KT4 ....20 C2
Paddock Gdns NRWD SE19 ......8 A3
Paddock Wk WARL CR6 ....56 B4
Padua Rd PGE/AN SE20 ....9 G3
Pageant Wk CROY/NA CRO 3 G4
Page Crs CROY/NA CRO.............35 H1
Pagehurst Rd CROY/NA CRO ...27 E1
Paget Av SUT SM1.....................23 F4
Pain's Cl MTCM CR4..................14 B1
Paisley Rd CAR SM5..................23 F2
Palace Gn CROY/NA CRO..........38 B3
Palace Gv NRWD SE19 ....8 D4
Palace Rd NRWD SE19 ....8 D4
Palace Sq NRWD SE19 ....8 D4
Palace Vw CROY/NA CRO 28 E5
Palestine Gv WIM/MER SW19 ....5 F5
Palmer Av CHEAM SM3.............29 H5
Palmer Cl WWKM BR4...............29 F5
Palmersfield Rd BNSTD SM7.....42 C4
Palmers Rd STRHM/NOR SW16 ...15 F1
Palmerston Gv WIM/MER SW19 ...4 E4
Palmerston Rd CAR SM5...........23 H5
 CROY/NA CRO..........................16 B4
 SUT SM1...............................33 E1
 WIM/MER SW19 ....4 C4
Pampisford Rd PUR/KEN CR8....45 G1
Pams Wy HOR/WEW KT19 ....20 D3
Panton Cl CROY/NA CRO 25 H2
Papermill Cl CAR SM5 ....24 A5
The Parade CAR SM5................33 H1
 CROY/NA CRO..........................15 G5
 CROY/NA CRO..........................35 F1
 EPSOM KT18..........................40 B3
 KWD/TDW/WH KT20 *..............51 E4
 PGE/AN SE20 *.........................9 G2
 SUT SM1...............................22 B4
 SYD SE26 *..............................9 H1
Parchmore Rd THHTH CR7.......15 H1
Parchmore Wy THHTH CR7......15 H1
Parfour Dr PUR/KEN CR8..........55 E1
Parish La PGE/AN SE20 ....9 H4
Park Av CAR SM5......................33 H2
 CHTM CR3 ....59 G4
 MTCM CR4 ....14 B1
 WWKM BR4............................29 E3
Park Av East EW KT17...............31 E2
Park Av West EW KT17..............31 E2
Park Cl CAR SM5.......................33 H2
Park Ct SYD SE26 *....................9 H1
Parkdale Crs WPK KT4 ....20 B4
Park End BMLY BR1 ....11 H5
Parker Cl CAR SM5....................33 H2
Parker Rd CROY/NA CRO 2 D6
Parkfields CROY/NA CRO 28 D1
Parkfields Cl CAR SM5...............24 A5
Parkgate Rd CAR SM5...............34 A1
Park Hl CAR SM5.......................33 H2
Park Hill Cl CAR SM5.................33 G1
Park Hill Ri CROY/NA CRO 40 D1
 EW KT17................................31 E2
 HAYES BR2.............................19 G1
 WLGTN SM6...........................34 B3
Parkhurst HOR/WEW KT19......30 A5
Parkhurst Rd SUT SM1..............23 F5
Parklands Rd TOOT SW17.........4 A5
Parklands Wy WPK KT4 ....20 C5
Park La CAR SM5.......................33 H2
 CHEAM SM3 ....32 A2
 CROY/NA CRO...........................2 B4
Parkleigh Rd WIM/MER SW19...12 D1
Park Ley Rd CTHM CR3..............56 D5
Park Rd BECK BR3 ....10 B4
 BNSTD SM7...........................42 D5
 CHEAM SM3..........................32 A3
 CTHM CR3.............................59 G3

Park View Dr MTCM CR4...........13 F1
Park View Rd CTHM CR3...........61 F2
Parkway EW KT17 *....................5 G2
Park Vis TOOT SW17 *...............5 G2
Parkway CROY/NA CRO.............39 E4
Parkwood Rd BECK BR3...........10 C4
Park Wood Cl BNSTD SM7.......41 H5
Park Wood Rd BNSTD SM7.......41 H5
Parkwood Rd WIM/MER SW19...4 B2
Park Wood Vw BNSTD SM7......50 C1
Parr Av EW KT17.......................31 F4
Parrs Cl SAND/SEL CR2.............36 B4
Parry Cl EW KT17......................31 E3
Parry Rd SNWD SE25................15 F2
Parsonage Cl WARL CR6............56 E1
Parsonsfield Cl BNSTD SM7......41 H5
Parsonsfield Rd BNSTD SM7.....50 D1
Parson's Md CROY/NA CRO........2 B1
Parthia Cl EPSOM KT18.............50 D5
Partridge Knoll PUR/KEN CR8...45 H2
Partridge Md BNSTD SM7..........41 G5
Paston Cl WLGTN SM6..............24 C4
Pathfield Rd STRHM/NOR SW16 ...6 D3
The Path WIM/MER SW19 ....4 D5
Patterdale Cl BMLY BR1 ....11 G3
Patterson Rd NRWD SE19 ....8 E3
Paul Gdns CROY/NA CRO.............3 J3
The Pavement WIM/MER SW19 *...4 B3
 WNWD SE27 *..........................8 A1
Pawleyne Cl PGE/AN SE20.........9 G3
Pawson's Rd CROY/NA CRO......16 A5
Paxton Pl WNWD SE27..............8 B1
Peabody Cl CROY/NA CRO........27 G2
Peace Cl SNWD SE25................16 C3
Peaches Cl BELMT SM2 ....32 A3
Peacock Gdns CROY/NA CRO...38 A5
Peak Hl SYD SE26 ....9 G1
Peak Hill Av SYD SE26...............9 G1
Peak Hill Gdns SYD SE26............9 G1
Peaks Hill PUR/KEN CR8...........35 E5
Peaks Hill Ri PUR/KEN CR8.......35 E5
Peall Rd CROY/NA CRO.............15 F5
Pearce Cl MTCM CR4................14 A1
Peartree Av TOOT SW17.............5 H5
Pear Tree Cl MTCM CR4............13 G1
Peartree Cl SAND/SEL CR2.......47 F4
Pegasus Rd CROY/NA CRO........35 G2
Pelham Rd PGE/AN SE20..........17 G1
 WIM/MER SW19 ....4 C4
Pellings Cl HAYES BR2..............19 G2
Pelton Av BELMT SM2...............32 D5
Pembroke Cl BNSTD SM7.........51 H2
Pembroke Rd MTCM CR4..........14 A1
 SNWD SE25...........................16 C3
Pembury Av WPK KT4................21 E2
Pembury Cl COUL/CHIP CR5.....44 A4
 HAYES BR2.............................28 E1
Pembury Rd SNWD SE25..........17 E3
Pemdevon Rd CROY/NA CRO...25 G1
Pendennis Rd STRHM/NOR SW16...7 H1
Pendle Rd STRHM/NOR SW16....6 B3
Penfold Cl CROY/NA CRO..........25 G4
Penge La PGE/AN SE20 ....9 H2
Penge Rd SNWD SE25...............17 E2
Penistone Rd STRHM/NOR SW16...7 E4
Pennycroft SAND/SEL CR2........38 A4
Penrith Cl BECK BR3.................10 D5
Penrith Rd THHTH CR7.............16 A1
Penrith St STRHM/NOR SW16...6 C3
Penshurst Gn HAYES BR2..........19 H1
Penshurst Rd THHTH CR7.........15 H4
Penshurst Wy BELMT SM2.........32 C3
Pentlands Cl MTCM CR4...........14 B2
Pentney Rd WIM/MER SW19.....4 A5
Penwortham Rd SAND/SEL CR2...46 D1
 STRHM/NOR SW16.....................6 B3
Pepper Cl CTHM CR3................59 G5
Peppercorn Cl THHTH CR7.......16 B1
Peppermint Cl CROY/NA CRO...25 E1
Percy Gdns WPK KT4 ....20 A5
Percy Rd MTCM CR4.................24 A1
 PGE/AN SE20.............................9 H5
 SNWD SE25...........................16 D4
Peregrine Gdns CROY/NA CRO...28 A3
Perry How WPK KT4 ....20 D2
Persfield Ms EW KT17 *.............30 D5
Persfield Rd EW KT17................31 E5
Pershore Gv CAR SM5...............23 F4
Perth Rd BECK BR3...................19 E1
Peterborough Rd CAR SM5........13 G5
Petersfield Crs COUL/CHIP CR5...45 G5
Petersham Cl SUT SM1..............32 D2
Petersham Ter CROY/NA CRO *...25 E4
Peterwood Wy CROY/NA CRO...25 F3
Petworth Rd COUL/CHIP CR5....53 G4
Pevensey Rd TOOT SW17............5 F1
Pharaoh Cl MTCM CR4..............24 A4
Pheasant Cl PUR/KEN CR8........45 H3
Philip Gdns CROY/NA CRO........28 B3
Philips Cl MTCM CR4.................24 A2
Phipp's Bridge Rd MTCM CR4....13 F2
Phoenix Cl WWKM BR4.............29 F3
Phoenix Rd PGE/AN SE20 ....9 G3
Pickering Gdns SNWD SE25......16 D5
Pickhurst Gn HAYES BR2...........29 H1
Pickhurst La HAYES BR2............19 H5
Pickhurst Md HAYES BR2...........29 H1

Pickhurst Pk HAYES BR2...........19 G5
Pickhurst Ri WWKM BR4............29 F2
Picquets Wy BNSTD SM7..........51 E1
Pikes Hl EW KT17......................40 C3
Pilgrim Cl MRDN SM4................22 D1
Pilgrim Hl WNWD SE27...............8 A1
Pilgrim's Wy SAND/SEL CR2......36 D2
Pincott Rd WIM/MER SW19........5 E5
Pine Av WWKM BR4..................28 D2
Pine Cl PGE/AN SE20...................9 G5
 PUR/KEN CR8.........................55 E2
Pine Coombe CROY/NA CRO.....38 C4
Pine Crs CAR SM5.....................33 E5
Pine Gv WIM/MER SW19 ....4 B2
Pine Pl EW KT17.......................41 H4
Pine Rdg CAR SM5....................34 A4
The Pines NRWD SE19 *.............7 H3
 PUR/KEN CR8.........................44 B5
Pine Wk BELMT SM2.................33 F5
 BNSTD SM7...........................52 D2
 CTHM CR3.............................59 G2
Pinewood Cl CROY/NA CRO......28 A4
Pinfold Rd STRHM/NOR SW16...7 E1
Pipers Gdns CROY/NA CRO.......28 B2
Pipewell Rd CAR SM5................13 G5
Pippin Cl CROY/NA CRO............28 B2
Piquet Rd PGE/AN SE20............17 G1
Pirbright Crs CROY/NA CRO......39 E2
Pitcairn Rd MTCM CR4..............5 H4
Pitlake CROY/NA CRO..................2 C4
Pitt Crs WIM/MER SW19.............4 D1
Pitt Pl EW KT17 *......................40 C4
Pitt Rd EW KT17.......................40 C4
 THHTH CR7...........................16 A3
Pittville Gdns SNWD SE25........17 E2
Pit Wood Gn
 KWD/TDW/WH KT20 ....50 C5
Pixton Wy CROY/NA CRO..........38 B3
Placehouse La COUL/CHIP CR5...54 B4
Plantagenet Cl HOR/WEW KT19...30 A5
Plantation La WARL CR6............57 E4
Plawsfield Rd BECK BR3............10 C5
Playgreen Wy CAT SE6..............10 B4
Playground Cl BECK BR3...........17 H1
Pleasant Gv CROY/NA CRO........28 B4
Plesman Wy WLGTN SM6..........35 E4
Pleydell Av NRWD SE19 ....8 D4
Pleydell Gdns NRWD SE19 *........8 D4
Plough La CROY/NA CRO............26 E5
 WIM/MER SW19 ....4 D2
 WLGTN SM6...........................35 E1
Plough Lane Cl WLGTN SM6......35 E1
Plough Rd HOR/WEW KT19 ......30 B3
Plummer La MTCM CR4.............14 C1
Plumpton Wy CAR SM5.............23 G4
Pollard Rd MRDN SM4...............13 H4
Pollards Crs STRHM/NOR SW16...15 E2
Pollards Hl East
 STRHM/NOR SW16...................15 F2
Pollards Hl North
 STRHM/NOR SW16...................15 F2
Pollards Hl South
 STRHM/NOR SW16...................15 E2
Pollards Hl West
 STRHM/NOR SW16...................15 E1
Pollards Wood Rd
 STRHM/NOR SW16...................15 E1
Polworth Rd STRHM/NOR SW16...7 E2
Pond Cottage La BECK BR3........28 C2
Pondfield Rd HAYES BR2...........28 E1
 PUR/KEN CR8.........................54 D1
Pond Hill Gdns CHEAM SM3 *....32 A2
Pool Cl BECK BR3.....................10 D5
Poole Rd HOR/WEW KT19 *......30 B2
Pope Cl WIM/MER SW19 *...........5 F3
Popes Gv CROY/NA CRO............28 B4
Popinjays Rw CHEAM SM3 *......31 H1
Poplar Av MTCM CR4.................5 H5
Poplar Crs HOR/WEW KT19......30 A2
Poplar Dr EW KT17....................41 H4
Poplar Farm Cl HOR/WEW KT19...30 A2
Poplar Rd CHEAM SM3..............22 C1
 WIM/MER SW19 ....12 C1
Poplar Rd South
 WIM/MER SW19 ....12 C2
Poplar Wk CROY/NA CRO............2 C1
 CTHM CR3.............................59 G3
Poppy Cl WLGTN SM6...............24 D5
Poppy La CROY/NA CRO............27 E5
Porchester Md BECK BR3..........10 D5
Porchfield Cl BELMT SM2..........32 D5
Porthcawe Rd SYD SE26...........10 A1
Portland Cl WPK KT4.................21 F1
Portland Cots CROY/NA CRO *...26 B3
Portland Pl EW KT17.................40 C2
 SNWD SE25...........................17 E3
Portland Place Flats EW KT17 *...40 C2
Portland Rd MTCM CR4.............13 G1
 SNWD SE25...........................17 E3
Portley La CTHM CR3................59 G1
Portley Wood Rd CTHM CR3.....59 H1
Portnalls Cl COUL/CHIP CR5.....53 F1
Portnalls Ri COUL/CHIP CR5......53 G1
Portnalls Rd COUL/CHIP CR5.....53 F2
Portway EW KT17.....................31 E4
Portway Crs EW KT17................31 E4
Postmill Cl CROY/NA CRO.........28 A4
Potter Cl MTCM CR4.................14 B1
Potters Cl CROY/NA CRO..........28 A3
Potter's La STRHM/NOR SW16....6 D4
Poulter Pk MTCM CR4 *.............13 G5
Poulton Av SUT SM1.................33 H1
Pound La HOR/WEW KT19 ....40 B1
Pound Rd BNSTD SM7...............50 C5
Pound St CAR SM5....................33 H1
Prentis Rd STRHM/NOR SW16....6 D1
Prestbury Crs BNSTD SM7........52 D1
Preston Dr HOR/WEW KT19 ......30 C2
Preston La KWD/TDW/WH KT20...50 C5
Preston Rd NRWD SE19 ....7 H3
Prestwood Gdns CROY/NA CRO...26 A1
Pretoria Rd STRHM/NOR SW16...6 B3
Price Rd CROY/NA CRO..............35 H1

Prickley Wd HAYES BR2............29 H2
Priddy's Yard CROY/NA CRO.......2 C3
Pridham Rd THHTH CR7............16 B3
Priestley Rd MTCM CR4.............14 A1
Primrose Cl CAT SE6.................11 E2
 WLGTN SM6...........................24 C2
Primrose La CROY/NA CRO........27 G2
Primrose Wk EW KT17..............30 D5
Prince Charles Wy WLGTN SM6...24 B4
Prince Georges Rd
 WIM/MER SW19 ....5 F5
Prince of Wales' Rd SUT SM1.....23 F5
Prince Rd SNWD SE25..............16 C4
Princes Av CAR SM5.................33 H3
 SAND/SEL CR2........................47 E5
Princes Cl SAND/SEL CR2..........47 F5
Princes Rd PGE/AN SE20...........9 G3
 WIM/MER SW19 ....4 D3
Princess Rd CROY/NA CRO........16 A5
Princes St SUT SM1..................23 G5
Princes Wy CROY/NA CRO.........35 F1
 WWKM BR4............................29 H5
Princethorpe Rd SYD SE26 *......9 J6
Pringle Gdns PUR/KEN CR8......35 F5
 STRHM/NOR SW16...................6 D7
Prior Av BELMT SM2.................33 J2
Priory Av CHEAM SM3...............21 H5
 WIM/MER SW19 ....4 A5
Priory Cl BECK BR3...................18 A2
 CHEAM SM3...........................21 H5
 WIM/MER SW19 ....4 A5
Priory Gdns SNWD SE25...........16 D3
Priory Rd CHEAM SM3...............21 H5
 CROY/NA CRO..........................25 G1
The Priory CROY/NA CRO *........25 G4
Proctor Cl MTCM CR4.................6 A5
Progress Wy CROY/NA CRO.......25 G2
Promenade de Verdun
 PUR/KEN CR8.........................44 D1
Prospect Cl SYD SE26...............9 H6
Prospect Pl EW KT17................40 C3
Provincial Ter PGE/AN SE20 *......9 J3
Pruffin Cl CROY/NA CRO.............2 C1
Pump House Cl HAYES BR2.......19 F1
Purberry Gv EW KT17................30 D5
Purberry Shot EW KT17 *...........30 D5
Purcell Cl PUR/KEN CR8............46 A4
Purley Bury Av PUR/KEN CR8....46 B1
Purley Bury Cl PUR/KEN CR8.....46 B1
Purley Downs Rd PUR/KEN CR8...36 A5
Purley Hl PUR/KEN CR8.............45 H2
Purley Knoll PUR/KEN CR8........45 F1
Purley Oaks Rd SAND/SEL CR2...46 B3
Purley Pde PUR/KEN CR8 *........45 G1
Purley Park Rd PUR/KEN CR8....45 H1
Purley Ri PUR/KEN CR8.............45 F2
Purley Rd SAND/SEL CR2..........45 H3
Purley Vale PUR/KEN CR8..........45 H3
Purley Wy CROY/NA CRO...........25 F1
 PUR/KEN CR8.........................55 F5
Pye Cl CTHM CR3......................59 F5
Pylbrook Rd SUT SM1...............22 C4
Pytchley Crs NRWD SE19 ....8 A3

Q

Quadrant Rd THHTH CR7...........15 H3
The Quadrant BELMT SM2.........33 F2
 RYNPK SW20...........................12 B6
Quail Gdns CROY/NA CRO..........38 A5
Quarry Park Rd SUT SM1............32 B2
Quarry Ri SUT SM1...................32 B2
Queen Adelaide Rd
 PGE/AN SE20............................9 G3
Queen Anne's Gdns
 MTCM CR4 *..........................13 H2
Queen Elizabeth Gdns
 MRDN SM4.............................12 C6
Queen Elizabeth's Dr
 CROY/NA CRO..........................39 F5
Queen Elizabeth's Wk
 WLGTN SM6...........................24 D5
Queenhill Rd SAND/SEL CR2.....37 F5
Queen Mary Rd NRWD SE19 ......8 B3
Queen Mary's Av CAR SM5........33 H3
Queens Acre CHEAM SM3.........31 H5
Queens Cl WLGTN SM6.............34 B1
Queens Ct BELMT SM2 *............42 C1
Queensland Av WIM/MER SW19...4 C5
Queensmead Av EW KT17.........31 F5
Queen's Mead Rd HAYES BR2....19 H1
Queen's Rd BECK BR3...............59 G3
Queen's Pk MRDN SM4.............12 E6
Queen's Rd BECK BR3...............18 A1
 BELMT SM2...........................32 C1
 CROY/NA CRO.........................15 H5
 MRDN SM4.............................12 C3
 MTCM CR4 ....13 F1
 WIM/MER SW19 ....4 D2
 WLGTN SM6...........................34 B1
Queensthorpe Ms SYD SE26 *....9 H1
Queensthorpe Rd SYD SE26......9 H1
Queen St CROY/NA CRO............35 F2
Queenswood Av THHTH CR7.....15 G2
 WLGTN SM6...........................24 D5
Quicks Rd WIM/MER SW19........4 D1
Quinton Av RYNPK SW20..........12 A5
Quinton Cl BECK BR3................19 E2
 WLGTN SM6...........................24 B5

R

Rackham Ms STRHM/NOR SW16...14 E1
Radcliffe Gdns CAR SM5............33 G4
Radcliffe Rd CROY/NA CRO..........3 H3
Radnor Cl MTCM CR4................14 C2
Radnor Wk CROY/NA CRO.........28 A4
Raglan Ct SAND/SEL CR2 *........36 C3
Railway Ap WLGTN SM6 *...........34 B1
Railway Cots BNSTD SM7 *.........42 C4
 WIM/MER SW19 *......................4 D2
Raleigh Av WLGTN SM6.............24 D2
Raleigh Dr BRYLDS KT5.............20 E1
Raleigh Gdns MTCM CR4...........13 J2
Raleigh Rd PGE/AN SE20..........17 H1
Ralph Perring Ct BECK BR3 *......18 B3
Rama Cl STRHM/NOR SW16........6 E5
Rambler Cl STRHM/NOR SW16...14 A1
Rame Cl TOOT SW17...................5 H1
Ramones Ter MTCM CR4 *..........5 J3
Ramsdale Rd TOOT SW17...........5 H1
Ramsey Pl CTHM CR3................59 F2
Ramsey Rd THHTH CR7.............15 F4
Randlesdown Rd CAT SE6.........10 C2
Randolph Rd EW KT17...............41 E4
Ranfurly Rd SUT SM1................22 C4
Ranmore Av CROY/NA CRO...........3 K4
Ranmore Rd BELMT SM2...........32 A5
Rathbone Sq CROY/NA CRO *......2 D5
Ravensbourne Av HAYES BR2....18 E4
Ravensbury Av MRDN SM4........13 G5
Ravensbury Gv MTCM CR4.........13 G2
Ravensbury La MTCM CR4.........13 G2
Ravenscar Rd BMLY BR1...........11 H2
Ravens Cl HAYES BR2................19 F1
Ravenscroft Rd BECK BR3.........17 G2
Ravensdale Gdns NRWD SE19...8 A3
Ravensfield Gdns
 HOR/WEW KT19.......................30 C3
Ravenshead Cl SAND/SEL CR2...47 F5
Ravensmead Rd HAYES BR2......18 C4
Ravens Wold PUR/KEN CR8.......55 H3
Ravenswood Av WWKM BR4......29 F4
Ravenswood Crs WWKM BR4.....29 F4
Ravenswood Rd CROY/NA CRO...2 B4
Rawlings Cl BECK BR3................19 E5
Rawlins Cl SAND/SEL CR2..........48 A2
Rawnsley Av MTCM CR4............13 G3
Rayleigh Av SAND/SEL CR2........36 E4
Rayleigh Rd WIM/MER SW19 .....4 C3
Raymead Av THHTH CR7...........15 G4
Raymond Cl SYD SE26...............9 J6
Raymond Rd BECK BR3.............17 G4
 WIM/MER SW19 ....4 C2
Rays Rd WWKM BR4.................19 F5
The Readens BNSTD SM7..........52 D2
Reading Rd SUT SM1................33 G1
Reads Rest La
 KWD/TDW/WH KT20.................51 J4
Recovery St TOOT SW17.............5 H2
Recreation Rd HAYES BR2 *........19 F1
Recreation Wy MTCM CR4.........14 C1
Rectory Gdns BECK BR3 *..........17 H2
Rectory Gn BECK BR3...............17 H2
Rectory Gv CROY/NA CRO...........2 B3
Rectory La BNSTD SM7..............51 H5
 TOOT SW17............................5 H2
 WLGTN SM6...........................24 C2
Rectory Orch WIM/MER SW19.....4 A4
Rectory Pk SAND/SEL CR2........47 E4
Rectory Rd BECK BR3................17 J2
 SUT SM1...............................22 C5
Redbarn Cl PUR/KEN CR8..........46 A1
Redclose Av MRDN SM4............13 F4
Reddington Cl SAND/SEL CR2...46 C2
Reddons Rd BECK BR3...............9 J6
Reddown Rd COUL/CHIP CR5....53 H3
Redford Av COUL/CHIP CR5.......52 E2
 THHTH CR7...........................15 F3
 WLGTN SM6...........................34 D2
Redgrave Cl SNWD SE25...........17 E2
Red House Rd CROY/NA CRO.....25 G1
Redlands COUL/CHIP CR5..........53 J3
Red Lodge Rd WWKM BR4.........29 F1
Redroofs Cl BECK BR3...............18 C1
Redstart Cl CROY/NA CRO..........39 F5
Redvers Rd WARL CR6...............57 E3
Redwing Cl SAND/SEL CR2.........48 A2
Redwing Rd WLGTN SM6............35 E4
Redwood Cl PUR/KEN CR8.........45 J1
Reedham Dr PUR/KEN CR8........45 F2
Reedham Park Av
 PUR/KEN CR8.........................55 F4
Rees Gdns CROY/NA CRO..........16 C5
Reeves Cnr CROY/NA CRO...........2 B4
Regal Ct MTCM CR4..................14 A1
Regal Crs WLGTN SM6...............24 B3
Regency Ms BECK BR3...............18 B1
Regency Wk CROY/NA CRO........28 B1
Regent Pde BELMT SM2 *..........33 G1
Regent Pl WIM/MER SW19 *........4 E1
Regents Cl CTHM CR3................59 F2
 SAND/SEL CR2........................47 E4
Regina Rd SNWD SE25..............17 E3
Reid Av CTHM CR3....................59 F3
Reid Cl COUL/CHIP CR5..............53 F2
Reigate Av SUT SM1..................23 H2
Reigate Rd EPSOM KT18............40 D5
 EW KT17................................41 E5
Reigate Wy WLGTN SM6............35 E1
Rembrandt Ct HOR/WEW KT19...30 D4
Rendle Cl CROY/NA CRO............16 D3
Renmark St TOOT SW17.............5 H1
Renown Cl CROY/NA CRO............2 B3
Repton Cl CAR SM5...................33 G2
Repton Ct BECK BR3.................18 B1
Reservoir Cl THHTH CR7............16 B2
Restmor Wy WLGTN SM6...........24 A3
The Retreat THHTH CR7.............16 B2
 WPK KT4................................21 E1

Rd SUT SM1.....32 B2
oke Rd WIM/MER SW19....4 A1
d CAR SM5.....13 C5
Rd CAR SM5.....13 F5
nd Dr NRWD SE19.....8 D4
ds CI CAR SM5.....23 H2
/MER SW19.....5 F5
as Rd NWMAL KT3.....20 B1
ds Wy CROY/NA CRO.....3 H6
old Wy WLGTN SM6.....35 E4
ald MTCM CR4.....14 A1
dale Rd
M/MER SW19.....6 B2
s Cots CAR SM5 *.....7 F2
s Fld HOR/WEW KT19.....30 B4
d Av COUL/CHIP CR5.....44 A4
ds Av EW KT17.....21 E5
nd Ln STRHM/NOR SW20.....4 A4
nd CI STRHM/NOR CR4.....40 C4
nd Ln CROY/NA CR0.....25 E4
nd Rd COUL/CHIP CR5.....44 B5
/NA CRO.....27 H5
d Av EW KT17.....15 H3
o Hill Rd COUL/CHIP CR5.....53 F2
dings CTHM CR3.....59 H5
down Av PUR/KEN CR8.....46 A2
down Rd PUR/KEN CR8.....36 A5
angley SAND/SEL CR2.....37 E5
o Rd COUL/CHIP CR5.....53 F2
/NA CRO.....13 G5
k WLGTN SM6.....34 D5
d CHEAM SM3.....22 B2
CR4.....6 B4
ge COUL/CHIP CR5.....45 E4
KEN CR8.....40 A2
HOR/WEW KT19.....40 A2
ngeway CROY/NA CR0.....25 F4
ell CI SYD SE26.....10 B1
pl WIM/MER SW19.....4 A3
SAND/SEL CR2.....33 F3
ngs EPSOM KT18.....47 E3
17.....30 D4
TDW/WH KT20.....51 F5
d HAYES BR2.....19 H2
e.....56 C3
/MER SW19.....4 A4
d PGE/AN SE20.....9 F5
rd CROY/NA CR0.....37 G2
e CROY/NA CRO.....25 C4
ale Rd
M/NOR SW16.....6 D2
nd Rd SUT SM1.....23 F5
d CI BECK BR3.....10 A4
ad Av CROY/NA CR0.....25 E1
CROY/NA CRO.....39 E2
gh Dr WPK KT4.....21 E1
EW KT17.....30 D5
/SEL CR2.....37 C4
ns CAR SM5.....24 A3
ove Pk BECK BR3.....10 B5
e Dr BELMT SM2.....32 D5
me Dr HOR/WEW KT19.....30 B4
ds HAYES BR2.....11 H4
d CI WLGTN SM6.....24 B4
e Dr MTCM CR4.....13 C4
Ms CROY/NA CRO *.....25 E4
e Rd TOOT SW17.....20 A5
er Gdns CROY/NA CR0.....3 H4
CR3.....59 G2
er Rd CAR SM5.....23 H5
k MRDN SM4.....13 F5
t Wy CROY/NA CRO.....15 E5
MTCM CR4.....13 F1
mpton Rd
/SEL CR2.....36 C2
M/NOR SW16.....7 G1
SYD SE26.....8 D1
unt Rd NRWD SE19.....8 B8
Gdns NRWD SE19.....8 C1
dns CROY/NA CRO.....16 C5
l WIM/MER SW19.....4 A3
d MTCM CR4.....13 G1
WLGTN SM6.....35 E3
CTHM CR3.....59 F5
PUR/KEN CR8.....54 D1
o COUL/CHIP CR5.....54 D3
WALL CR6.....57 F3
d PUR/KEN CR8.....45 H1
d Rd PUR/KEN CR8.....45 H1
d MTCM CR4.....13 C2
WIM/MER SW19.....4 A4
d Wy SUT SM1.....32 D1
d Rd CROY/NA CR0.....28 A2
I SAND/SEL CR2.....17 C5
ce CI WLGTN SM6.....35 E3
rst Av HAYES BR2.....19 G3
rst Gdns BECK BR3.....19 G3
NRWD SE19.....8 B3
y CROY/NA CRO.....2 B2
Gdns CHEAM SM3.....22 C1
M/MER SW19.....4 A4
ST WNWD SE27.....8 B1
s BECK BR3.....18 B4
ery
/NOR SW16 *.....7 F3
CTHM CR3.....58 C4
I BELMT SM2.....32 D5
ne Rd TOOT SW17.....15 H2

Rookwood Av WLGTN SM6.....24 D5
Roper Wy MTCM CR4.....14 A1
Rosamund CI SAND/SEL CR2.....3 F7
Rose Av MRDN SM4.....13 E4
  MTCM CR4.....5 H5
Rosebank EPSOM KT18.....40 A4
  PGE/AN SE20.....9 F4
Rosebery Av EW KT17.....40 A4
  THHTH CR7.....16 A1
Rosebery Gdns SUT SM1.....22 D5
Rosebery Pde EW KT17 *.....30 D3
Rosebery Rd SUT SM1.....22 D5
Rosebriars CTHM CR3.....59 C5
Rose Bushes EW KT17.....50 C1
Rosecourt Rd CROY/NA CR0.....15 F5
Rosedale Rd EW KT17.....31 E1
Rosedene Av CROY/NA CR0.....25 E1
  MRDN SM4.....12 C4
Rose End WPK KT4.....21 H3
Rosefield CI CAR SM5.....33 C1
Rose HI SUT SM1.....22 D3
Rosehill Av SUT SM1.....22 D3
Rosehill Court Pde MRDN SM4 *..23 E1
Rosehill Farm Meadow
  BNSTD SM7.....42 D5
Rosehill Gdns SUT SM1.....22 D3
Rose Hill Pk West SUT SM1.....23 E2
Rosemary CI CROY/NA CR0.....25 E1
Rosemead Av MTCM CR4.....14 C2
Roseneath Ct CTHM CR3 *.....60 A5
Rosenheath PI STRHM/NOR SW16.....7 C4
The Rosery CROY/NA CR0.....17 H5
Rose Wk WWKM BR4.....29 F5
Rosewell CI PGE/AN SE20.....9 F4
Rosewood Gv SUT SM1.....23 E3
Rosewood Ter PGE/AN SE20 *.....9 F4
Roslyn CI MTCM CR4.....13 C1
Rossdale SUT SM1.....33 C1
Rossetti Gdns COUL/CHIP CR5.....54 B2
Rossignol Gdns CAR SM5.....24 A3
Rosslyn CI WWKM BR4.....29 H4
Ross Pde WLGTN SM6.....34 C5
Ross Rd SNWD SE25.....16 C2
  WLGTN SM6.....34 C2
Rosswood Gdns WLGTN SM6.....34 C2
Rostella Rd TOOT SW17.....5 F1
Rostrevor Rd WIM/MER SW19.....4 E2
Rotherfield Rd CAR SM5.....24 A5
Rotherhill Av STRHM/NOR SW16.....6 D3
Rothermere Rd CROY/NA CR0.....35 F1
Rotherwood CI WIM/MER SW19.....4 E1
Rothesay Av RYNPK SW20.....12 A1
Rothesay Rd SNWD SE25.....16 B3
Rothschild St WNWD SE27.....7 H1
Rougemont Av MRDN SM4.....13 E3
Round Gv CROY/NA CR0.....27 H1
Roundwood Av BNSTD SM7.....41 H5
Roundwood Wy BNSTD SM7.....41 H5
Rouse Gdns DUL SE21.....8 C1
Rowan CI STRHM/NOR SW16.....6 C5
Rowan Crs STRHM/NOR SW16.....6 C5
Rowan Gdns CROY/NA CR0.....3 K4
Rowan Rd EPSOM KT18.....50 B4
Rowan Rd STRHM/NOR SW16.....14 C3
Rowan Ter PGE/AN SE20 *.....9 E5
  WIM/MER SW19 *.....4 E5
Rowden Rd BECK BR3.....10 A5
  HOR/WEW KT19.....30 C3
Rowdown Crs CROY/NA CR0.....39 F4
Rowland Wy WIM/MER SW19.....4 D5
Rowley Ct CTHM CR3.....59 E2
Roxburgh Rd WNWD SE27.....7 H2
Roxton Gdns CROY/NA CR0.....38 B2
Royal Av WPK KT4.....20 D5
Royal CI WPK KT4.....20 D5
Royal Dr EPSOM KT18.....50 B3
Royston Av SUT SM1.....24 D5
Royston Rd PGE/AN SE20.....9 H5
Ruden Wy EW KT17.....41 F5
The Ruffetts SAND/SEL CR2.....37 F3
Ruffetts Wy
  KWD/TDW/WH KT20.....51 H2
Rugby La BELMT SM2.....31 H4
Ruislip St TOOT SW17.....5 H1
Runes CI MTCM CR4.....13 F3
Runnymede WIM/MER SW19.....5 F5
Runnymede Crs
  STRHM/NOR SW16.....6 D5
Rural Wy STRHM/NOR SW16.....6 B4
Rushden CI NRWD SE19.....8 A5
Rushmead CI CROY/NA CR0.....3 J6
Rushmere Ct WPK KT4.....21 E5
Rushmon PI CHEAM SM3.....32 A2
Rusholme Gv NRWD SE19.....8 B4
Rushy Meadow La CAR SM5.....23 G3
Ruskin Dr WPK KT4.....21 F5
Ruskin Rd CAR SM5.....34 A1
  CROY/NA CR0.....2 B2
Ruskin Wy WIM/MER SW19.....13 F1
Russel CI BECK BR3.....18 D2
Russell Green CI PUR/KEN CR8.....35 G5
Russell HI PUR/KEN CR8.....45 G1
Russell Hill PI PUR/KEN CR8.....45 H1
Russell Hill Rd PUR/KEN CR8.....45 H1
Russell Rd MTCM CR4.....13 G2
  WIM/MER SW19.....4 B2
Russell Wy SUT SM1.....32 D1
Russet Dr CROY/NA CR0.....28 A2
Rusthall CI CROY/NA CR0.....17 C5
Rustic Av STRHM/NOR SW16.....6 B4
Rustington Wk MRDN SM4.....22 B1
Rutford Rd STRHM/NOR SW16.....7 E2
Rutherford CI BELMT SM2.....33 F2
Rutherwyke CI EW KT17.....31 F2
Rutland Dr MRDN SM4.....22 C1
Rutland Gdns CROY/NA CR0.....3 H7
Rutland Ga HAYES BR2.....19 H3
Rutland Rd WIM/MER SW19.....5 F3
Rutlish Rd WIM/MER SW19.....4 C5
Rutter Gdns MTCM CR4.....13 F3
Ruxley La HOR/WEW KT19.....30 B1

Ruxton CI COUL/CHIP CR5.....44 C5
Rydal CI PUR/KEN CR8.....46 B3
Rydal Dr WWKM BR4.....29 G3
Rydal Mt HAYES BR2 *.....19 H5
Rydal Rd STRHM/NOR SW16.....6 D2
Rydons La COUL/CHIP CR5.....55 E5
Rydon's Wood CI
  COUL/CHIP CR5.....55 E5
Ryecroft Rd STRHM/NOR SW16.....7 G3
Ryefield Rd NRWD SE19.....8 A3
Ryelands CI CTHM CR3.....59 G1
Rylandes Rd SAND/SEL CR2.....37 F4
Rymer Rd CROY/NA CR0.....26 C1
Ryves Cots MTCM CR4 *.....14 A1

S

Sackville Rd BELMT SM2.....32 C3
Sadler CI MTCM CR4.....13 H1
Saffron CI CROY/NA CR0.....15 E5
Sainsbury Rd NRWD SE19.....8 C2
St Agatha's Gv CAR SM5.....23 H2
St Alban Gv CAR SM5.....23 G1
St Albans Rd SUT SM1.....22 B5
St Amunds CI CAT SE6.....10 C1
St Andrews Rd CAR SM5.....55 E5
  COUL/CHIP CR5.....53 F1
  CROY/NA CR0.....2 C6
St Ann's Wy CROY/NA CR0.....35 H2
St Arvans CI CROY/NA CR0.....3 H4
St Aubyn's Av WIM/MER SW19.....4 A2
St Aubyn's Rd NRWD SE19.....8 D3
St Augustine's Av
  SAND/SEL CR2.....36 A3
St Barnabas CI BECK BR3.....19 E1
St Barnabas Rd MTCM CR4.....6 A4
  SUT SM1.....33 F1
St Bartholomew's La SYD SE26.....9 G1
St Benet's Gv CAR SM5.....23 E1
St Bernards CROY/NA CR0.....3 G5
St Bernards CI WNWD SE27.....8 B1
St Christopher's Ms WLGTN SM6.....34 C1
St Clair Dr WPK KT4.....21 F4
St Clair's Rd CROY/NA CR0.....3 G3
St Cloud Rd WNWD SE27.....8 A1
St Cyprian's St TOOT SW17.....5 H1
St David's COUL/CHIP CR5.....54 B2
St David's CI WWKM BR4.....29 F5
St Denis Rd WNWD SE27.....8 B1
St Denys CI PUR/KEN CR8.....35 H5
St Dunstan's Hi SUT SM1.....22 B5
St Dunstan's Rd SNWD SE25.....16 C3
St Edwards CI CROY/NA CR0.....39 H2
St Elizabeth Dr EPSOM KT18.....40 A4
St George's Gdns EW KT17.....31 E1
St George's Rd BECK BR3.....10 D5
  MTCM CR4.....14 B2
  WIM/MER SW19.....4 B2
  WLGTN SM6.....34 B1
St George's Wk CROY/NA CR0.....2 D3
St Gothard Rd WNWD SE27.....8 B1
St Helen's Crs STRHM/NOR SW16 *.....7 F4
St Helen's Rd
  STRHM/NOR SW16.....15 F1
St Helier Av MRDN SM4.....22 D2
St Hugh's Rd PGE/AN SE20.....9 F5
St James Av EW KT17.....40 D1
  SUT SM1.....32 C1
St James CI EPSOM KT18.....40 C4
St James Ga CTHM CR3 *.....60 A2
St James Rd CAR SM5.....23 G4
  MTCM CR4.....6 A5
  PUR/KEN CR8.....45 H3
  SUT SM1.....32 C2
St James's Av BECK BR3.....18 A2
St James's CI TOOT SW17 *.....6 A2
St James's Pk CROY/NA CR0.....26 B2
St James's Rd CROY/NA CR0.....2 A2
St Johns Av EW KT17.....40 D2
St Johns Cots PGE/AN SE20 *.....9 G4
St John's Hi PUR/KEN CR8.....54 C2
St John's Rd CAR SM5.....23 G4
  CROY/NA CR0.....2 B4
  PGE/AN SE20.....9 G4
  SUT SM1.....22 C3
  WIM/MER SW19.....4 A4
St Julian's CI STRHM/NOR SW16.....7 H4
St Julian's Farm Rd WNWD SE27.....7 G1
St Katharines Rd CTHM CR3.....60 A5
St Kitts Ter SE19.....8 C2
St Lawrence Wy CTHM CR3.....59 F3
St Leonard's Rd CROY/NA CR0.....2 A3
  EPSOM KT18.....50 C4
St Leonard's Wk
  STRHM/NOR SW16.....15 F1
St Louis Rd WNWD SE27.....8 A1
St Luke's St CWTH.....17 F5
St Luke's Rd CTHM CR3.....59 F4
St Margaret's Av CHEAM SM3.....22 A4
St Margarets Dr EPSOM KT18.....40 B5
St Mark's Pl WIM/MER SW19 *.....4 B3
St Marks Rd EPSOM KT18.....50 C5
  MTCM CR4.....14 A1
  SNWD SE25.....17 E3
St Martin's Av EPSOM KT18.....40 C4
St Martin's CI EW KT17 *.....40 D3
St Martin's La BECK BR3.....18 B4
St Mary Av WLGTN SM6.....24 A4
St Mary's Av HAYES BR2.....19 G2
St Mary's CI EW KT17.....30 D5
St Mary's Mt CTHM CR3.....59 H4
St Mary's Rd SAND/SEL CR2.....36 B5
  SNWD SE25.....17 E3
  WIM/MER SW19.....4 A2
  WPK KT4.....20 D5
St Michaels CI WPK KT4.....20 D3
St Michael's Rd CROY/NA CR0.....2 D1
  CTHM CR3.....59 F2
  WLGTN SM6.....34 C2

St Nicholas Glebe TOOT SW17.....6 A1
St Nicholas Rd SUT SM1.....32 D1
St Nicholas Wy SUT SM1.....22 D5
St Normans Wy EW KT17.....31 E5
St Olave's Wk
  STRHM/NOR SW16.....14 C1
St Oswald's Rd
  STRHM/NOR SW16.....7 H5
St Paul's CI CAR SM5.....23 G1
St Paul's Rd THHTH CR7.....16 A2
St Peter's Rd CROY/NA CR0.....2 E7
St Peter's St SAND/SEL CR2.....36 B1
St Philip's Av WPK KT4.....21 F5
St Saviour's Rd CROY/NA CR0.....16 A5
Saints CI WNWD SE27.....7 H1
St Stephen's Crs THHTH CR7.....15 G2
St Theresa CI EPSOM KT18.....40 A4
St Vincent CI WNWD SE27.....7 H2
Salcombe Dr MRDN SM4.....21 H2
Salcot Crs CROY/NA CR0.....39 E5
Salcott Rd CROY/NA CR0.....25 H2
Salem PI CROY/NA CR0.....2 B5
Salisbury Av SUT SM1.....32 B2
Salisbury CI WPK KT4.....20 D5
Salisbury Rd CAR SM5.....33 H1
  CROY/NA CR0.....17 E5
  HOR/WEW KT19.....20 B5
  WIM/MER SW19.....4 A4
Salmons La WEST CTHM CR3.....55 C5
Salmons La West CTHM CR3.....55 C5
Saltash CI SUT SM1.....22 B5
Salterford Rd TOOT SW17.....6 A3
Salter's HI NRWD SE19.....8 B2
Salvador TOOT SW17.....5 G2
Samos Rd PGE/AN SE20.....17 F1
Sandbourne Av
  WIM/MER SW19.....12 D2
Sandersfield Rd BNSTD SM7.....42 C5
Sanders De STRHM/NOR SW16 *.....7 F3
Sanderstead Court Av
  SAND/SEL CR2.....47 E3
Sanderstead HI SAND/SEL CR2.....46 C1
Sanderstead Rd SAND/SEL CR2.....36 B3
Sandfield PI THHTH CR7.....15 H2
Sandfield Rd THHTH CR7.....15 H2
Sandhills WLGTN SM6.....24 D5
Sandhurst CI SAND/SEL CR2.....36 C4
Sandhurst Wy SAND/SEL CR2.....36 C3
Sandiford Rd CHEAM SM3.....22 B3
Sandiland Crs HAYES BR2.....29 H5
Sandilands CROY/NA CR0.....27 E4
Sandmartin Wy MTCM CR4.....24 A2
Sandon CI ESH/CLAY KT10.....18 A5
Sandown Dr CAR SM5.....34 A4
Sandown Rd COUL/CHIP CR5.....53 E1
  SNWD SE25.....17 F4
Sandpiper Rd SAND/SEL CR2.....47 H1
  SUT SM1.....32 C1
Sandpit Rd BMLY BR1.....11 G2
Sandpits Rd CROY/NA CR0.....27 H5
Sandringham Av RYNPK SW20.....4 A5
Sandringham Rd CROY/NA CR0.....16 A4
  WPK KT4.....21 E4
Sandrock PI CROY/NA CR0.....27 H5
Sandy Hill Rd WLGTN SM6.....34 C4
Sandy La BELMT SM2.....32 A4
  MTCM CR4.....6 A5
Sandy La North WLGTN SM6.....34 D1
Sandy La South WLGTN SM6.....34 C4
Sandy Wy CROY/NA CR0.....28 A4
Sangley Rd SNWD SE25.....16 C3
Saracen CI CROY/NA CR0.....16 B5
Savile Gdns CROY/NA CR0.....3 K3
Saville Rw HAYES BR2.....29 H2
Sawtry CI CAR SM5.....23 F1
Saxonbury CI MTCM CR4.....13 F3
Saxon Rd BMLY BR1.....11 H4
  CROY/NA CR0.....16 B4
Scarborough CI BELMT SM2.....32 B5
Scarbrook Rd CROY/NA CR0.....2 C5
Scawen CI CAR SM5.....24 A5
Scotsdale CI BELMT SM2.....32 A3
Scotshall La WARL CR6.....49 E5
Scott CI HOR/WEW KT19.....30 A1
  STRHM/NOR SW16.....7 F5
Scotts Av HAYES BR2.....19 F1
Scotts Farm Rd HOR/WEW KT19.....30 A2
Scott's La HAYES BR2.....29 G3
Seabrook Dr WWKM BR4.....29 G3
Seaforth Gdns HOR/WEW KT19.....20 B5
Searchwood Rd WARL CR6.....56 B3
Seaton Rd MTCM CR4.....13 G1
Seddon Rd MRDN SM4.....23 E3
Sedgehill Rd CAT SE6.....10 D2
Sedgewood CI HAYES BR2.....29 H1
Seeley Dr DUL SE21.....8 C1
Seely Rd TOOT SW17.....6 A3
Sefton Rd CROY/NA CR0.....27 E2
  HOR/WEW KT19.....30 B5
Selborne Rd CROY/NA CR0.....3 H5
Selby Gn CAR SM5.....23 G1
Selby Rd CAR SM5.....23 G1
  PGE/AN SE20.....17 E1
Selcroft Rd PUR/KEN CR8.....45 H2
Selhurst New Rd SNWD SE25.....16 C5
Selhurst PI CROY/NA CR0.....16 C5
Selhurst Rd SNWD SE25.....16 C5
Selkirk Rd TOOT SW17.....5 G1
Sellincourt Rd TOOT SW17.....5 H3
Sellindge CI BECK BR3.....10 B4
Selsdon Av SAND/SEL CR2.....36 B2
Selsdon Crs SAND/SEL CR2.....37 G5
Selsdon Park Rd SAND/SEL CR2.....38 B4
Selsdon Rd SAND/SEL CR2.....36 B1
  CROY/NA CR0.....15 F4
Selwood Rd CHEAM SM3.....22 B2
  CROY/NA CR0.....27 G3
Semley Rd STRHM/NOR SW16.....15 E1
Seneca Rd THHTH CR7.....16 A3
Senga Rd WLGTN SM6.....24 A2
Senhouse Rd CHEAM SM3.....21 H4

Seven Acres CAR SM5.....23 G3
Sevenoaks CI BELMT SM2.....32 C5
Seward Rd BECK BR3.....17 H1
Seymour Rd CAR SM5.....23 G1
  EW KT17.....31 G4
  MRDN SM4.....22 C3
Seymour Ms EW KT17.....31 E5
Seymour PI SNWD SE25.....17 G3
Seymour Rd CAR SM5.....34 A1
  MTCM CR4.....24 A1
Seymour Ter PGE/AN SE20.....9 F5
Seymour Vls PGE/AN SE20.....9 F5
Shadbolt CI WPK KT4.....20 D5
Shaftesbury Rd BECK BR3.....18 E1
  CAR SM5.....23 F5
Shaldon Dr MRDN SM4.....12 A4
Shamrock Rd CROY/NA CR0.....15 E5
Shannon Wy BECK BR3.....10 D5
Shap Crs CAR SM5.....23 H2
Sharland Cl THHTH CR7.....15 H5
Sharon CI HOR/WEW KT19.....40 A5
Shaw CI EW KT17.....40 D2
  SAND/SEL CR2.....46 D2
Shaw Crs SAND/SEL CR2.....46 C2
Shawford Rd HOR/WEW KT19.....30 B2
Shawley Crs EPSOM KT18.....50 C3
Shawley Wy EPSOM KT18.....50 C3
Shaw Wy WLGTN SM6.....34 D5
Shaxton Crs CROY/NA CR0.....39 E4
Shearing Dr MRDN SM4.....12 A4
Shearwater Rd SUT SM1.....32 B1
Sheenewood SYD SE26.....9 F2
Sheen Wy WLGTN SM6.....35 F1
Sheephouse Wy NWMAL KT3.....20 C1
Sheldon CI PGE/AN SE20.....9 F5
Sheldon St CROY/NA CR0.....2 C6
Sheldrick CI MTCM CR4.....13 F1
Shelford Ri NRWD SE19.....8 C4
Shelley CI BNSTD SM7.....41 H5
  COUL/CHIP CR5.....54 B2
Shelley Wy WIM/MER SW19.....5 F3
Shelton Av WARL CR6.....56 C3
Shelton CI WARL CR6.....56 C3
Shelton Rd WIM/MER SW19.....14 A1
Shenfield CI COUL/CHIP CR5.....53 F4
Shepherds Wy SAND/SEL CR2.....37 H3
Shepley CI CAR SM5.....24 B3
Sheraton Dr HOR/WEW KT19.....40 A3
Sherborne CI EPSOM KT18.....50 C3
Sherborne Rd CAR SM5.....23 G1
Sherborne Rd CHEAM SM3.....22 C3
Sherbrooke Wy WPK KT4.....21 F1
Shere Av BELMT SM2.....31 G5
Sheridan Rd WIM/MER SW19.....4 B5
Sheridan Wk CAR SM5.....33 H1
Sheridan Wy BECK BR3.....10 B5
Sheringham Rd PGE/AN SE20.....17 F1
Sherwood Av STRHM/NOR SW16.....6 D4
Sherwood Park Rd MTCM CR4.....14 C3
  SUT SM1.....32 C1
Sherwood Rd COUL/CHIP CR5.....53 C1
  CROY/NA CR0.....27 G1
  WIM/MER SW19.....4 A4
Sherwood Wy WWKM BR4.....29 E3
Shinners CI SNWD SE25.....17 E4
Shire Ct EW KT17.....30 D3
Shirley Av BELMT SM2.....31 H5
  COUL/CHIP CR5.....54 D4
  CROY/NA CR0.....27 C2
  SUT SM1.....33 E1
Shirley Church Rd
  CROY/NA CR0.....27 H4
Shirley Crs BECK BR3.....18 A3
Shirley Hills Rd CROY/NA CR0.....37 H1
Shirley Oaks Rd CROY/NA CR0.....27 H2
Shirley Park Rd CROY/NA CR0.....27 F2
  WLGTN SM6.....34 C4
Shirley Rw SNWD SE25 *.....17 E1
Shirley Wy CROY/NA CR0.....28 B4
Shoel HI HOR/WEW KT19.....55 F1
Shoreham CI CROY/NA CR0.....17 E5
Shortcroft Rd EW KT17.....30 D5
Shortlands Gdns HAYES BR2.....19 G1
Shortlands Gv HAYES BR2.....19 F2
Shortlands Rd HAYES BR2.....19 F2
Shorts Rd CAR SM5.....23 C5
Shotfield WLGTN SM6.....34 B2
Shott CI SUT SM1.....33 E1
Shrewsbury Rd BECK BR3.....18 A2
  CAR SM5.....23 G1
Shreveton Rd TOOT SW17 *.....5 H4
Shroffold Rd BMLY BR1.....11 C1
Shropshire CI MTCM CR4.....15 E3
Shrubbery Rd
  STRHM/NOR SW16.....7 E1
Shrubland Gv WPK KT4.....21 G4
Shrubland Rd BNSTD SM7.....51 F1
Shrublands Av CROY/NA CR0.....28 C5
Sibthorp Rd MTCM CR4 *.....13 H1
Sibton Rd CAR SM5.....23 G1
Siddons Rd CROY/NA CR0.....25 H1
Sidney Rd BECK BR3.....17 G5
  SNWD SE25.....17 E4
Silbury Av MTCM CR4.....5 C5
Silverdale FSTH SE23.....9 H1
Silverdale CI SUT SM1.....22 B5
Silver La PUR/KEN CR8.....46 A4
  WWKM BR4.....29 F3
Silverleigh Rd THHTH CR7.....15 F5
Silvermere Rw SNWD SE25 *.....17 F1
Silverwood CI BECK BR3.....10 C4
  CROY/NA CR0.....38 B4
Simms CI CAR SM5.....23 G3
Simone Dr PUR/KEN CR8.....55 E1
Sinclair Dr BELMT SM2.....32 D5
Singleton CI CROY/NA CR0.....26 A1
  WIM/MER SW19.....5 F4
Sir Cyril Black Wy
  WIM/MER SW19.....4 B4
Sirdar Rd MTCM CR4.....6 A3
Sissinghurst CI BMLY BR1.....11 G2
Sissinghurst Rd CROY/NA CR0.....27 E1
Skid Hill La WARL CR6.....49 H5

Slines New Rd *CTHM* CR3 ....56 D5
Slines Oak Rd *CTHM* CR3 ....57 G4
Sloane Wk *CROY/NA* CR0 ....18 B5
Smallwood Rd *TOOT* SW17 ....5 F1
Smitham Bottom La
 CTHM CR3 ....44 D2
Smitham Downs Rd
 COUL/CHIP CR5 ....45 E3
Snowdown Cl *PGE/AN* SE20 ....9 G5
Soloms Court Rd
 COUL/CHIP CR5 ....52 D2
Somerfield Cl
 KWD/TDW/WH KT20 ....51 E4
Somerset Cl *HOR/WEW* KT19 ....30 C5
Somerset Gdns
 STRHM/NOR SW16 ....15 F2
Somerton Cl *PUR/KEN* CR8 ....54 C1
Somerville Rd *PGE/AN* SE20 ....9 F4
Songhurst Cl *CROY/NA* CR0 ....15 F5
Sonning Rd *CROY/NA* CR0 ....17 E5
Soper Dr *CTHM* CR3 ....59 F3
Sorrel Bank *CROY/NA* CR0 ....38 A5
Sorrento Rd *SUT* SM1 ....22 D4
Southampton Row *MTCM* CR4 ....15 E4
South Av *CAR* SM5 ....34 A3
The South Border
 PUR/KEN CR8 ....44 D1
Southbridge Pl *CROY/NA* CR0 ....2 C6
Southbridge Rd *CROY/NA* CR0 ....2 C6
Southbrook Rd
 STRHM/NOR SW16 ....7 E5
Southcote Rd *SAND/SEL* CR2 ....36 C5
 SNWD SE25 ....17 F4
Southcroft Av *WWKM* BR4 ....29 E3
Southcroft Rd
 STRHM/NOR SW16 ....6 B3
Southdown Rd *CAR* SM5 ....34 A4
 CTHM CR3 ....61 D2
South Dr *BELMT* SM2 ....32 A5
 BNSTD SM7 ....43 G3
 COUL/CHIP CR5 ....44 D6
South Eden Park Rd *BECK* BR3 ....18 D5
South End *CROY/NA* CR0 ....2 D7
Southend La *CAT* SE6 ....10 C1
Southend Rd *BECK* BR3 ....10 C5
Southern Av *SNWD* SE25 ....16 D2
Southey Rd *WIM/MER* SW19 ....4 C4
Southey St *PGE/AN* SE20 ....9 H4
Southfields Rd *GDST* RH9 ....61 H5
South Gdns *WIM/MER* SW19 ....5 H4
South Hill Rd *HAYES* BR2 ....19 G2
Southholme Cl *NRWD* SE19 ....8 C5
Southlands Cl *COUL/CHIP* CR5 ....54 B2
South Lodge Av *MTCM* CR4 ....15 H3
South Md *HOR/WEW* KT19 ....30 D3
South Norwood HI *SNWD* SE25 ....16 C1
South Oak Rd *STRHM/NOR* SW16 ....7 F1
South Pde *WLGTN* SM6 * 34 C2
South Park Hill Rd
 SAND/SEL CR2 ....36 B1
South Park Rd *WIM/MER* SW19 ....4 C3
South Rd *CAR* SM5 ....33 G4
South Rd *WIM/MER* SW19 ....5 F5
South St *EPSOM* KT18 ....40 B3
South V *NRWD* SE19 ....8 C3
Southview Cl *TOOT* SW17 ....6 A2
South View Ct *NRWD* SE19 * 8 A4
Southview Gdns *WLGTN* SM6 ....34 C5
Southview Rd *BMLY* BR1 ....11 F1
 CTHM CR3 ....61 H4
 WARL CR6 ....66 B5
Southviews *SAND/SEL* CR2 ....37 H4
Southville Cl *HOR/WEW* KT19 ....30 B4
South Wk *WWKM* BR4 ....29 G4
Southwater Cl *BECK* BR3 ....10 D4
South Wy *CAR* SM5 ....33 F5
 CROY/NA CR0 ....24 C5
Southway *WLGTN* SM6 ....24 C5
Southwell Rd *CROY/NA* CR0 ....15 G5
Southwood Av *COUL/CHIP* CR5 ....44 C5
Southwood Cl *WPK* KT4 ....21 H2
Southwood Dr *BRYLDS* KT5 ....20 A1
Sovereign Cl *PUR/KEN* CR8 ....35 F5
Spa Cl *NRWD* SE19 ....8 C5
Spa HI *THHT* CR7 ....8 B5
Spalding Rd *TOOT* SW17 ....6 B2
Sparrow Farm Rd *EW* KT17 ....21 E5
Speakers Ct *CROY/NA* CR0 * 26 B2
Speke Rd *THHTH* CR7 ....16 B1
Speldhurst Cl *HAYES* BR2 ....19 H4
Spencer Rd *WIM/MER* SW19 * 4 A5
Spencer Hill Rd *WIM/MER* SW19 ....4 A4
Spencer Pl *CROY/NA* CR0 ....26 B1
Spencer Rd *BMLY* BR1 ....11 H4
 CTHM CR3 ....59 F1
 MTCM CR4 ....14 A1
 MTCM CR4 ....24 A1
 SAND/SEL CR2 ....2 C6
Spices Yd *CROY/NA* CR0 ....2 D6
Spindlewood Gdns
 CROY/NA CR0 ....3 F6
Spinney Cl *BECK* BR3 ....18 C6
 WPK KT4 ....21 H2
Spinney Gdns *NRWD* SE19 ....8 D4
The Spinney *CHEAM* SM3 ....21 G5
 EPSOM KT18 ....50 B4
 PUR/KEN CR8 ....45 H1
Spooner Wk *WLGTN* SM6 ....34 C1
Springbourne Ct *BECK* BR3 ....11 E5
Springclose La *CHEAM* SM3 ....32 A2
Springfield Av *RYNPK* SW20 ....12 B2
Springfield Gdns *WWKM* BR4 ....28 D3
Springfield Ri *SYD* SE26 ....9 F1
Springfield Rd *EW* KT17 ....31 G5
 SYD SE26 ....9 F2
 THHT CR7 ....8 A5
 WIM/MER SW19 ....4 B2
 WLGTN SM6 ....34 B1
Spring Gdns *WLGTN* SM6 ....34 C1
Spring Gv *MTCM* CR4 ....6 A5
Spring HI *SYD* SE26 ....9 G1
Springhurst Cl *CROY/NA* CR0 ....28 B5
Spring La *SNWD* SE25 ....17 F5

Spring Park Av *CROY/NA* CR0 ....27 H3
Springpark Dr *BECK* BR3 ....19 E2
Spring Park Rd *CROY/NA* CR0 ....27 H3
Spring St *EW* KT17 ....30 D4
Springwell Rd
 STRHM/NOR SW16 ....6 C6
Sprucedale Gdns *CROY/NA* CR0 ....27 H5
 PUR/KEN CR8 ....35 E4
The Square *CAR* SM5 ....34 A1
The Squerryes *CTHM* CR3 ....59 G1
Squires Ct *WIM/MER* SW19 ....4 C2
Squirrels La *WPK* KT4 ....20 D3
Squirrel's Wy *EPSOM* KT18 ....40 B5
Stable Ms *WNWD* SE27 ....7 H4
Staddon Cl *BECK* BR3 ....18 A3
Staddon Ct *BECK* BR3 ....18 A3
Stafford Cl *CHEAM* SM3 ....32 A2
 CTHM CR3 ....59 H3
Stafford Gdns *CROY/NA* CR0 ....35 F1
Stafford Rd *CROY/NA* CR0 ....35 F1
 CTHM CR3 ....59 H3
 WLGTN SM6 ....34 C2
Stagbury Av *COUL/CHIP* CR5 ....52 C3
Stagbury Cl *COUL/CHIP* CR5 ....52 C3
Stag Leys Cl *BNSTD* SM7 ....43 G5
Stainbank Rd *MTCM* CR4 ....14 B2
Staines Av *CHEAM* SM3 ....21 H3
Staiths Wy *KWD/TDW/WH* KT20 ....50 B5
Stambourne Wy *NRWD* SE19 ....8 A4
 WWKM BR4 ....28 D2
Stamford Dr *HAYES* BR2 ....19 H3
Stane Cl *WIM/MER* SW19 ....4 D4
Stane Wy *EW* KT17 ....31 E5
Stanford Rd *STRHM/NOR* SW16 ....15 E1
The Stanfords *EW* KT17 ....40 D2
Stanford Wy *STRHM/NOR* SW16 ....14 D1
Stanger Rd *SNWD* SE25 ....17 E4
Stanhope Gv *BECK* BR3 ....18 B4
Stanhope Rd *CAR* SM5 ....34 A3
 CROY/NA CR0 ....2 E6
Stanley Av *BECK* BR3 ....19 E2
Stanley Cl *COUL/CHIP* CR5 ....54 B2
Stanley Gdns *MTCM* CR4 * 6 A3
 SAND/SEL CR2 ....47 E2
 WLGTN SM6 ....34 C2
Stanley Gv *THHTH* CR7 ....15 C5
Stanley Park Rd *CAR* SM5 ....33 H3
 WLGTN SM6 ....34 B2
Stanmore Gdns *SUT* SM1 ....23 E4
Stanmore Ter *BECK* BR3 ....18 C1
Stannet Wy *WLGTN* SM6 ....24 C5
Stansted Cl *HAYES* BR2 ....19 H4
Stanstead Rd *CTHM* CR3 ....59 G4
Stanthorpe Cl
 STRHM/NOR SW16 * 7 E2
Stanthorpe Rd
 STRHM/NOR SW16 * 7 E2
Stanton Cl *WPK* KT4 ....21 H2
Stanton Rd *CROY/NA* CR0 ....26 A1
Stanton Wy *SYD* SE26 ....9 G2
Staplehurst Rd *CAR* SM5 ....33 G3
Stapleton Gdns *CROY/NA* CR0 ....35 G3
Starling Cl *CROY/NA* CR0 ....18 A5
Starrock La *COUL/CHIP* CR5 ....53 F4
Starrock Rd *COUL/CHIP* CR5 ....53 F4
Station Ap *BECK* BR3 ....10 A5
 BELMT SM2 ....32 A3
 BELMT SM2 ....32 D5
 CAR SM5 ....10 B2
 COUL/CHIP CR5 ....53 H1
 CROY/NA CR0 ....53 H1
 CTHM CR3 ....56 A2
 EW KT17 ....31 F5
 HOR/WEW KT19 ....30 D1
 HOR/WEW KT19 ....40 D3
 PUR/KEN CR8 * 45 G2
 SAND/SEL CR2 ....36 B4
 STRHM/NOR SW16 ....7 E2
Station Approach Rd
 COUL/CHIP CR5 ....44 D5
Station Av *CTHM* CR3 ....60 A4
 HOR/WEW KT19 ....30 C4
Station Est *BECK* BR3 ....17 H3
Station Garage Ms
 STRHM/NOR SW16 * 6 D5
Station Pde *BECK* BR3 * 17 H3
 BELMT SM2 ....32 C5
Station Rd *BELMT* SM2 ....32 C5
 CAR SM5 ....23 H5
 CROY/NA CR0 ....55 H3
 CTHM CR3 ....55 H3
 CTHM CR3 ....61 E2
 HAYES BR2 ....19 G1
 PGE/AN SE20 ....9 H5
 PUR/KEN CR8 ....46 A4
 SNWD SE25 ....16 D3
 WIM/MER SW19 ....4 A3
 WWKM BR4 ....29 E5
Station Wy *CHEAM* SM3 ....32 A2
Station Yd *PUR/KEN* CR8 ....45 H1
Stavordale Rd *CAR* SM5 ....23 E1
Stayton Rd *SUT* SM1 ....22 C4
Steep HI *CROY/NA* CR0 ....3 G6
Steeple Cl *WIM/MER* SW19 ....4 A1
Steers Md *MTCM* CR4 ....6 A5
Stella Rd *TOOT* SW17 ....5 H3
Stembridge Rd *PGE/AN* SE20 ....17 F1
Sterry Dr *HOR/WEW* KT19 ....30 B3
Steve Biko La *CAT* SE6 ....10 D1
Stevens Cl *BECK* BR3 ....10 C3
Stevens Pl *PUR/KEN* CR8 ....45 H3
Steyning Cl *PUR/KEN* CR8 ....54 D1

Stiby Wy *COUL/CHIP* CR5 ....53 G2
Stirling Av *WLGTN* SM6 ....35 E5
Stirling Cl *BNSTD* SM7 ....51 F2
 STRHM/NOR SW16 ....6 C5
Stirling Dr *CTHM* CR3 ....59 E1
Stites Hill Rd *COUL/CHIP* CR5 ....54 D5
Stoats Nest Rd *COUL/CHIP* CR5 ....54 A3
Stockbury Rd *CROY/NA* CR0 ....17 G5
Stockhams Cl *SAND/SEL* CR2 ....36 B5
Stockport Rd *STRHM/NOR* SW16 ....14 D5
Stodart Rd *PGE/AN* SE20 ....9 G5
Stokes Rd *CROY/NA* CR0 ....17 H5
Stonecot Cl *MRDN* SM4 ....22 D2
Stonecot HI *MRDN* SM4 ....22 A2
Stonecroft Wy *CROY/NA* CR0 ....25 E1
Stoneleigh Broadway *EW* KT17 ....31 E4
Stoneleigh Crs *HOR/WEW* KT19 ....31 E1
Stoneleigh Park Av
 CROY/NA CR0 ....17 H5
Stoneleigh Park Rd
 HOR/WEW KT19 ....30 D2
Stone Md *SAND/SEL* CR2 ....23 C1
Stone Park Av *BECK* BR3 ....18 C5
Stone Pl *WPK* KT4 ....21 E3
Stone Rd *HAYES* BR2 ....19 H4
Stone's Rd *EW* KT17 ....40 C1
Stoneyfield Rd *COUL/CHIP* CR5 ....54 B2
Stoney La *NRWD* SE19 ....8 C3
Storrington Rd *CROY/NA* CR0 ....26 D2
Stoughton Av *CHEAM* SM3 ....31 H1
Stowell Av *CROY/NA* CR0 ....39 F5
Stratford Rd *THHTH* CR7 ....15 G3
Strathbrook Rd
 STRHM/NOR SW16 ....7 F1
Strathdale *STRHM/NOR* SW16 ....7 F2
Strathearn Rd *SUT* SM1 ....32 C1
 WIM/MER SW19 ....4 B2
Strathmore Cl *CTHM* CR3 ....59 G1
Strathmore Rd *CROY/NA* CR0 ....2 F1
 WIM/MER SW19 ....4 D4
Strathyre Av *STRHM/NOR* SW16 ....15 G2
Stratton Av *WLGTN* SM6 ....34 D4
Stratton Cl *WIM/MER* SW19 ....12 B1
Stratton Rd *WIM/MER* SW19 ....12 C1
Strawberry La *CAR* SM5 ....23 H4
Straw Cl *CTHM* CR3 ....59 E3
Streatham Common
 STRHM/NOR SW16 * 6 D4
Streatham Common North
 STRHM/NOR SW16 ....7 F2
Streatham Common South
 STRHM/NOR SW16 ....7 E3
Streatham Gn
 STRHM/NOR SW16 * 7 E1
Streatham High Rd
 STRHM/NOR SW16 ....6 D4
Streatham V *STRHM/NOR* SW16 ....6 C5
Streeters La *WLGTN* SM6 ....24 D4
Stretton Rd *CROY/NA* CR0 ....26 C1
Strond Green Gdns
 CROY/NA CR0 ....27 G1
Strond Green Wy *CROY/NA* CR0 ....27 G1
Stroudes Cl *WPK* KT4 ....20 D1
Stroud Green Wy *CROY/NA* CR0 ....17 G5
Stuart Crs *CROY/NA* CR0 ....28 B4
Stuart Pl *MTCM* CR4 ....5 H5
Stuart Rd *THHTH* CR7 ....16 A3
 WARL CR6 ....56 B5
Stubbs Wy *WIM/MER* SW19 ....5 F5
Studland Rd *SYD* SE26 ....9 E2
Stumps Hill La *BECK* BR3 ....10 C5
Styles Wy *BECK* BR3 ....19 E3
Succomb's HI *CTHM* CR3 ....56 B5
Succombs Pl *WARL* CR6 ....56 B5
Sudbury Gdns *CROY/NA* CR0 ....3 H6
Suffield Cl *SAND/SEL* CR2 ....47 H2
Suffield Rd *PGE/AN* SE20 ....17 G1
Suffolk Rd *SNWD* SE25 ....16 D3
 WPK KT4 ....20 D5
Sultan St *BECK* BR3 ....17 H1
Summerene Cl
 STRHM/NOR SW16 ....6 C4
Summers Av *WIM/MER* SW19 ....6 A5
Summers Ct *BELMT* SM2 ....32 C3
Summerswood Cl
 PUR/KEN CR8 ....55 F1
Summerville Gdns *SUT* SM1 ....32 B2
Summit Wy *NRWD* SE19 ....8 C3
Sumner Gdns *CROY/NA* CR0 ....25 G2
Sumner Rd *CROY/NA* CR0 ....25 H2
Sumner Rd South *CROY/NA* CR0 ....25 G2
Sunbury Rd *CHEAM* SM3 ....21 H4
Sundale Av *SAND/SEL* CR2 ....37 G5
Sundial Av *SNWD* SE25 ....16 D1
Sundown Av *SAND/SEL* CR2 ....47 G1
Sundridge Rd *CROY/NA* CR0 ....26 D2
Sunken Rd *CROY/NA* CR0 ....37 G1
Sunkist Wy *WLGTN* SM6 ....35 E4
Sunlight Cl *WIM/MER* SW19 * 5 E3
Sunningdale Rd *SUT* SM1 ....22 D4
Sunny Bank *SNWD* SE25 ....16 D1
 WARL CR6 ....57 E2
Sunnycroft Rd *SNWD* SE25 ....16 D1
Sunnydene Rd *PUR/KEN* CR8 ....45 H3
Sunnydene St *SYD* SE26 ....9 G2
Sunnyhill Rd *STRHM/NOR* SW16 ....7 E1
Sunnyhurst Cl *SUT* SM1 ....22 C6
Sunnymede Av *CAR* SM5 ....43 F1
 HOR/WEW KT19 ....30 C4
Sunny Nook Gdns
 SAND/SEL CR2 * 36 B2
Sunny Ri *CTHM* CR3 ....59 F4
Sunnyside *WIM/MER* SW19 ....4 A3
Sunset Gdns *SNWD* SE25 ....16 C1
Sunshine Wy *MTCM* CR4 ....13 H1
Surrey Gv *SUT* SM1 ....23 F4
Surrey Mt *WNWD* SE27 ....7 G3
Surrey St *CROY/NA* CR0 ....2 C5
Surridge Gdns *NRWD* SE19 ....8 B5

Sussex Rd *CAR* SM5 ....33 H2
 MTCM CR4 * 15 E4
 SAND/SEL CR2 ....36 B4
 WWKM BR4 ....28 D2
Sussex Ter *PGE/AN* SE20 * 9 G4
Sutherland Dr *WIM/MER* SW19 ....5 F5
Sutherland Gdns *WPK* KT4 ....21 F2
Sutherland Rd *CROY/NA* CR0 ....25 G1
Sutton Cl *BECK* BR3 ....10 D5
Sutton Common Rd
 CHEAM SM3 ....22 B1
Sutton Ct *BELMT* SM2 ....33 E3
Sutton Court Rd *BELMT* SM2 ....33 E2
Sutton Gdns *CROY/NA* CR0 ....16 D4
Sutton Gv *SUT* SM1 ....33 F1
Sutton La *BNSTD* SM7 ....43 D5
Sutton Park Rd *SUT* SM1 ....32 D2
Swain Cl *STRHM/NOR* SW16 ....6 B5
Swain Rd *THHTH* CR7 ....16 A4
Swains Rd *MTCM* CR4 ....5 H4
Swallowdale *SAND/SEL* CR2 ....37 H4
Swallow Gdns
 STRHM/NOR SW16 ....6 D2
Swanley Av *PUR/KEN* CR8 ....63 E1
Swiftsden Wy *BMLY* BR1 ....11 G3
Swinburne Crs *CROY/NA* CR0 ....17 G5
Sycamore Cl *CAR* SM5 ....23 H5
 SAND/SEL CR2 ....38 C5
Sycamore Gdns *MTCM* CR4 ....13 F1
Sycamore Ri *EW* KT17 ....44 H4
Sydenham Av *SYD* SE26 ....9 F2
Sydenham Rd *CROY/NA* CR0 ....2 E1
 SYD SE26 ....9 G1
Sydenham Station Ap *SYD* SE26 ....9 G1
Sydney Av *PUR/KEN* CR8 ....45 E3
Sydney Rd *SUT* SM1 ....22 C5
Sylvan Cl *SAND/SEL* CR2 ....37 F5
Sylvan HI *NRWD* SE19 ....8 C5
Sylvan Rd *NRWD* SE19 ....8 D5
Sylvan Wy *WWKM* BR4 ....29 G5
Sylverdale Rd *PGE/AN* SE20 * 2 A4
 PUR/KEN CR8 ....45 H3

T

Tabarin Wy *EW* KT17 ....50 C1
Tabor Gdns *CHEAM* SM3 ....32 B2
Tabor Gv *WIM/MER* SW19 ....4 A4
Taffy's How *MTCM* CR4 ....13 G2
Tait Rd *CROY/NA* CR0 ....26 C1
Talbot Rd *CAR* SM5 ....34 A1
 THHTH CR7 ....16 B3
Talisman Sq *SYD* SE26 ....9 E1
Talisman Wy *EW* KT17 ....50 C1
Tall Elms Cl *HAYES* BR2 ....19 F2
Tall Trees *STRHM/NOR* SW16 ....15 F2
Tamesis Gdns *WPK* KT4 ....20 C3
Tamworth La *MTCM* CR4 ....14 B2
Tamworth Pk *MTCM* CR4 ....14 C3
Tamworth Pl *CROY/NA* CR0 ....2 C3
Tandridge Gdns *SAND/SEL* CR2 ....46 D5
Tandridge Rd *WARL* CR6 ....56 D4
Tanfield Rd *CROY/NA* CR0 ....2 C6
Tangier Wy *KWD/TDW/WH* KT20 ....51 F2
Tangier Wd *KWD/TDW/WH* KT20 ....51 E5
Tanglewood Cl *CROY/NA* CR0 ....27 G4
Tankerton Ter *CROY/NA* CR0 * 25 F1
Tankerville Rd
 STRHM/NOR SW16 ....6 D4
Tannery Cl *CROY/NA* CR0 ....17 H4
Tannsfeld Rd *SYD* SE26 ....9 H2
Tapestry Cl *BELMT* SM2 ....32 D4
Taplow Ct *MTCM* CR4 ....13 G3
Tara Pk *COUL/CHIP* CR5 ....52 D5
Tarragon Gv *SYD* SE26 ....9 H3
Tarrington Cl
 STRHM/NOR SW16 * 6 D1
Tate Rd *SUT* SM1 ....32 C1
Tattenham Corner Rd
 EPSOM KT18 ....50 A3
Tattenham Crs *EPSOM* KT18 ....50 A3
Tattenham Gv *EPSOM* KT18 ....50 B4
Tattenham Wy
 KWD/TDW/WH KT20 ....51 E2
Taunton Av *CHEAM* SM3 ....31 H1
Taunton Cl *CHEAM* SM3 ....22 C2
Taunton La *COUL/CHIP* CR5 ....54 C4
Tavern Cl *CAR* SM5 ....23 G1
Tavistock Crs *MTCM* CR4 ....15 E3
Tavistock Gv *CROY/NA* CR0 ....26 A1
Tavistock Rd *CAR* SM5 ....23 F2
 CROY/NA CR0 ....26 B2
Tayles Hill Dr *EW* KT17 ....30 D5
Taylor Rd *WIM/MER* SW19 ....5 G4
 WLGTN SM6 ....34 B3
Taylor's La *SYD* SE26 ....9 E2
Teal Cl *SAND/SEL* CR2 ....47 H1
Tealing Dr *HOR/WEW* KT19 ....20 D5
Teasel Cl *CROY/NA* CR0 ....27 H3
Tedder Rd *SAND/SEL* CR2 ....37 H3
Teddington Cl *HOR/WEW* KT19 ....30 B5
Teesdale Gdns *SNWD* SE25 ....16 C1
Teevan Cl *CROY/NA* CR0 ....27 E1
Teevan Rd *CROY/NA* CR0 ....27 E1
Telegraph Tr *WLGTN* SM6 ....44 A1
Telford Cl *NRWD* SE19 ....8 D5
Temple Av *CROY/NA* CR0 ....28 B4
Templecombe Wy *MRDN* SM4 ....12 A4
Temple Cl *CROY/NA* CR0 * 2 F6
 HOR/WEW KT19 ....40 B2
Templeton Cl *THHTH* CR7 ....15 H5
Temple Wy *SUT* SM1 ....23 F4
Tennison Cl *COUL/CHIP* CR5 ....54 D5
Tennison Rd *SNWD* SE25 ....16 D3
Tennyson Rd *PGE/AN* SE20 ....9 H4
 WIM/MER SW19 ....5 E3

Tenterden Gdns *CROY/NA* CR0 ....17 E5
Tenterden Rd *CROY/NA* CR0 ....17 E5
Tewkesbury Rd *CAR* SM5 ....23 F5
Thakeham Cl *SYD* SE26 ....9 E2
Thames Down Link
 CHSGTN KT9 ....
Thanescroft Gdns
 CROY/NA CR0 ....
Thanet Pl *CROY/NA* CR0 ....2 C5
Tharp Rd *WLGTN* SM6 ....34 D1
Thayers Farm Rd *BECK* BR3 ....17 G1
Theobald Rd *CROY/NA* CR0 ....2 B3
Therapia La *CROY/NA* CR0 ....14 D5
Theresa's Wk *SAND/SEL* CR2 ....36 B3
Thesiger Rd *PGE/AN* SE20 ....9 H5
Thicket Crs *SUT* SM1 ....23 F3
Thicket Gv *PGE/AN* SE20 ....9 E5
Thicket Rd *PGE/AN* SE20 ....9 E5
 SUT SM1 ....23 F3
Thicket Ter *PGE/AN* SE20 * 9 E5
Thirlmere Ri *BMLY* BR1 ....11 H1
Thirlmere Rd *STRHM/NOR* SW16 ....15 E5
Thirsk Rd *MTCM* CR4 ....6 A4
 SNWD SE25 ....16 B3
Thistlewood Crs *CROY/NA* CR0 ....39 E5
Thomas Av *CTHM* CR3 ....59 E5
Thomas Dean Rd *SYD* SE26 * 9 A1
Thomas Wall Cl *SUT* SM1 ....32 D1
Thompson Cl *CHEAM* SM3 ....22 A4
Thomson Crs *CROY/NA* CR0 ....25 G1
Thorburn Wy *WIM/MER* SW19 ....13 G1
Thorn Ct *BELMT* SM2 * 33 E3
Thorncroft Cl *COUL/CHIP* CR5 ....54 C4
Thorncroft Rd *SUT* SM1 ....32 D1
Thorndon Gdns *HOR/WEW* KT19 ....30 C3
Thorndyke Cl *SUT* SM1 ....32 D1
Thorne's Cl *BECK* BR3 ....19 F1
Thornhill Rd *CROY/NA* CR0 ....26 A1
Thornlaw Rd *WNWD* SE27 ....7 F4
Thornsett Pl *PGE/AN* SE20 ....17 G1
Thornsett Rd *PGE/AN* SE20 ....17 G1
 WIM/MER SW19 ....4 C5
Thornsett Ter *PGE/AN* SE20 * 17 G1
Thornton Cl *CROY/NA* CR0 ....25 G2
Thornton Crs *COUL/CHIP* CR5 ....54 D5
Thornton Dene *BECK* BR3 ....18 C2
Thornton HI *WIM/MER* SW19 ....3 H2
Thornton Rd *CAR* SM5 ....23 F5
 THHTH CR7 ....15 G1
Thornton Rw *THHTH* CR7 ....15 G3
Thornville Gv *MTCM* CR4 ....13 E1
Thorold Cl *SAND/SEL* CR2 ....38 B5
Thorpe Cl *CROY/NA* CR0
 SYD SE26 * 9 G2
Thorpe Cl *TOOT* SW17 ....6 A1
Thorsden Wy *NRWD* SE19 * 8 B5
Thrale Rd *STRHM/NOR* SW16 ....6 D1
Throwley Rd *SUT* SM1 ....32 D2
Throwley Wy *SUT* SM1 ....32 D1
Thrupp Cl *MTCM* CR4 ....6 C6
Thurbarn Rd *CAT* SE6 ....10 D1
Thurleston Av *MRDN* SM4 ....12 A3
Thurnham Wy
 KWD/TDW/WH KT20 ....51 F1
Thursley Crs *CROY/NA* CR0 ....28 B5
Thurso St *TOOT* SW17 ....5 H1
Tideswell Rd *CROY/NA* CR0 ....28 A1
Tiepigs La *WWKM* BR4 ....29 F4
Tilehurst Rd *CHEAM* SM3 ....32 A3
Tilford Av *CROY/NA* CR0 ....28 A5
Tilia Cl *SUT* SM1 ....32 C3
Tillingbourne Wy *CTHM* CR3 ....
Tillingdown La *CTHM* CR3 ....61 G2
Timbercroft *HOR/WEW* KT19 ....30 B3
Timber Hill Rd *CTHM* CR3 ....60 B4
Timberling Gdns *SAND/SEL* CR2 ....36 B4
Timberslip Dr *WLGTN* SM6 ....34 D4
The Timbers *CHEAM* SM3 * 31 H2
Times Sq *SUT* SM1 * 32 D1
Tindale Cl *SAND/SEL* CR2 ....46 C5
Tintagel Cl *EW* KT17 ....40 D3
Tintern Cl *WIM/MER* SW19 ....5 E2
Tintern Rd *CAR* SM5 ....23 E1
Tipton Dr *CROY/NA* CR0 ....3 G6
Tirlemont Rd *SAND/SEL* CR2 ....36 A3
Tirrell Rd *CROY/NA* CR0 ....15 H5
Tisbury Rd *STRHM/NOR* SW16 ....15 E5
Titchfield Rd *CAR* SM5 ....23 E5
Tithepit Shaw La *SAND/SEL* CR2 ....
 WARL CR6 ....
Tiverton Cl *CROY/NA* CR0 ....26 D1
Tivoli Rd *WNWD* SE27 ....7 H4
Tollers La *COUL/CHIP* CR5 ....54 C5
Tollhouse La *WLGTN* SM6 ....34 C5
Tolworth Ri North *BRYLDS* KT5 ....20 B1
Tolworth Ri South *BRYLDS* KT5 ....20 B1
Tomlin Cl *HOR/WEW* KT19 ....40 B5
Tonbridge Cl *BNSTD* SM7 ....44 D4
Tonfield Rd *CHEAM* SM3 ....22 B6
Tonstall Rd *HOR/WEW* KT19 ....40 B5
Tooting Bec Gdns
 STRHM/NOR SW16 ....6 D1
Tooting High St *TOOT* SW17 ....6 A1
Tooting High St *TOOT* SW17 * ....
Tootswood Rd *HAYES* BR2 ....19 G1
Top Pk *BECK* BR3 ....19 G3
Tormead La *SUT* SM1 ....
Torridge Rd *THHTH* CR7 ....15 H3
Torrington Gv *MRDN* SM4 ....12 C4
Torrington Wy *MRDN* SM4 ....12 B4
Torr Rd *PGE/AN* SE20 ....9 H4
Torwood La *CTHM* CR3 ....59 F3
Totterdown St *TOOT* SW17 * 5 H1
Totton Rd *THHTH* CR7 ....15 G2
Tovil Cl *PGE/AN* SE20 ....17 F1
Tower Cl *PGE/AN* SE20 ....9 G5
The Towers *PUR/KEN* CR8 ....
Tower Vw *CROY/NA* CR0 ....28 A1
Townend *CTHM* CR3 ....
Town End Cl *CTHM* CR3 ....

...h Wy CROY/NA CR0 ....16 D5
...e Rd RYNPK SW20 ....4 A5
...cery BNSTD SM7 ....42 D5
...ar Av WPK KT4 ....21 H2
...ar Rd WIM/MER SW19 ....4 A4
...ar Rd THHTH CR7 ....15 G4
...ell Rd EPSOM KT18 ....40 D5
...ry Pth MTCM CR4 ....13 G5
...ll Rd WNWD SE27 ....7 H1
...gs WARL CR6 ....56 A5
...ev CI NRWD SE19 ....8 D5
...Gdns NRWD SE19 ....8 B5
...ne Rd PGE/AN SE20 ....17 F1
...in DR WARL CR6 ....56 C1
...me Ter PGE/AN SE20 ....9 F4
...ie La SUT SM1 ....21 G4
...I BMLY BR1 ....11 G3
...an Rd TOOT SW17 ....5 H3
...CI HAYES BR2 ....29 H1
...iry Rd SYD SE26 ....9 H2
...I SAND/SEL CR2 ....5 J6
...ns PGE/AN SE20 * 9 G5
...n WIM/MER SW19 ....1 J4
...a Rd BMLY BR1 ....11 H1
...Av CROY/NA CR0 ....25 E5
...ury Rd SYD SE26 ....9 G5
...d Rd WNWD SE27 ....7 G2
...y WPK KT4 ....21 H2
...I BNSTD SM7 ....42 A5
...SM3 ....31 H1
.../CHIP CR5 ....54 C3
...CR2 ....47 F5
...SM6 ....24 B1
...dns WWKM BR4 ....29 E4
...NRWD SE19 * 8 D4
...SW19 ....5 G4
...BECK BR3 ....19 E2
...SE19 ....8 A3
...SE25 ....17 F4
...Rd CROY/NA CR0 ....16 B5
...CROY/NA CR0 ....27 H2
...MTCM CR4 ....23 H1
...BECK BR3 ....19 E2
...wood Rd BNSTD SM7 ....51 E1
...Gdns SNWD SE25 ....16 C1
...Rd CROY/NA CR0 ....3 H1
...Scrubbs Rd
...CR3 * 56 A5
...Oak CI NRWD SE19 * 8 B5
...I STRHM/NOR SW16 ....15 E1
...Av MTCM CR4 ....5 H5
...s BELMT SM2 ....32 D3
...d NWMAL KT3 ....20 B1
...Meadow Wy BECK BR3 ....10 D5
...ne CI SAND/SEL CR2 ....4 B6
...e La SUT SM1 ....33 E1
...e Link CROY/NA CR0 ....3 H3
...ne CI SAND/SEL CR2 ....38 A5
...ie Rd CAR SM5 ....34 B3
...e Rd STRHM/NOR SW16 ....15 E1
...t NRWD SE19 ....8 D2
...uth Rd MTCM CR4 ....6 A4

U

... Gv MTCM CR4 ....6 A5
... Rd WNWD SE27 ....7 G1
... ne Rd
... CHTH CR3 ....6 C1
... r Crs COUL/CHIP CR5 ....54 A1
... CHTH CR3 ....61 G3
... ood CROY/NA CR0 ....39 E2
... ood Ct CTHM CR3 ....59 H4
... ood Rd CTHM CR3 ....59 G5
... t TOOT SW17 ....5 H4
... CROY/NA CR0 ....26 A1
... CROY/NA CR0 ....38 D4
... SE27 ....9 G3
... y WIM/MER SW19 ....5 F3
... rd Rd CAR SM5 ....33 F3
... CR3 ....57 G5
... / SEL CR2 ....36 B1
... BECK BR3 ....18 C1
... Rd PUR/KEN CR8 ....55 E2
... Wy EPSOM KT18 ....50 C3
... ulah HI NRWD SE19 ....6 B6
... urt Rd CTHM CR3 ....61 G3
... VEW KT19 ....40 A1
... unnymans BNSTD SM7 ....42 B4
... mers End Rd
... BR3 ....18 A3
... East MTCM CR4 ....13 H1
... West MTCM CR4 ....13 H1
... SNWD SE25 ....16 C3
... gh St EW KT17 ....40 C3
... ulgrave Rd BELMT SM2 ....32 A3
... iory Down Rd CAR SM5 ....44 A3
... es BNSTD SM7 ....42 B2
... WLGTN SM6 ....34 D3
... wleywood BNSTD SM7 ....42 B4
... Isdon Rd
... /SEL CR2 ....36 D4
... irley Rd CROY/NA CR0 ....27 G4
... ooting Rd TOOT SW17 ....5 H4
... rnon Rd SUT SM1 ....33 F1

Upper Woodcote Village
    PUR/KEN CR8 ....44 D3
Upton Dene BELMT SM2 ....32 D3
Upton Rd THHTH CR7 ....16 B1
Upwood Rd STRHM/NOR SW16 ....7 E5
Uvedale CI CROY/NA CR0 ....49 F1
Uvedale Crs CROY/NA CR0 ....49 F1

V

Valan Leas HAYES BR2 ....19 G3
Vale CI COUL/CHIP CR5 ....45 E4
Valentyne CI CROY/NA CR0 ....49 G1
Vale Rd MTCM CR4 ....14 D2
    SUT SM1 ....22 D5
    WPK KT4 ....20 D4
Valeswood Rd BMLY BR1 ....11 H2
The Vale COUL/CHIP CR5 ....45 E4
    CROY/NA CR0 ....27 H3
Valleyfield Rd STRHM/NOR SW16 ....7 F2
Valley Gdns WIM/MER SW19 ....5 F4
Valley Rd HAYES BR2 ....19 G1
    PUR/KEN CR8 ....46 B5
    STRHM/NOR SW16 ....7 F1
    WIM/MER SW19 ....5 F3
Valley View Gdns PUR/KEN CR8 ....46 C5
Valley Wk CROY/NA CR0 ....27 G5
Valnay St TOOT SW17 ....5 H2
Vancouver CI HOR/WEW KT19 ....40 A1
Van Dyck Av NWMAL KT3 ....20 B1
Vanguard CI CROY/NA CR0 ....2 A1
    THHTH CR7 ....15 H3
Vanguard Wy CROY/NA CR0 ....3 J6
    WLGTN SM6 ....35 E4
Vant Rd TOOT SW17 ....5 H2
Varley Wy MTCM CR4 ....13 F1
Vauxhall Gdns SAND/SEL CR2 ....36 A2
Veals Md MTCM CR4 ....5 C5
Vectis Rd TOOT SW17 ....6 B3
Vectis Rd TOOT SW17 ....5 F3
Vellum Dr CAR SM5 ....24 A4
Venner Rd SYD SE26 ....9 G3
Ventnor Rd BELMT SM2 ....32 D3
Verdayne Av CROY/NA CR0 ....27 H2
Verdayne Gdns WARL CR6 ....56 C1
Vermont Rd NRWD SE19 ....8 B5
    SUT SM1 ....23 F1
Vernon CI HOR/WEW KT19 ....30 A2
Vernon Dr CTHM CR3 ....59 G5
Vernon Rd SUT SM1 ....33 E1
Vernon Wk KWD/TDW/WH KT20 ....50 D5
Veronica Gdns MTCM CR4 ....6 C5
Versailles Rd PGE/AN SE20 ....9 E4
Verulam Av PUR/KEN CR8 ....44 C2
Vicarage CI WPK KT4 ....20 C2
Vicarage Ct BECK BR3 * 18 A2
Vicarage Dr BECK BR3 ....10 C5
Vicarage Gdns MTCM CR4 ....13 G2
Vicarage Rd CROY/NA CR0 ....25 G4
    SUT SM1 ....23 F4
Vicars Oak Rd NRWD SE19 ....8 C5
Vickers Ct BECK BR3 * 19 E1
Victoria Av SAND/SEL CR2 ....36 A5
    WLGTN SM6 ....24 A4
Victoria Crs NRWD SE19 ....8 C5
    WIM/MER SW19 ....4 B4
Victoria PI EW KT17 ....40 C2
Victoria Rd COUL/CHIP CR5 ....44 D5
    MTCM CR4 ....5 J4
    SUT SM1 ....33 F1
Victor Rd PGE/AN SE20 ....9 H4
Victory Pl NRWD SE19 * 8 C3
Victory Rd WIM/MER SW19 ....5 E4
Vigilant CI SYD SE26 ....9 E1
Village Gdns EW KT17 ....30 D5
Village Rd BELMT SM2 ....32 B5
Village Wy BECK BR3 ....18 C1
    SAND/SEL CR2 ....47 E3
Villiers Gv BELMT SM2 ....31 H4
Villiers Rd BECK BR3 ....17 H1
Vincennes Est WNWD SE27 ....8 B1
Vincent Av CAR SM5 ....43 F1
Vincent Rd COUL/CHIP CR5 ....53 G1
    CROY/NA CR0 ....26 C4
Vincents CI COUL/CHIP CR5 ....52 D5
Vine CI SUT SM1 ....23 E4
Vineyard Hill Rd
    WIM/MER SW19 ....4 C1
Viney Bank CROY/NA CR0 ....38 B4
Violet CI CHEAM SM3 ....22 A2
    WLGTN SM6 ....24 B3
Violet Gdns CROY/NA CR0 ....35 H1
Violet La CROY/NA CR0 ....35 H2
Virginia Rd THHTH CR7 ....7 H5
Volta Wy CROY/NA CR0 ....25 F2
Voss Ct STRHM/NOR SW16 ....7 F3
Vulcan Wy CROY/NA CR0 ....39 G5
    WLGTN SM6 ....35 E4

W

Waddington Av COUL/CHIP CR5 ....54 C4
Waddington CI COUL/CHIP CR5 ....54 D4
Waddington Wy NRWD SE19 ....8 A5
Waddon CI CROY/NA CR0 ....25 G3
Waddon Court Rd
    CROY/NA CR0 ....25 G5
Waddon Marsh Wy
    CROY/NA CR0 ....25 G2
Waddon New Rd CROY/NA CR0 ....2 A4
Waddon Park Av CROY/NA CR0 ....25 G5
Waddon Rd CROY/NA CR0 ....2 A4
Waddon Wy CROY/NA CR0 ....35 G2
Wadhurst CI PGE/AN SE20 ....17 F1

Wagtail Gdns SAND/SEL CR2 ....37 H5
Wagtail Wk BECK BR3 ....19 E4
Wakefield Gdns NRWD SE19 ....8 C4
Walburton Rd PUR/KEN CR8 ....44 C3
Waldegrave Rd NRWD SE19 ....8 D4
Waldegrove CROY/NA CR0 ....3 G5
Waldemar Av WIM/MER SW19 ....4 J2
Walden Gdns THHTH CR7 ....15 F3
Waldo PI WIM/MER SW19 ....5 G4
Waldorf CI SAND/SEL CR2 ....35 H4
Waldron Gdns HAYES BR2 ....19 F2
Waldronhyrst CROY/NA CR0 ....2 B7
The Waldrons CROY/NA CR0 ....2 B6
Wales Av CAR SM5 ....33 H1
Waleton Acres WLGTN SM6 * 34 C2
Walham Ri WIM/MER SW19 ....4 B3
Walkfield Dr EPSOM KT18 ....50 B2
Wallace Crs CAR SM5 ....33 H1
Wallace Flds EW KT17 ....40 C3
    CTHM CR3 ....59 H3
Walnut CI CAR SM5 ....33 H1
    EPSOM KT18 ....40 D5
Walnut Gv BNSTD SM7 ....41 H4
Walnut Ms BELMT SM2 ....33 E3
Walnut Tree Av MTCM CR4 * 13 G2
Walnut Tree CI BNSTD SM7 ....42 C2
Walpole Av COUL/CHIP CR5 ....52 D4
Walpole Rd CROY/NA CR0 ....2 E2
    WIM/MER SW19 ....5 F3
Walsh Crs CROY/NA CR0 ....49 G2
Walsingham Gdns
    HOR/WEW KT19 ....20 C5
Walsingham Rd CROY/NA CR0 ....39 E5
    MTCM CR4 ....13 G4
Walter's Rd SNWD SE25 ....16 C3
Waltham Rd CAR SM5 ....23 F2
    CTHM CR3 ....60 B2
Walton Av CHEAM SM3 ....22 A4
Walton Gn CROY/NA CR0 ....38 D4
Walton Wy MTCM CR4 ....14 C3
Wandle Bank CROY/NA CR0 ....25 E3
    WIM/MER SW19 ....5 F3
Wandle Ct HOR/WEW KT19 ....5 F3
Wandle Court Gdns
    CROY/NA CR0 ....25 E4
Wandle Rd CROY/NA CR0 ....25 E4
    MRDN SM4 ....13 H4
    WLGTN SM6 ....24 B3
Wandle Side CROY/NA CR0 ....25 E4
    WLGTN SM6 ....24 B4
Wandle Wy MTCM CR4 ....13 H4
Warbank CI CROY/NA CR0 ....39 G5
Warbank Crs CROY/NA CR0 ....39 G5
Ward CI SAND/SEL CR2 ....36 C1
Warde La WARL CR6 ....56 C1
Warham Rd SAND/SEL CR2 ....36 A1
Waring St WNWD SE27 ....8 C2
Warlingham Rd THHTH CR7 ....15 H3
Warminster Rd SNWD SE25 ....17 E1
Warminster Sq SNWD SE25 ....17 E1
Warminster Wy MTCM CR4 ....6 B5
Warner Av CHEAM SM3 ....22 A3
Warner Rd BMLY BR1 * 11 H4
Warnham Court Rd CAR SM5 ....33 J5
Warren Av BELMT SM2 ....32 B5
    BMLY BR1 ....11 G4
    SAND/SEL CR2 ....37 H3
Warren Dr South BRYLDS KT5 ....20 H2
Warren Md BNSTD SM7 ....41 G5
Warren Pk WARL CR6 ....56 D3
Warren Park Rd SUT SM1 ....33 F2
Warren Rd BNSTD SM7 ....41 H4
    CROY/NA CR0 ....26 D4
    PUR/KEN CR8 ....45 H2
    CAR SM5 ....33 H4
The Warren CAR SM5 ....33 H4
    HOR/WEW KT19 ....20 B5
Warrington Rd CROY/NA CR0 ....2 A5
Warwick Gdns THHTH CR7 * 15 G3
Warwick Rd COUL/CHIP CR5 ....44 D5
    PGE/AN SE20 ....17 F2
    SUT SM1 ....33 F1
    THHTH CR7 ....15 G2
Washington Rd WPK KT4 ....21 F3
Watcombe Rd SNWD SE25 ....17 F4
Waterer Gdns
    KWD/TDW/WH KT20 ....51 E3
Waterer Ri WLGTN SM6 ....34 D2
Waterfall Cots WIM/MER SW19 ....5 G3
Waterfall Rd WIM/MER SW19 ....5 F3
Waterfall Ter TOOT SW17 ....5 G3
Waterfield CI WARL CR6 ....56 B4
Waterfield Gdns SNWD SE25 ....16 C3
Waterfield Gn
    KWD/TDW/WH KT20 ....50 B5
Waterhouse La PUR/KEN CR8 ....55 E4
Waterloo PI CAR SM5 * 23 J4
Waterloo Rd HOR/WEW KT19 ....40 B3
    SUT SM1 ....33 G1
Waterman Sq PGE/AN SE20 ....9 H4
Water Md CROY/NA CR0 ....55 D2
Watermead La MTCM CR4 ....6 A4
Watermead Rd CAT SE6 ....11 E1
Watermens Sq PGE/AN SE20 * 9 H4
Watermill Wy WIM/MER SW19 ....5 J4
Watersedge HOR/WEW KT19 ....20 A5
Waterside Av BECK BR3 ....18 A4
Waterside Wy TOOT SW17 ....5 E1
Water Tower HI CROY/NA CR0 ....2 B6
Wates Wy MTCM CR4 ....13 H5
Watlings CI CROY/NA CR0 ....27 H2
Watlington Gv SYD SE26 ....10 A2
Watneys Rd MTCM CR4 ....14 D4
Watson Av CHEAM SM3 ....22 A3
Wattenden Rd PUR/KEN CR8 ....54 D1
Wavel PI SYD SE26 ....9 E1
Waverley Av SUT SM1 ....23 F5
Waverley Rd EW KT17 ....31 F1
    SNWD SE25 ....17 F3
Waverley Wy CAR SM5 ....33 G2

Waynflete Av CROY/NA CR0 ....2 A5
Wayside CROY/NA CR0 * 38 D2
Wealdstone Rd CHEAM SM3 ....22 B3
Weaver Wk WNWD SE27 ....7 H1
Wedgwood Wy NRWD SE19 ....8 A4
Weighton Rd PGE/AN SE20 ....17 F1
Weihurst Gdns SUT SM1 ....33 F1
Welbeck CI EW KT17 ....31 E3
Welbeck Rd CAR SM5 ....23 G2
Welcomes Cots CTHM CR3 * 61 G3
Welcomes Rd PUR/KEN CR8 ....46 A5
Welford PI WIM/MER SW19 ....4 A1
Welham Rd TOOT SW17 ....6 A3
Welhouse Rd CAR SM5 ....23 G2
Well CI STRHM/NOR SW16 ....7 F1
Wellesford CI BNSTD SM7 ....51 F2
Wellesley Court Rd
    CROY/NA CR0 ....2 E3
Wellesley Gv CROY/NA CR0 ....2 E3
Wellesley Rd BELMT SM2 ....33 E2
    CROY/NA CR0 ....2 D2
Well Farm Rd CTHM CR3 ....56 A4
Wellfield Gdns CAR SM5 ....33 G5
Wellfield Rd STRHM/NOR SW16 ....7 F1
Wellhouse Rd BECK BR3 ....18 B3
Wellington Av WPK KT4 ....21 G4
Wellington Dr PUR/KEN CR8 ....55 F5
Wellington Rd CROY/NA CR0 ....25 H1
    CTHM CR3 ....59 E2
Wells CI SAND/SEL CR2 ....36 C1
Wellwood CI COUL/CHIP CR5 ....45 G1
Wendling Rd CAR SM5 ....23 F2
The Wend COUL/CHIP CR5 ....44 D4
Wentworth CI MRDN SM4 ....22 C1
Wentworth Rd CROY/NA CR0 ....25 G1
Wentworth Wy SAND/SEL CR2 ....47 G5
Wermbee Rd SNWD SE25 ....17 E3
Wessex Av WIM/MER SW19 ....12 C1
Wessex Ct BECK BR3 * 10 A5
Wessex Ter MTCM CR4 * 13 G4
West Av WLGTN SM6 ....35 E1
Westbourne Av CHEAM SM3 ....22 A3
Westbourne Rd CROY/NA CR0 ....16 D5
    SYD SE26 ....9 H5
Westbrook Rd THHTH CR7 ....8 B5
Westbury CI CTHM CR3 * 55 H3
Westbury Rd BECK BR3 ....18 A2
    CROY/NA CR0 ....16 D5
    TOOT SW17 ....6 B1
Westcombe Av CROY/NA CR0 ....15 E5
Westcote Rd STRHM/NOR SW16 ....6 D2
Westcott CI CROY/NA CR0 ....38 D4
Westcott Wy BELMT SM2 ....31 G5
Westcroft Gdns MRDN SM4 ....12 B2
Westcroft Rd CAR SM5 ....24 B4
West Dr BELMT SM2 ....31 H4
    CAR SM5 ....33 F5
    KWD/TDW/WH KT20 ....50 D3
    TOOT SW17 ....6 B1
Westerham CI BELMT SM2 * 32 C5
Westerley Crs SYD SE26 * 10 B2
Western Rd MTCM CR4 ....13 G1
    SUT SM1 ....32 C1
Westfield SAND/SEL CR2 ....46 B3
Westfield CI SUT SM1 ....22 B5
Westfield Rd BECK BR3 ....18 B1
    CROY/NA CR0 ....2 A2
    MTCM CR4 ....13 G1
    SUT SM1 ....22 B5
West Gdns EW KT17 ....30 C5
    WIM/MER SW19 ....5 G3
Westgate Rd BECK BR3 ....11 E5
    SNWD SE25 ....17 G4
Westhall Pk WARL CR6 ....56 C4
Westhall Rd WARL CR6 ....56 A5
West HI HOR/WEW KT19 ....40 A3
    SAND/SEL CR2 ....36 C4
West Hill Av HOR/WEW KT19 ....40 A2
Westland Dr HAYES BR2 ....29 H5
Westlands Ct EPSOM KT18 ....40 A5
Westleigh Av COUL/CHIP CR5 ....53 E1
West Md HOR/WEW KT19 ....30 C2
Westmead Rd SUT SM1 ....23 F5
Westminster Av THHTH CR7 ....15 H1
Westminster Rd SUT SM1 ....23 F3
Westmoreland Dr BELMT SM2 ....32 D4
Westmoreland Rd HAYES BR2 ....19 G4
Westmoreland Ter
    PGE/AN SE20 ....9 F4
Westmorland CI
    HOR/WEW KT19 ....30 C5
Westmorland Wy MTCM CR4 ....14 D5
West Oak BECK BR3 ....11 F5
Weston CI COUL/CHIP CR5 ....54 B5
Weston Dr CTHM CR3 ....59 E1
    CTHM CR3 ....60 A4
Weston Gv BMLY BR1 ....11 H5
Weston Rd BMLY BR1 ....11 H5
    EW KT17 ....40 C1
Westover CI BELMT SM2 ....32 D4
Westow HI NRWD SE19 ....8 C5
Westow St NRWD SE19 ....8 C5
West Parkside WARL CR6 ....56 D4
West St CAR SM5 ....23 H5
    CROY/NA CR0 ....2 D6
    EPSOM KT18 ....40 A3
    EW KT17 ....30 C5
    SUT SM1 ....32 D1
West Street La CAR SM5 ....23 H5
West Street Rd EW KT17 ....30 D5
West View Av CTHM CR3 ....55 H3
West View Rd WARL CR6 ....56 B4
West Wy CAR SM5 ....33 F5
West Wy WWKM BR4 ....28 A3
Westway CTHM CR3 ....59 F2
West Way Gdns CROY/NA CR0 ....27 H3
Westways HOR/WEW KT19 ....20 D5
Westwell Rd STRHM/NOR SW16 ....7 E3
Westwell Road Ap
    STRHM/NOR SW16 ....7 E3
Westwood Av NRWD SE19 ....8 A5
Westwood HI SYD SE26 ....9 E2

Westwood PI SYD SE26 * 9 E2
Westwood Rd COUL/CHIP CR5 ....53 H3
Wettern CI SAND/SEL CR2 ....36 C5
Weybourne PI SAND/SEL CR2 ....36 B5
Weybridge Rd THHTH CR7 ....15 G3
Wey Ct HOR/WEW KT19 ....20 A5
Weymouth Ct BELMT SM2 * 32 D3
Wharfedale Gdns
    STRHM/NOR SW16 ....15 F3
Wharncliffe Gdns SNWD SE25 ....16 C1
Wharncliffe Rd SNWD SE25 ....16 B1
Whatley Av RYNPK SW20 ....4 B6
Wheathill Rd PGE/AN SE20 ....17 F1
Wheat Knoll PUR/KEN CR8 ....55 E1
Wheatstone CI WIM/MER SW19 ....5 F5
Whelan Wy WLGTN SM6 ....24 D4
Whimbrel CI PUR/KEN CR8 ....46 B1
Whinfell CI STRHM/NOR SW16 ....6 D2
Whitby Gdns SUT SM1 ....23 F3
Whitby Rd SUT SM1 ....23 F3
White Bridge Av MTCM CR4 ....13 E3
Whitecroft CI BECK BR3 ....19 E5
Whitecroft Wy BECK BR3 ....19 E5
Whitefield Av PUR/KEN CR8 ....54 C1
Whitefoot La CAT SE6 ....11 H1
Whitegate Wy
    KWD/TDW/WH KT20 ....50 B5
Whitehall PI CAR SM5 ....24 B5
Whitehall Rd THHTH CR7 ....15 G4
White Hi SAND/SEL CR2 ....36 B5
White Horse Dr EPSOM KT18 ....40 A4
Whitehorse La SNWD SE25 ....16 C3
Whitehorse Rd CROY/NA CR0 ....16 B4
White Knobs Wy CTHM CR3 ....60 A5
Whiteley Rd NRWD SE19 ....8 C4
White Ldg NRWD SE19 ....9 H4
White Lodge CI BELMT SM2 ....33 E5
White Oak Dr BECK BR3 ....19 E1
Whiteoaks BNSTD SM7 ....42 D3
Whitethorn Av COUL/CHIP CR5 ....44 A5
Whitethorn Gdns CROY/NA CR0 ....27 F3
Whitford Gdns MTCM CR4 ....13 G2
Whitgift Av SAND/SEL CR2 ....36 A1
Whitgift St CROY/NA CR0 ....2 C5
Whitland Rd CAR SM5 ....23 F2
Whitmead CI SAND/SEL CR2 ....36 B2
Whitmore Rd BECK BR3 ....18 B2
Whitmores CI EPSOM KT18 ....40 A5
Whitstable PI CROY/NA CR0 ....10 B5
Whitstone La BECK BR3 ....18 D4
Whittaker Rd CHEAM SM3 ....22 A4
Whittlebury CI CAR SM5 ....33 H5
Westcroft Rd SNWD SE25 ....16 C2
Whitworth Rd SNWD SE25 ....16 C2
Whytebeam Vw CTHM CR3 ....55 H3
Whytecliffe Rd North
    PUR/KEN CR8 ....45 H1
Whytecliffe Rd South
    PUR/KEN CR8 ....45 G2
Whyteleafe Hi CTHM CR3 ....55 H3
Whyteleafe Rd CTHM CR3 ....59 G1
Wickers Oake NRWD SE19 * 8 D1
The Wicket CROY/NA CR0 ....38 C1
Wickham Av CHEAM SM3 .... * 31 G1
    CROY/NA CR0 ....28 A3
Wickham Cha WWKM BR4 ....29 F1
Wickham Ct WWKM BR4 ....29 F5
Wickham Court Rd WWKM BR4 ....29 F5
Wickham Crs WWKM BR4 ....29 F5
Wickham Rd BECK BR3 ....18 D2
    CROY/NA CR0 ....27 G3
Wickham Wy BECK BR3 ....19 E4
Wide Wy STRHM/NOR SW16 ....14 D2
Wigmore Rd CAR SM5 ....23 F2
Wilbury Av BELMT SM2 ....32 B5
Wilcox Rd SUT SM1 * 22 D5
Wildwood Ct PUR/KEN CR8 ....46 B5
Wilhelmina Av COUL/CHIP CR5 ....53 G4
Wilkins CI MTCM CR4 ....13 F3
Wilkinson Gdns NRWD SE19 ....8 C5
Wilks Gdns CROY/NA CR0 ....27 G3
Willett Rd THHTH CR7 ....15 G4
Willey Broom La CTHM CR3 ....58 C5
Willey La CTHM CR3 ....59 E5
William Booth Rd PGE/AN SE20 ....9 E5
William Rd CTHM CR3 ....59 G2
    SUT SM1 ....33 E1
    WIM/MER SW19 .... * 4 A4
Williams La MRDN SM4 ....13 E5
Williams Ter CROY/NA CR0 ....35 G3
William St CAR SM5 ....23 G4
Willis Av BELMT SM2 ....33 G2
Willis Rd CROY/NA CR0 ....26 A1
Willmore End WIM/MER SW19 ....4 D5
The Willow Centre MTCM CR4 ....13 H4
Willow La MTCM CR4 ....13 H4
Willow Lea WARL CR6 ....56 B4
Willow Mt CROY/NA CR0 * 3 H5
Willow Rd WLGTN SM6 ....34 B3
Willows Av MRDN SM4 ....12 D4
The Willows BECK BR3 * 10 C5
    CROY/NA CR0 ....9 F5
Willowtree Wy
    STRHM/NOR SW16 ....7 G5
Willow Vw WIM/MER SW19 ....13 G1
Willow Wk CHEAM SM3 ....22 B2
Willow Wy HOR/WEW KT19 ....30 B2
Wilmar Gdns WWKM BR4 ....28 D2
Wilmot Cots BNSTD SM7 * 42 D5
Wilmot Rd CAR SM5 ....23 H5
    PUR/KEN CR8 ....45 G2
Wilmot Wy BNSTD SM7 ....42 C2
Wilson Av MTCM CR4 ....5 G4
Wilson CI SAND/SEL CR2 ....36 B1
Wilton Crs WIM/MER SW19 ....4 B4
Wilton Gv WIM/MER SW19 ....4 B4
Wilton Rd WIM/MER SW19 ....4 B4
Wiltshire Rd THHTH CR7 ....15 G2
Wimbledon Br WIM/MER SW19 ....4 B3
Wimbledon Hill Rd
    WIM/MER SW19 ....4 A3

Wimbledon Rd *TOOT* SW17 ....5 E1
Wimborne Cl *EW* KT17 ....40 C3
  WPK KT4 ....21 G2
Wimborne Wy *BECK* BR3 ....17 H2
Wimshurst Cl *CROY/NA* CR0 ....25 E2
Winchcombe Rd *CAR* SM5 ....23 F4
Winchelsey Ri *SAND/SEL* CR2 ....36 D2
Winchester Cl *HAYES* BR2 ....19 H2
Winchester Cl *EW* KT17 ....19 H2
Winchester Rd *HAYES* BR2 ....19 H2
Winchfield Rd *SYD* SE26 ....10 A2
Windall Cl *BNSTD* SM7 ....34 A3
Windborough Rd *CAR* SM5 ....34 A3
Windermere Av
  WIM/MER SW19 ....12 D2
Windermere Rd
  COUL/CHIP CR5 ....45 E5
  CROY/NA CR0 ....26 D2
  STRHM/NOR SW16 ....8 A1
  WWKM BR4 ....29 G3
Windfield Cl *SYD* SE26 ....9 H1
Windham Av *CROY/NA* CR0 ....39 F5
The Windings *SAND/SEL* CR2 ....46 D1
Windmill Av *EW* KT17 ....40 D1
Windmill Cl *CTHM* CR3 ....59 E1
  EW KT17 ....40 D2
Windmill End *EW* KT17 ....40 D2
Windmill Gv *CROY/NA* CR0 ....26 A1
Windmill La *EW* KT17 ....40 D2
Windmill Rd *CROY/NA* CR0 ....26 A1
  MTCM CR4 ....14 C4
Windsor Av *CHEAM* SM3 ....22 A4
  WIM/MER SW19 ....5 E5
Windsor Cl *WNWD* SE27 ....8 A1
Windsor Gdns *CROY/NA* CR0 ....25 E4
Windsor Gv *WNWD* SE27 ....8 A1
Windsor Rd *THHTH* CR7 ....15 H1
  WPK KT4 ....21 E3
Windycroft Cl *PUR/KEN* CR8 ....44 D5
Wingate Crs *CROY/NA* CR0 ....15 E5
Wings Cl *SUT* SM1 ....22 C5
Winifred Rd *COUL/CHIP* CR5 ....53 E1
  WIM/MER SW19 ....4 C5
Winkworth Pl *BNSTD* SM7 ....42 B4
Winkworth Rd *BNSTD* SM7 ....42 C4
Winlaton Rd *BMLY* BR1 ....11 F1
Winterbourne Rd *THHTH* CR7 ....15 G3
Winton Wy *STRHM/NOR* SW16 ....7 G2
Wisbeach Rd *CROY/NA* CR0 ....16 A4
Wisborough Rd *SAND/SEL* CR2 ....36 D4
Witham Rd *PGE/AN* SE20 ....9 E1
Witherby Cl *SAND/SEL* CR2 ....36 C1
Witley Crs *CROY/NA* CR0 ....39 E2

Wittersham Rd *BMLY* BR1 ....11 H2
Wiverton Rd *SYD* SE26 ....9 G3
Woburn Av *PUR/KEN* CR8 ....45 G1
Woburn Cl *WIM/MER* SW19 ....5 E5
Woburn Rd *CAR* SM5 ....23 G2
  CROY/NA CR0 ....26 A2
Woldingham Rd *CTHM* CR3 ....56 B5
The Wold *CTHM* CR3 ....61 G2
Wolfington Rd *WNWD* SE27 ....7 H1
Wolseley Rd *MTCM* CR4 ....24 A1
Wolsey Cl *WPK* KT4 ....21 E5
Wolsey Crs *CROY/NA* CR0 ....39 E4
  MRDN SM4 ....22 B1
Wonersh Wy *BELMT* SM2 ....31 H4
Wontford Rd *PUR/KEN* CR8 ....45 F5
Woodbastwick Rd *SYD* SE26 ....9 H5
Woodbine Gv *PGE/AN* SE20 ....9 F4
Woodbine La *WPK* KT4 ....21 F4
Woodbourne Gdns *WLGTN* SM6 ....34 B3
Woodbury Cl *CROY/NA* CR0 ....3 K3
Woodbury Dr *BELMT* SM2 ....33 E5
Woodcote Av *THHTH* CR7 ....15 G3
  WLGTN SM6 ....34 B4
Woodcote Cl *EPSOM* KT18 ....40 B4
Woodcote End *EPSOM* KT18 ....40 B5
Woodcote Gn *WLGTN* SM6 ....34 C4
Woodcote Green Rd
  EPSOM KT18 ....40 B4
Woodcote Grove Rd
  EPSOM KT18 ....40 B4
Woodcote House Ct
  COUL/CHIP CR5 ....44 D5
Woodcote House Ct
  EPSOM KT18 ....40 B5
Woodcote La *PUR/KEN* CR8 ....44 D1
Woodcote Ms *WLGTN* SM6 ....34 B2
Woodcote Pk *COUL/CHIP* CR5 * 44 B5
Woodcote Park Av
  PUR/KEN CR8 ....44 C1
Woodcote Pl *WNWD* SE27 * 7 H2
Woodcote Rd *WLGTN* SM6 ....34 B2
Woodcote Valley Rd
  PUR/KEN CR8 ....44 D5
Wood Crest *BELMT* SM2 * 33 E5
Woodcrest Rd *PUR/KEN* CR8 ....45 E5
Woodcroft Rd *THHTH* CR7 ....15 H4
Woodend *NRWD* SE19 ....8 A3
  SUT SM1 ....23 E5
The Wood End *WLGTN* SM6 ....34 B5
Wooderson Cl *SNWD* SE25 ....16 C3
Woodfield Av *CAR* SM5 ....34 A2
Woodfield Cl *COUL/CHIP* CR5 ....54 A2
  NRWD SE19 ....8 A4
Woodfield Hl *COUL/CHIP* CR5 ....53 F4

The Woodfields *SAND/SEL* CR2 ....46 D1
Woodgate Dr *STRHM/NOR* SW16 ....6 D4
Woodgavil *BNSTD* SM7 ....51 F1
Woodhatch Spinney
  COUL/CHIP CR5 ....54 A1
Woodhyrst Gdns *PUR/KEN* CR8 ....45 H5
Woodland Cl *HOR/WEW* KT19 * 30 C2
  NRWD SE19 ....8 C3
Woodland Gdns *SAND/SEL* CR2 ....47 G1
Woodland Gv *CROY/NA* CR0 ....35 G5
Woodland Hl *NRWD* SE19 ....8 C3
Woodland Rd *NRWD* SE19 ....8 C2
  THHTH CR7 ....15 G3
Woodlands Av *WPK* KT4 ....20 D3
Woodlands Gdns *EPSOM* KT18 ....50 C2
Woodlands Gv *COUL/CHIP* CR5 ....52 B5
Woodlands Rd *WLGTN* SM6 ....8 A4
  WLGTN SM6 ....34 B4
Woodland Wy *CROY/NA* CR0 ....28 A2
  MRDN SM4 ....12 B3
  MTCM CR4 ....6 A4
  PUR/KEN CR8 ....45 E4
  WWKM BR4 ....29 E4
Wood La *CTHM* CR3 ....59 F4
  KWD/TDW/WH KT20 ....51 G4
Woodlea Dr *HAYES* BR2 ....19 G2
Woodley Cl *TOOT* SW17 ....5 H4
Woodley La *SUT* SM1 ....23 G4
Wood Lodge La *WWKM* BR4 ....29 G1
Woodman Rd *COUL/CHIP* CR5 ....53 G1
Woodmansterne La *BNSTD* SM7 ....42 D5
Woodmansterne Rd *CAR* SM5 ....44 C5
  COUL/CHIP CR5 ....44 C5
  STRHM/NOR SW16 ....6 C4
Woodmansterne St *BNSTD* SM7 ....48 C5
Woodmere Av *CROY/NA* CR0 ....27 H1
Woodmere Cl *CROY/NA* CR0 ....27 H1
Woodmere Gdns *CROY/NA* CR0 ....27 H1
Woodmere Wy *BECK* BR3 ....19 F4
Woodnook Rd
  STRHM/NOR SW16 ....6 B2
Woodpecker Mt *CROY/NA* CR0 ....38 A4
Woodplace Cl *COUL/CHIP* CR5 ....53 G4
Woodplace La *COUL/CHIP* CR5 ....53 G5
Woodside *WIM/MER* SW19 ....4 B2
Woodside Av *SNWD* SE25 ....17 F5
Woodside Cl *BRYLDS* KT5 ....20 A1
  CTHM CR3 ....59 G4
Woodside Court Rd
  CROY/NA CR0 ....27 E1
Woodside Gn *CROY/NA* CR0 ....27 E1
  SNWD SE25 ....17 F5
Woodside Pk *SNWD* SE25 ....17 E5

Woodside Rd *PUR/KEN* CR8 ....45 E3
  SNWD SE25 ....17 F5
  SUT SM1 ....23 E4
Woodside Wy *CROY/NA* CR0 ....17 C5
  MTCM CR4 ....6 B5
Woodstock Av *CHEAM* SM3 ....22 C1
Woodstock Gdns *BECK* BR3 ....10 D5
Woodstock Ri *CHEAM* SM3 ....22 B2
Woodstock Rd *CAR* SM5 ....34 A1
  COUL/CHIP CR5 ....53 F1
  CROY/NA CR0 ....2 C6
Woodstock Wy *MTCM* CR4 ....14 C1
Woodstone Av *EW* KT17 ....31 E1
Wood St *MTCM* CR4 ....24 A1
Woodsyre *SYD* SE26 ....8 D1
Woodvale Av *SNWD* SE25 ....16 D2
Woodview *SAND/SEL* CR2 ....47 F4
Woodville Rd *MRDN* SM4 ....12 C5
  THHTH CR7 ....16 B2
Worbeck Rd *PGE/AN* SE20 ....17 F1
Worcester Cl *CROY/NA* CR0 ....28 B5
  MTCM CR4 ....14 A1
Worcester Gdns *WPK* KT4 ....20 A4
Worcester Park Rd *WPK* KT4 ....20 A4
Worcester Rd *BELMT* SM2 ....32 C3
  WIM/MER SW19 ....4 C3
Wordsworth Av *PUR/KEN* CR8 ....46 B5
Wordsworth Dr *CHEAM* SM3 ....21 G5
Wordsworth Rd *PGE/AN* SE20 ....9 H4
  WLGTN SM6 ....34 C3
Worple Rd *EPSOM* KT18 ....40 C4
  WIM/MER SW19 ....4 A4
Worple Road Ms
  WIM/MER SW19 ....4 B5
Worslade Rd *TOOT* SW17 ....5 F1
Worsley Bridge Rd *CAT* SE6 ....10 B2
Worthfield Cl *HOR/WEW* KT19 ....30 B3
Worthington Cl *MTCM* CR4 ....14 B3
Wortley Rd *CROY/NA* CR0 ....25 G1
Wotton Wy *BELMT* SM2 ....31 E5
Wrayfield Rd *CHEAM* SM3 ....21 H4
Wray Rd *BELMT* SM2 ....32 B4
Wren Cl *SAND/SEL* CR2 ....37 H5
Wrenthorpe Rd *BMLY* BR1 ....11 G1
Wrights Rd *SNWD* SE25 ....16 C2
Wright's Rw *CAR* SM5 ....24 B5
Wrythe Green Rd *CAR* SM5 ....23 H4
Wrythe Green Rd *CAR* SM5 ....23 H4
Wrythe La *CAR* SM5 ....23 G2
Wyche Gv *SAND/SEL* CR2 ....36 A3
Wychwood Av *THHTH* CR7 ....15 H2
Wycliffe Rd *WIM/MER* SW19 ....4 D3
Wydenhurst Rd *CROY/NA* CR0 ....27 E1

Wyeths Ms *EW* KT17 * ....
Wyeth's Rd *EW* KT17 ....
Wyncote Wy *SAND/SEL* CR2 ....
Wyndham Cl *BELMT* SM2 ....
Wyndhurst Cl *SAND/SEL* CR2 ....
Wynton Gdns *SNWD* SE25 ....
Wyvern Rd *PUR/KEN* CR8 ....

Y

Yarborough Rd *WIM/MER* SW1
Yarbridge Cl *BELMT* SM2 * ....
Yenston Cl *MRDN* SM4 ....
Yeomanry Cl *EW* KT17 ....
Yewbank Cl *PUR/KEN* CR8 ....
Yewdale Cl *BMLY* BR1 ....
Yewlands Cl *BNSTD* SM7 ....
Yew Tree Bottom Rd *EW* KT17 ....
Yew Tree Cl *COUL/CHIP* CR5 ....
  WPK KT4 ....
Yew Tree Dr *CTHM* CR3 ....
Yew Tree Gdns *EPSOM* KT18 ....
Yewtree Rd *BECK* BR3 ....
Yew Tree Wk *PUR/KEN* CR8 ....
York Cl *MRDN* SM4 ....
Yorke Ga *CTHM* CR3 ....
York Rd *BELMT* SM2 ....
  CROY/NA CR0 ....
Yorkshire Rd *MTCM* CR4 ....
York St *MTCM* CR4 ....

Z

Zermatt Rd *THHTH* CR7 ....
Zig Zag Rd *PUR/KEN* CR8 ....
Zion Pl *THHTH* CR7 ....
Zion Rd *THHTH* CR7 ....

Index - featured places

Abbey Industrial Estate
  MTCM CR4 ....13 H4
Abbey Mills
  WIM/MER SW19 ....5 E5
Abbey Primary School
  MRDN SM4 ....22 C1
Abbey Trading Estate
  SYD SE26 ....10 A2
Abbotsbury Primary School
  MRDN SM4 ....12 C4
Aberdour School
  KWD/TDW/WH KT20 ....51 F3
Acumen (Anglo School) Ltd
  NRWD SE19 ....8 C4
Addington Business Centre
  CROY/NA CR0 ....39 G5
The Addington Golf Club
  CROY/NA CR0 ....38 B4
Addington High School
  CROY/NA CR0 ....49 G2
Addington Palace Golf Club
  CROY/NA CR0 ....38 A2
Addiscombe Cricket Club
  CROY/NA CR0 ....27 E4
Aerodrome Hotel
  CROY/NA CR0 ....35 G2
Albany Clinic
  WIM/MER SW19 ....4 D4
Alexandra Infant School
  PGE/AN SE20 ....9 H4
Alexandra Junior School
  SYD SE26 ....9 H3
All Saints Benhilton CE
  Primary School *SUT* SM1 ....22 D4
All Saints CE Junior School
  NRWD SE19 ....8 C5
All Saints CE Primary School
  WIM/MER SW19 ....5 E4
Anerley Primary School
  PGE/AN SE20 ....9 E5
Anerley School
  PGE/AN SE20 ....9 U5
Applegarth Primary School
  MRDN SM4 ....38 D2
Aragon Primary School
  MRDN SM4 ....22 A1
The Archbishop Lanfranc
  School *CROY/NA* CR0 ....15 E5
Archbishop Tenisons
  CE School *CROY/NA* CR0 ....3 J5
Ashburton Community
  School *CROY/NA* CR0 ....27 F1
Ashburton Primary School
  CROY/NA CR0 ....17 F5
Ashgrove Trading Estate
  BMLY BR1 ....11 F5
Ashley Centre Shopping
  Precinct *HOR/WEW* KT19 ....40 B3
Atwood Primary School
  SAND/SEL CR2 ....47 E4

Audley Primary School
  CTHM CR3 ....59 G1
Auriol Junior School
  HOR/WEW KT19 ....20 D5
The Avenue Primary School
  BELMT SM2 ....32 C5
Back Care Clinic
  WPK KT4 ....21 E2
Balgowan Primary School
  BECK BR3 ....18 A1
Bandon Hill Cemetery
  WLGTN SM6 ....34 D1
Bandon Hill Primary School
  WLGTN SM6 ....34 D2
Banstead Athletic FC
  KWD/TDW/WH KT20 ....50 C5
Banstead Clinic
  BNSTD SM7 ....42 C5
Banstead County Junior
  School *BNSTD* SM7 ....42 B5
Banstead Downs Golf Club
  BELMT SM2 ....42 C1
Banstead Infant School
  BNSTD SM7 ....42 B5
Banstead Sports Centre
  KWD/TDW/WH KT20 ....50 C5
Banstead Village Clinic
  BNSTD SM7 ....42 D5
Barrow Hedges Primary
  School *CAR* SM5 ....33 G3
Beacon School
  BNSTD SM7 ....51 E2
Beaumont Primary School
  PUR/KEN CR8 ....45 F4
Beckenham Business Centre
  BECK BR3 ....10 A3
Beckenham Crematorium
  SNWD SE25 ....17 G2
Beckenham Cricket Club
  BECK BR3 ....10 D4
Beckenham Hospital
  BECK BR3 ....18 B1
Beckenham Leisure Centre
  BECK BR3 ....10 A5
Beckenham Place Park
  Golf Course *BECK* BR3 ....10 D3
Beckenham RFC
  BECK BR3 ....18 A3
Beckenham Town FC
  BECK BR3 ....18 C4
Beckmead School
  BECK BR3 ....28 C2
Beddington Infants School
  WLGTN SM6 ....34 C1
Beddington Medical Centre
  CROY/NA CR0 ....25 E5
Beddington Park Primary
  School *CROY/NA* CR0 ....24 D4
Beddington Trading Estate
  CROY/NA CR0 ....25 E2

Bedington Infant School
  WLGTN SM6 ....24 C5
Beech House School
  SAND/SEL CR2 ....36 D5
Beecholme Primary School
  MTCM CR4 ....6 B5
Benedict Primary School
  MTCM CR4 ....13 F2
Bensham Manor School
  THHTH CR7 ....16 A4
Benson Primary School
  CROY/NA CR0 ....28 A4
Bethel Temple
  STRHM/NOR SW16 ....6 D1
Bethlem Royal Hospital
  BECK BR3 ....28 C1
Beulah Infant & Nursery
  School *THHTH* CR7 ....16 A1
Beverley Trading Estate
  MRDN SM4 ....21 H1
Bishop Challoner School
  HAYES BR2 ....19 F1
Bishop Gilpin Primary School
  WIM/MER SW19 ....4 B2
Bishop Thomas Grant School
  STRHM/NOR SW16 ....7 F2
Blenheim Business Centre
  MTCM CR4 ....5 H5
Blenheim High School
  HOR/WEW KT19 ....30 B5
Blenheim Shopping Centre
  PGE/AN SE20 ....9 G4
Bond Primary School
  MTCM CR4 ....13 H1
Bonus Pastor School
  BMLY BR1 ....11 G1
Boundary Business Park
  MTCM CR4 ....13 F1
Bourne Hall Health Centre
  EW KT17 ....30 D4
Bourne Hall Museum
  EW KT17 ....30 D4
The Bridge Leisure Centre
  SYD SE26 ....10 B2
Brigstock Medical Centre
  THHTH CR7 ....15 H4
BRIT School for Performing
  Arts *SNWD* SE25 ....16 B5
Broadmead Primary School
  CROY/NA CR0 ....16 B5
Broadwater Primary School
  TOOT SW17 ....5 F1
Bromley Cemetery
  BMLY BR1 ....11 H4
Bromley College of Further
  & Higher Education
  BMLY BR1 ....11 H5
Bromley Court Hotel
  BMLY BR1 ....11 G3

Bromley Magistrates Court
  BMLY BR1 ....11 H5
Bromley Road Infant School
  BECK BR3 ....10 D5
Brookfield Primary School
  CHEAM SM3 ....22 A2
Brookmead Industrial Estate
  MTCM CR4 ....14 C1
Broomsleigh Business Park
  CAT SE6 ....10 B2
Burghwood Clinic
  BNSTD SM7 ....51 F1
Burnhill Business Centre
  BECK BR3 ....10 C5
Burnhill Business Centre
  BECK BR3 ....18 C1
Burnt Ash School
  BMLY BR1 ....11 H2
Byron Primary School
  COUL/CHIP CR5 ....54 A2
Camden Junior School
  CAR SM5 ....23 H3
The Canons Leisure Centre
  MTCM CR4 ....13 H3
Capital Business Centre
  MTCM CR4 ....13 H4
  SAND/SEL CR2 ....36 C2
Caplan Estate
  MTCM CR4 ....6 D5
Carew Manor School
  WLGTN SM6 ....24 D4
Carshalton AFC
  SUT SM1 ....23 G4
Carshalton College of FE
  CAR SM5 ....23 H4
Carshalton High School
  for Boys *CAR* SM5 ....23 F3
Carshalton High School
  for Girls *CAR* SM5 ....23 G3
Carshalton War Memorial
  Hospital *CAR* SM5 ....33 H1
Castle Hill Primary School
  CROY/NA CR0 ....39 E2
The Caterham Dene Hospital
  CTHM CR3 ....59 H3
Catford Wanderers Sports
  Club *CAT* SE6 ....11 E1
Cator Park School for Girls
  BECK BR3 ....10 A4
centrale Shopping Centre
  CROY/NA CR0 ....2 C2
Central Medical Centre
  MRDN SM4 ....13 E3
Centre Court Shopping Centre
  WIM/MER SW19 ....4 B5
Chaffinch Business Park
  BECK BR3 ....17 H2
Chalk Lane Hotel
  EPSOM KT18 ....40 B5

Chandos Business Centre
  WLGTN SM6 ....
Cheam Common J&I School
  WPK KT4 ....
Cheam Fields Primary School
  CHEAM SM3 ....
Cheam High School
  CHEAM SM3 ....
Cheam Leisure Centre
  CHEAM SM3 ....
Cheam Park Farm Junior
  School *CHEAM* SM3 ....
Cheam Sports Club
  BELMT SM2 ....
Chelsea Fields Industrial
  Estate *WIM/MER* SW19 ....
Chipstead Golf Club
  COUL/CHIP CR5 ....
Chipstead Valley Primary
  School *COUL/CHIP* CR5 ....
Christ Church Primary School
  PUR/KEN CR8 ....
Christian Meeting Hall
  BECK BR3 ....
Churchfields Primary School
  BECK BR3 ....
Clare House Primary School
  BECK BR3 ....
Clifton Hill School
  CTHM CR3 ....
Clocktower
  CROY/NA CR0 ....
College Fields Business Centre
  WIM/MER SW19 ....
Collingwood Preparatory
  School *WLGTN* SM6 ....
Coloma Convent Girls School
  CROY/NA CR0 ....
Colonnades Leisure Park
  CROY/NA CR0 ....
Colours Sports Club
  SUT SM1 ....
Coney Hall School
  HAYES BR2 ....
Connaught Business Centre
  CROY/NA CR0 ....
  MTCM CR4 ....
Coulsdon CE Primary School
  COUL/CHIP CR5 ....
The Coulsdon Eye Clinic
  COUL/CHIP CR5 ....
Coulsdon High School
  COUL/CHIP CR5 ....
Coulsdon Manor Hotel
  COUL/CHIP CR5 ....
Coulsdon Sixth Form College
  COUL/CHIP CR5 ....
Courtwood Primary School
  CROY/NA CR0 ....

Index – featured P...

Primary School
  /M CR4 ...13 H3
Green School
  /M CR4 ...13 G2
Hurst Golf Club
  /SEL CR2 ...36 D2
ane Primary School
  D SE27 ...8 A1
Airport Industrial
  e CROY/NA CR0 ...35 G5
Cemetery
  /M CR7 ...15 F4
Clocktower Cinema
  /NA CR0 ...2 D4
College
  /NA CR0 ...2 E3
Fairfield Halls Cinema
  /NA CR0 ...2 E4
FC
  SE25 ...17 G4
High Junior School
  SAND/SEL CR2 ...47 F1
Indoor Bowling Club
  /SEL CR2 ...36 A1
Magistrates Court
  /NA CR0 ...2 E5
Mosque & Islamic
  re THHTH CR7 ...15 C5
Road Industrial
  e SNWD SE25 ...17 G3
Sports Arena
  e SNWD SE25 ...17 G4
Palace FC
  urst Park) SNWD SE25 ...16 C3
Palace Museum
  D SE19 ...8 D3
ports Ground
  BR3 ...10 C5
ton Cemetery
  KT4 ...21 F3
ton CP School
  KT4 ...20 D4
ton Golf Club
  D SM7 ...42 A3
House Primary School
  /M CR4 ...24 A2
House School
  /SEL CR2 ...35 H4
Infant School
  e6 ...16 C1
Junior School
  D SE25 ...16 C1
College of Art
  D SE27 ...7 H1
e School
  /WEW KT19 ...30 A3
ean Cinema
  /NA CR0 ...2 D4
vingstone Primary
  n J&I School /NA CR0 ...26 D1
ord College
  l CR3 ...59 H1
hire Primary School
  T SM2 ...33 E3
ster Primary School
  KT4 ...21 G2
rry Primary School
  / BR1 ...11 G1
m Health Centre
  / BR1 ...11 C1
ew Primary School
  D SE19 ...8 A4
ead Hotel
  SM5 ...24 B5
ald Primary School
  /MER SW19 ...4 B4
Junior School
  /NA CR0 ...35 H1
siness Park
  /N SM6 ...24 A3
Primary School
  M/NOR SW16 ...6 C5
rey Museum
  l CR3 ...59 H4
m County Infants
  ol EPSOM KT18 ...40 A4
m Sports Club
  /WEW KT19 ...40 A2
ourne Primary School
  TH CR7 ...16 A4
Estate
  /WEW KT19 ...40 A3
n High School
  /NA CR0 ...28 A1
e Child Health Clinic
  SW17 ...6 A4
siness Park
  17 ...40 C1
College
  17 ...41 E4
County & Magistrates
  e EPSOM KT18 ...40 B3
L Ewell High School
  /WEW KT19 ...30 A2
eneral Hospital
  /M KT18 ...40 A5
olf Club
  17 ...41 E5
ealth Clinic
  KT18 ...40 C3

Epsom Primary School
  HOR/WEW KT19 ...40 B1
Epsom Sports Club
  EPSOM KT18 ...40 B5
Eversley Medical Centre
  THHTH CR7 ...15 G5
Ewell Athletics Track
  HOR/WEW KT19 ...30 B2
Ewell Castle Junior School
  EW KT17 ...30 D4
Ewell Castle School
  EW KT17 ...31 E4
Ewell Grove Infant School
  EW KT17 ...30 D4
Express by Holiday Inn
  CROY/NA CR0 ...2 C3
  WIM/MER SW19 ...5 F4
Fairchildes Primary School
  CROY/NA CR0 ...49 G2
Fairfield Halls
  CROY/NA CR0 ...2 E4
Fairview Medical Centre
  STRHM/NOR SW16 ...7 E5
Farleigh Court Golf Club
  WARL CR6 ...48 C2
Farleigh Primary School
  WARL CR6 ...56 D2
Farleigh Rovers FC
  WARL CR6 ...57 F1
Felnex Trading Estate
  WLGTN SM6 ...24 A3
First Quarter Business Park
  HOR/WEW KT19 ...40 C1
Follys End Christian High
  School SNWD SE25 ...16 C5
Forestdale Primary School
  CROY/NA CR0 ...38 A4
Foresters Primary School
  STRHM/NOR SW16 ...34 D2
Franciscan Primary School
  TOOT SW17 ...6 A1
Franklin Industrial Estate
  PGE/AN SE20 ...9 G5
Furzedown Primary School
  TOOT SW17 ...6 B3
Gardener Industrial Estate
  BECK BR3 ...10 A2
Garden Primary School
  MTCM CR4 ...14 D2
Garfield Primary School
  WIM/MER SW19 ...5 E3
Garth Primary School
  MRDN SM4 ...13 F4
The Garth Road Industrial
  Centre MRDN SM4 ...21 G1
Gateway Business Centre
  BECK BR3 ...10 A3
Gilbert Scott Primary School
  SAND/SEL CR2 ...38 A3
Glebe School
  WWKM BR4 ...29 F2
Glenthorne High School
  CHEAM SM3 ...22 C2
Glyn Technology School
  EW KT17 ...40 D1
Gonville Primary School
  THHTH CR7 ...15 F4
Good Shepherd RC Primary
  School BMLY BR1 ...11 H1
  CROY/NA CR0 ...38 D3
Gorringe Park Primary School
  MTCM CR4 ...14 B5
Grace Business Centre
  MTCM CR4 ...13 H5
Grand Avenue Primary School
  BRYLDS KT5 ...20 A1
Granton Primary School
  STRHM/NOR SW16 ...6 C4
Graveney School
  TOOT SW17 ...6 B3
Greenacre School for Girls
  BNSTD SM7 ...43 E3
Green Lane Primary School
  WPK KT4 ...21 F1
Greenshaw High School
  SUT SM1 ...23 E3
Greenvale Primary School
  SAND/SEL CR2 ...47 H1
Green Wrythe Primary School
  CAR SM5 ...13 F5
Gresham Primary School
  SAND/SEL CR2 ...46 D2
Greyhound Hotel
  SUT SM1 ...33 H1
Hackbridge Primary School
  WLGTN SM6 ...24 A2
Haling Manor High School
  CROY/NA CR0 ...35 H3
Hamilton Road Industrial
  Estate WNWD SE27 ...8 B1
Hampton Road Industrial Park
  CROY/NA CR0 ...16 A5
Hamsey Green Infant School
  WARL CR6 ...56 B1
Hamsey Green Junior School
  WARL CR6 ...56 B1
Harris City Technology College
  NRWD SE19 ...5 H2
Haseltine Primary School
  CAT SE6 ...10 B1
Haslemere Primary School
  MTCM CR4 ...13 F1
Hatfeild Primary School
  MRDN SM4 ...12 A5
Hawes Down Clinic
  WWKM BR4 ...29 F3
Hawes Down Primary School
  WWKM BR4 ...29 F2
Hawkins Clinic
  EW KT17 ...41 G5
The Hayes Primary School
  PUR/KEN CR8 ...54 D1
Heavers Farm Primary School
  SNWD SE25 ...16 D4

Henderson Hospital
  BELMT SM2 ...32 C4
Highfield Infant School
  HAYES BR2 ...19 G3
Highfield Junior School
  HAYES BR2 ...19 G3
Highview Primary School
  WLGTN SM6 ...35 E1
Hillbrook Primary School
  TOOT SW17 ...5 H1
Hillcroft Primary School
  CTHM CR3 ...59 G3
Hillcross Primary School
  MRDN SM4 ...12 B3
HM Prison
  BELMT SM2 ...43 E2
Holiday Inn
  SUT SM1 ...32 D2
Holy Trinity CE Junior School
  WLGTN SM6 ...24 C5
Holy Trinity Primary School
  WIM/MER SW19 ...4 C3
Homefield Preparatory School
  SUT SM1 ...32 C1
Horton Hospital
  HOR/WEW KT19 ...40 A1
Horton Park Golf & Country
  Club HOR/WEW KT19 ...30 A3
Howard Primary School
  CROY/NA CR0 ...2 C7
HSBC Sports Club
  BECK BR3 ...10 A3
Immanuel CE Primary School
  STRHM/NOR SW16 ...7 E3
Innkeeper's Lodge
  BECK BR3 ...18 C5
  SAND/SEL CR2 ...36 A2
James Dixon Primary School
  PGE/AN SE20 ...9 E4
John Ruskin College
  SAND/SEL CR2 ...38 A3
The John Wernham College
  EW KT17 ...41 E1
Joseph Hood Primary School
  RYNPK SW20 ...12 A1
Julians Primary School
  STRHM/NOR SW16 ...7 G1
Jurys Inn Hotel
  CROY/NA CR0 ...2 D2
Kangley Business Centre
  SYD SE26 ...10 B2
Kelsey Park School
  BECK BR3 ...18 C2
Kenley Primary School
  PUR/KEN CR8 ...55 G1
Kenley Sports Club
  PUR/KEN CR8 ...46 A4
Kensington Ave Primary
  School THHTH CR7 ...7 G5
Keston Primary School
  COUL/CHIP CR5 ...54 C4
Kiln Park Business Centre
  EW KT17 ...40 C1
Kimpton Industrial Estate
  CHEAM SM3 ...22 B3
Kingsley Primary School
  CROY/NA CR0 ...25 F2
Kings School of English
  BECK BR3 ...18 B1
Kingswood Primary School
  WNWD SE27 ...8 B1
Knollmead Primary School
  WPK KT4 ...20 A3
Laine Theatre Arts
  EW KT17 ...40 C3
Laker Industrial Estate
  BECK BR3 ...10 A2
Laleham Lea School
  PUR/KEN CR8 ...35 E5
Lambeth Cemetery
  TOOT SW17 ...5 E2
Lambeth Crematorium
  TOOT SW17 ...5 E1
Lamont Business Centre
  BECK BR3 ...25 E1
Langley Park Girls School &
  Sports Centre BECK BR3 ...18 D4
Langley Park Golf Club
  BECK BR3 ...19 F5
Langley Park School for Boys
  BECK BR3 ...18 D5
Le Meridien Selsdon Park
  Hotel & Golf Course
  SAND/SEL CR2 ...47 G1
Lewin Mead Community
  Mental Health Centre
  STRHM/NOR SW16 ...6 D3
Lewis Clinic
  CAR SM5 ...24 A5
Liberty Middle School
  MTCM CR4 ...13 C1
Lifecare NHS Trust
  CTHM CR3 ...59 G3
Lifetimes Museum
  CROY/NA CR0 ...2 D4
Linden Bridge School
  WPK KT4 ...20 C4
The Link Day Primary School
  CROY/NA CR0 ...25 E5
The Link Secondary School
  CROY/NA CR0 ...25 F5
Links Primary School
  TOOT SW17 ...6 A3
Lodge School
  PUR/KEN CR8 ...44 D2
Lombard Business Park
  CROY/NA CR0 ...25 F1
  WIM/MER SW19 ...13 E1
London Ladies & Girls FC
  CAT SE6 ...10 D2
London Lane Clinic
  BMLY BR1 ...11 H4
London Living Theatre
  SYD SE26 ...9 H1

London Road Medical Centre
  THHTH CR7 ...15 G5
Lonesome Primary School
  MTCM CR4 ...14 B1
The Longcroft Clinic
  BNSTD SM7 ...43 E4
Longmead Business Centre
  HOR/WEW KT19 ...40 B1
Longmead Industrial Estate
  HOR/WEW KT19 ...40 B1
Lower Sydenham Industrial
  Estate CAT SE6 ...10 B2
Lynton Preparatory School
  EW KT17 ...40 D1
Malcolm Primary School
  PGE/AN SE20 ...9 G4
Malden Manor Junior School
  NWMAL KT3 ...20 C1
Malden Parochial Primary
  School WPK KT4 ...20 C2
Malden Road Baths
  CHEAM SM3 ...21 H5
Malmesbury Primary School
  MRDN SM4 ...23 E1
Manor Drive Health Centre
  WPK KT4 ...20 D2
Manor Park Primary School
  SUT SM1 ...33 E1
Maple House Independent
  Montessori THHTH CR7 ...16 A3
Maple House School
  THHTH CR7 ...16 A2
Marden Lodge Primary School
  CTHM CR3 ...56 B5
Margaret Roper Catholic
  Primary School
  PUR/KEN CR8 ...35 G5
Marion Vian Primary School
  BECK BR3 ...17 H4
Mayday University Hospital
  THHTH CR7 ...15 H5
The Mead Infant School
  HOR/WEW KT19 ...20 D4
Melrose Special School
  MTCM CR4 ...13 G2
Merland Rise Primary School
  EPSOM KT18 ...50 C4
Merton Abbey Primary School
  WIM/MER SW19 ...4 D5
Merton Adult College
  RYNPK SW20 ...12 A2
Merton College
  MRDN SM4 ...12 B5
Merton Industrial Park
  WIM/MER SW19 ...5 E5
Merton Park Primary School
  WIM/MER SW19 ...12 B1
Metro Business Centre
  SYD SE26 ...10 B3
Metropolitan Police Hayes
  Sports Club HAYES BR2 ...29 H3
Mill Green Business Park
  MTCM CR4 ...23 H1
Mill Lane Trading Estate
  CROY/NA CR0 ...25 F4
Mitcham Cricket Club
  MTCM CR4 ...13 G3
Mitcham Golf Club
  MTCM CR4 ...14 A4
Mitcham Industrial Estate
  MTCM CR4 ...6 A5
Mitcham Road Crematorium
  THHTH CR7 ...15 E4
Mitcham Vale High School
  MTCM CR4 ...14 C1
Mollison Drive Health Centre
  WLGTN SM6 ...35 E5
Monks Hill Sports Centre
  SAND/SEL CR2 ...37 H3
Monks Orchard Primary
  School CROY/NA CR0 ...17 H4
Morden First School
  MRDN SM4 ...12 C4
Morden Hall Medical Centre
  WIM/MER SW19 ...12 D2
Morden Hall Park NT
  WIM/MER SW19 ...13 E3
Morden Park Pool
  MRDN SM4 ...12 B4
Morden Road Clinic
  WIM/MER SW19 ...12 D2
Muschamp Primary School
  CAR SM5 ...23 G3
National Sports Centre
  NRWD SE19 ...9 E3
Natural Therapy Clinic
  TOOT SW17 ...6 B2
Natwest Sports Club
  BECK BR3 ...10 B5
Nelson Hospital
  WIM/MER SW19 ...12 B1
Nelson Trading Estate
  WIM/MER SW19 ...4 D5
NE Surrey College of
  Technology EW KT17 ...41 E1
New Addington Pools &
  Fitness Centre
  CROY/NA CR0 ...39 G5
New Woodlands School
  BMLY BR1 ...11 G1
Nonsuch High School for Girls
  EW KT17 ...31 H3
Nonsuch Industrial Estate
  EW KT17 ...31 G1
Nonsuch Primary School
  EW KT17 ...31 F1
Norbury Complementary
  Therapy Clinic
  STRHM/NOR SW16 ...7 F5
Norbury Health Centre
  STRHM/NOR SW16 ...15 F1
Norbury Manor Primary School
  STRHM/NOR SW16 ...7 E5

Norbury Manor Secondary
  Girls School
  STRHM/NOR SW16 ...7 F5
Norbury Trading Estate
  STRHM/NOR SW16 ...15 F1
North Croydon Medical Centre
  THHTH CR7 ...15 H5
North Downs Golf Club
  GDST RH9 ...61 G5
Norwood Heights Shopping
  Centre NRWD SE19 ...8 C3
Norwood School
  WNWD SE27 ...8 A2
Oakfield Road Industrial Estate
  PGE/AN SE20 ...9 F4
Oak Lodge JMI School
  WWKM BR4 ...28 D1
Oaks Sports Centre
  CAR SM5 ...43 H1
Oakwood Independent School
  PUR/KEN CR8 ...45 H3
Odeon Cinema
  BECK BR3 ...18 C1
  EW KT17 ...40 C3
Odeon Cinema
  WIM/MER SW19 ...4 C1
Old Beckenhamian RFC
  WWKM BR4 ...29 F4
The Old Cottage Hospital
  THHTH CR7 ...40 D3
Oldfields Trading Estate
  SUT SM1 ...22 C4
Old Palace School
  CROY/NA CR0 ...2 B4
Old Wilsonians Sports Club
  WWKM BR4 ...29 G2
Orchard Business Centre
  SYD SE26 ...10 B2
Orchard Hill College of
  Further Education
  WLGTN SM6 ...33 H4
Orchard Way Primary School
  CROY/NA CR0 ...28 A1
Our Lady & St Phillip Neri
  Junior School
  SYD SE26 ...10 A1
Oval Primary School
  CROY/NA CR0 ...3 G1
Overton Grange School
  BELMT SM2 ...32 D4
Palmerston Business Centre
  SUT SM1 ...33 E1
Parchmore Medical Centre
  THHTH CR7 ...16 A2
Park Hill Junior School
  CROY/NA CR0 ...3 G5
The Patrick Doody Clinic &
  Health Centre
  WIM/MER SW19 ...4 C4
Paxton Primary School
  NRWD SE19 ...8 D3
Payne Clinic
  EW KT17 ...41 E3
Peall Road Industrial Estate
  CROY/NA CR0 ...15 F5
Pelham Primary School
  WIM/MER SW19 ...4 C4
Penwortham Primary School
  STRHM/NOR SW16 ...6 B3
Phoenix College
  MRDN SM4 ...12 D4
Pickhurst Infant School
  HAYES BR2 ...19 G5
Pickhurst Junior School
  HAYES BR2 ...19 H5
Pilton Estate
  CROY/NA CR0 ...2 B2
Pinnacles Cricket & Squash Club
  SUT SM1 ...32 C2
Pioneers Industrial Park
  CROY/NA CR0 ...25 E2
Pitwood Park Industrial Estate
  KWD/TDW/WH KT20 ...50 D5
Playhouse Cinema
  EPSOM KT18 ...40 B4
Playhouse Theatre
  EPSOM KT18 ...40 A3
Polka Theatre for Children
  WIM/MER SW19 ...4 D3
Poplar Primary School
  WIM/MER SW19 ...12 C2
Portland Medical Centre
  SNWD SE25 ...17 F4
Premier Lodge
  CROY/NA CR0 ...35 G2
  HOR/WEW KT19 ...30 C1
  KWD/TDW/WH KT20 ...51 E4
Priory CE Primary School
  WIM/MER SW19 ...4 D2
Priory Retail Park
  WIM/MER SW19 ...5 F4
Priory School
  BNSTD SM7 ...42 C5
Priory Special School
  SNWD SE25 ...16 D3
Progress Business Park
  CROY/NA CR0 ...25 F3
Purley Community Health
  Clinic PUR/KEN CR8 ...45 G1
Purley & District War
  Memorial Hospital
  PUR/KEN CR8 ...45 G1
Purley Downs Golf Club
  PUR/KEN CR8 ...46 B1
Purley John Fisher RFC
  COUL/CHIP CR5 ...54 C5
Purley Oaks Primary School
  SAND/SEL CR2 ...36 B5
Purley Pool
  PUR/KEN CR8 ...45 G1
Purley Secretarial &
  Language College
  PUR/KEN CR8 ...45 G1

Purley Sports Club
WLGTN SM6 ....34 D5
Queen Elizabeth Hospital
BNSTD SM7 ....52 A3
Queen Mary's Hospital for
Children *SUT* SM1 ....23 E2
Queen's Road Cemetery
CROY/NA CRO 16 A5
Rainbow Leisure Centre
EW KT17 ....40 C2
Rangefield Primary School
BMLY BR1 ....11 G2
Red Gates School
CROY/NA CRO 35 G1
Reedham Park School
PUR/KEN CR8 ....45 G4
Refuge Temple
STRHM/NOR SW16 ....7 E1
Regina Coeli RC Primary School
EW KT17 ....35 H3
The Retail Business Centre
EW KT19 ....30 D5
Ricards Lodge High School
WIM/MER SW19 ....4 B1
Riddlesdown High School
SAND/SEL CR2 ....46 C4
Ridgeway Primary School
SAND/SEL CR2 ....36 C4
Riverside Business Park
WIM/MER SW19 ....5 E5
Riverside Wandle Trading
Estate *MTCM* CR4 ....23 H1
Riverview CE Primary School
HOR/WEW KT19 ....20 A5
Roan Industrial Estate
MTCM CR4 ....5 G5
Robin Hood Infant School
SUT SM1 ....32 C1
Robin Hood Junior School
SUT SM1 ....32 D1
Robin Hood Lane Health
Centre *SUT* SM1 ....32 C1
Rockmount Primary School
NRWD SE19 ....8 A3
Roke Primary School
PUR/KEN CR8 ....46 A4
Roman Industrial Estate
CROY/NA CRO 26 C1
Rosebery School
EPSOM KT18 ....40 A4
Roundshaw J&I School
WLGTN SM6 ....35 E3
Royal Marsden Hospital
BELMT SM2 ....33 E5
Royal Russell School
CROY/NA CRO 37 F2
Royston Primary School
BECK BR3 ....9 H5
Rutlish School
RYNPK SW20 ....12 B1
Ryelands Primary School
SNWD SE25 ....17 F4
Safari Cinema
CROY/NA CRO 25 H2
St Andrews CE School
CROY/NA CRO 2 A5
St Annes Catholic Primary
School *BNSTD* SM7 ....51 G1
St Annes Special School
MRDN SM4 ....12 D4
St Anthonys Hospital
WPK KT4 ....21 H2
St Anthonys RC Primary
School *PGE/AN* SE20 ......9 F5
St Augustines RC Primary
School *SYD* SE26 ....9 G1
St Bartholomews CE Primary
School *SYD* SE26 ....9 G1
St Boniface RC Primary
School *TOOT* SW17 ....5 H2
St Ceciiias RC Primary School
WPK KT4 ....21 H3
St Chads RC Primary School
SNWD SE25 ....16 C4
St Christophers School
BECK BR3 ....19 E1
EPSOM KT18 ....40 C4
St Clements Primary School
EW KT17 ....30 D4
St Cyprians Greek Orthodox
Primary School
THHTH CR7 ....16 A1
St Davids College
WWKM BR4 ....28 D1
St Davids School
PUR/KEN CR8 ....45 F1
St Dunstans CE Primary
School *CHEAM* SM3 ....32 A2
St Ebba's Hospital
HOR/WEW KT19 ....30 A4
St Elpheges RC Primary
School *WLGTN* SM6 ....35 E2
St Francis Catholic School
CTHM CR3 ....59 H1
St Georges Hospital
TOOT SW17 ....5 G2
St Giles School
CROY/NA CRO 35 H2
St Helier Hospital
SUT SM1 ....23 E2
St James Medical Centre
CROY/NA CRO 26 B1

St James the Great RC
Primary School
THHTH CR7 ....15 H1
St Johns CE Primary School
CROY/NA CRO 27 H4
PGE/AN SE20 ....9 G4
St John the Baptist CE
Primary School
CAT SE6 ....11 E1
St Josephs Catholic Infant
School *NRWD* SE19 ....8 A3
St Josephs Catholic Primary
School *EPSOM* KT18 ......40 A4
St Josephs College
STRHM/NOR SW16 ....7 H3
St Josephs RC Junior School
STRHM/NOR SW16 ....7 H3
St Leonards CE Primary School
STRHM/NOR SW16 ....6 D2
St Lukes CE Primary School
WNWD SE27 ....8 A2
St Lukes School
THHTH CR7 ....15 G3
St Marks CE Primary School
SNWD SE25 ....17 E3
St Marks Primary School
MTCM CR4 ....13 H1
St Martins CE Junior School
EPSOM KT18 ....40 B5
St Marys Catholic Infant School
CROY/NA CRO 2 E1
St Mary's High School
CROY/NA CRO 26 A2
St Marys Infant School
CAR SM5 ....23 C5
St Marys Rc Infant School
CAR SM5 ....33 H1
St Marys RC Primary School
BECK BR3 ....11 E4
WIM/MER SW19 ....4 C4
St Michaels Sydenham CE
Primary School *SYD* SE26 ..10 A1
St Nicholas Centre
SUT SM1 ....32 D1
St Nicholas School
PUR/KEN CR8 ....45 F3
St Peter & Paul CE Infant
School *CTHM* CR3 ....58 C5
Ss Peter & Paul Rc Primary
School *MTCM* CR4 ....13 H3
St Peters Primary School
SAND/SEL CR2 ....36 B2
St Phillips Infant School
CROY/NA CRO 9 F1
St Philomenas Catholic High
School *CAR* SM5 ....33 G1
St Raphaels Hospice
WPK KT4 ....21 H3
St Thomas Becket RC Primary
School *SNWD* SE25 ....17 E5
St Thomas of Canterbury
Primary School
MTCM CR4 ....14 A2
Sanderstead Junior School
SAND/SEL CR2 ....36 B4
Saxon Business Centre
WIM/MER SW19 ....13 E1
Sayer Clinic
CROY/NA CRO 25 F5
Seaton House School
BELMT SM2 ....33 F5
Secombe Centre
SUT SM1 ....32 C1
Sedgehill School
CAT SE6 ....10 D2
Selhurst High School for Boys
SNWD SE25 ....16 B5
The Selhurst Medical Centre
SNWD SE25 ....16 C5
Sellincourt School
TOOT SW17 ....5 G3
Selsdon Community Centre
SAND/SEL CR2 ....37 F5
Selsdon High School
SAND/SEL CR2 ....37 H3
Selsdon Primary School
SAND/SEL CR2 ....37 G4
Selsdon Road Industrial Estate
SAND/SEL CR2 ....36 B3
Selsdon Wood Nature Reserve
CROY/NA CRO 48 A1
Shawley Primary School
EPSOM KT18 ....50 C3
Sherwood Park School
WLGTN SM6 ....24 D4
Sherwood School
MTCM CR4 ....14 C3
Shirley Clinic
CROY/NA CRO 27 G2
Shirley High School
CROY/NA CRO 27 H4
Shirley Oaks Hospital
CROY/NA CRO 27 G1
Shirley Park Golf Club
CROY/NA CRO 27 F3
Shirley Wanderers RFC
WWKM BR4 ....29 E5
Shotfield Health Clinic
WLGTN SM6 ....34 B2
Shree Ghanapathy Temple
WIM/MER SW19 ....5 E3

Shree Swaminarayan Temple
STRHM/NOR SW16 ....7 E5
Silver Wing Industrial Estate
CROY/NA CRO 35 F2
Singlegate Primary School
WIM/MER SW19 ....5 F4
Sloane Hospital
BECK BR3 ....11 F5
Smallwood Primary School
TOOT SW17 ....5 F1
Smitham Primary School
COUL/CHIP CR5 ....53 G1
South Croydon Medical
Centre *SAND/SEL* CR2 ..36 A3
South Croydon Sports Club
SAND/SEL CR2 ....36 C1
South Lewisham Health
Centre *CAT* SE6 ....11 E1
South London Crematorium
MTCM CR4 ....14 C1
South London Tamil School
CROY/NA CRO 26 A1
South Norwood Country Park
SNWD SE25 ....17 G3
South Norwood Hill Medical
Centre *SNWD* SE25 ....16 C1
South Norwood Medical
Centre *SNWD* SE25 ....16 C3
South Norwood Pools &
Fitness Centre *SNWD* SE25 ..17 E4
South Norwood Primary
School *SNWD* SE25 ....17 E4
South Park Hotel
SAND/SEL CR2 ....3 G7
South Thames College
TOOT SW17 ....5 G2
Sparrow Farm Community
Junior School
EW KT17 ....31 F1
Spring Park Primary School
CROY/NA CRO 28 C4
Squash and Badminton Club
WIM/MER SW19 ....4 A4
Stafford Cross Business Park
CROY/NA CRO 35 F1
Stanford Primary School
STRHM/NOR SW16 ....6 D5
Stanley Park High School
CAR SM5 ....34 A2
Stanley Park Junior School
CAR SM5 ....33 H5
Stanley Technical High School
SNWD SE25 ....16 D2
Stanton Square Industrial
Estate *CAT* SE6 ....10 B1
Stewart Fleming Primary
School *PGE/AN* SE20 ......17 G2
Stirling Way Industrial Estates
CROY/NA CRO 25 E1
Stowford College
SUT SM1 ....33 E3
Streatham & Croydon RFC
THHTH CR7 ....15 G4
Streatham Ice Rink
STRHM/NOR SW16 ....7 E2
Streatham Modern School
STRHM/NOR SW16 ....7 F3
Streatham Park Cemetery
MTCM CR4 ....14 C1
Streatham Swimming Pool
STRHM/NOR SW16 ....7 E2
Streatham Vale Sports Club
STRHM/NOR SW16 ....6 C4
Sunnydown School
CTHM CR3 ....59 H1
Sunnyhill Primary School
STRHM/NOR SW16 ....7 F1
Surrey Business Park
EW KT17 ....40 C1
Surrey Institute of Art &
Design *HOR/WEW* KT19 ..40 C3
EPSOM KT18 ....40 B4
Surrey National Golf Club
CTHM CR3 ....58 D3
Sutton Alternative Health
Centre *SUT* SM1 ....32 D1
Sutton Arena
CAR SM5 ....23 F1
Sutton Bowling Club
BELMT SM2 ....32 C4
Sutton Cemetery
CHEAM SM5 ....22 B3
Sutton Civic Centre
SUT SM1 ....32 D1
Sutton College of Learning
for Adults *SUT* SM1 ......32 D1
Sutton General Hospital
BELMT SM2 ....32 D5
Sutton Grammar School for
Boys *SUT* SM1 ....33 E1
Sutton High Junior School
SUT SM1 ....32 D2
Sutton High School for Girls
Gdst *SUT* SM1 ....32 C2
Sutton Magistrates Court
WLGTN SM6 ....34 B2
Sutton Superbowl
SUT SM1 ....32 D1
Sutton United FC
SUT SM1 ....22 C5
Sutton West Centre
SUT SM1 ....32 C1

Sydenham High School
Junior Dept *SYD* SE26 ....9 F1
Sydenham High School
(Secondary) *SYD* SE26 ....9 F2
Sydenham High School
Sports Ground *BECK* BR3 ..10 C2
Taberner House
CROY/NA CRO 2 D4
Tait Road Industrial Estate
CROY/NA CRO 26 B1
Tamworth Manor High School
STRHM/NOR SW16 ....14 D2
Tandem Centre
WIM/MER SW19 ....5 F5
Tattenham Health Centre
EPSOM KT18 ....50 B3
Thatched House Hotel
SUT SM1 ....32 B2
Theatre Centre
BECK BR3 ....18 D1
The Theatre on the Hill
CTHM CR3 ....59 C2
Therapia Trading Estate
CROY/NA CRO 24 D1
Thornton Heath Health
Centre *THHTH* CR7 ....16 A3
Thornton Heath Pools &
Fitness Centre
THHTH CR7 ....16 A2
Thornton Road Industrial
Estate *CROY/NA* CRO 15 E5
Times Square Shopping
Centre *SUT* SM1 ....32 D1
Tollgate Primary School
CROY/NA CRO 17 C5
Tooting Bec Athletics Track
TOOT SW17 ....6 B1
Tooting Leisure Centre
TOOT SW17 ....5 F1
Tooting & Mitcham United FC
MTCM CR4 ....14 B4
Tower Industrial Estate
SNWD SE25 ....17 E3
Travel Inn
EPSOM KT18 ....40 A4
SAND/SEL CR2 ....37 F1
Trident Business Centre
TOOT SW17 ....5 G4
Trinity School
CROY/NA CRO 27 G3
Tudor Lodge
PUR/KEN CR8 ....35 E5
Tweeddale Primary School
CAR SM5 ....23 F1
Two Bridges Business Park
SAND/SEL CR2 ....36 B2
UCI Cinema
SUT SM1 ....32 D1
The Ullswater Business Park
COUL/CHIP CR5 ....54 A1
Ullswater Trading Estate
COUL/CHIP CR5 ....54 A1
Unicorn Primary School
BECK BR3 ....18 D4
Valley Primary School
HAYES BR2 ....19 H1
Vestry Hall
MTCM CR4 ....13 H2
Victor Seymour Infant School
CAR SM5 ....23 H4
Virgo Fidelis Convent Schools
NRWD SE19 ....8 A1
VUE Cinema
CROY/NA CRO 25 F3
Vulcan Business Centre
CROY/NA CRO 39 C4
Waddon Clinic
CROY/NA CRO 35 G1
Waddon Infant School
CROY/NA CRO 35 G1
Waldorf Steiner School of
S W London
STRHM/NOR SW16 ....6 D1
Wallace Fields County Infant
School *EW* KT17 ....41 E3
Wallace Fields Junior School
EW KT17 ....41 E2
Wallington County Grammar
School *WLGTN* SM6 ......24 B4
Wallington High School for
Girls *WLGTN* SM6 ....34 B4
Wandle Trading Estate
MTCM CR4 ....23 H1
Wandle Valley School
CAR SM5 ....23 G1
Warehouse Theatre
CROY/NA CRO 2 E3
Warlingham Park School
WARL CR6 ....57 G1
Warlingham RFC & John
Fisher Sports Club
WARL CR6 ....56 B1
Warlingham School
WARL CR6 ....56 B1
Warlingham Sports Club
WARL CR6 ....56 D2
War Memorial Sports Ground
SUT SM1 ....23 G5
Warren Mead Infant School
BNSTD SM7 ....41 G5
Warren Mead Junior School
BNSTD SM7 ....41 H5

Watergate School
CAT SE6 11
Watermeads High School
MRDN SM4 ....
Wattenden Primary School
PUR/KEN CR8 ....
Westbourne Primary School
SUT SM1 ....
Westcroft Leisure Centre
CAR SM5 ....
West Dene School
PUR/KEN CR8 ....
West Ewell Infant School
HOR/WEW KT19 ....
West Thornton Primary School
CROY/NA CRO ....
West Wickham Swimming
Baths *WWKM* BR4 ....
Westwood Language College
for Girls *NRWD* SE19 ......
Whitehorse Manor Primary
School *THHTH* CR7 ....
Whitgift Almshouses
CRO/NA CRO ....
Whitgift School
SAND/SEL CR2 ....
Whitgift Shopping Centre
CROY/NA CRO ....
Whyteleafe Business Village
CTHM CR3 ....
Whyteleafe FC
CTHM CR3 ....
Whyteleafe School
CTHM CR3 ....
Wickham Court School
WWKM BR4 ....
Wickham Theatre
WWKM BR4 ....
Wide Way Health Clinic
MTCM CR4 ....
William Morris Primary School
MTCM CR4 ....
Willington School
WIM/MER SW19 ....
Willow Business Centre
MTCM CR4 ....
Wilson's School
WLGTN SM6 ....
Wimbledon Chase Primary
School *RYNPK* SW20 ......
Wimbledon (Gap Road)
Cemetery *WIM/MER* SW19 ..
Wimbledon High School
WIM/MER SW19 ....
Wimbledon House School
WIM/MER SW19 ....
Wimbledon Magistrates Court
WIM/MER SW19 ....
Wimbledon Recreation Centre
WIM/MER SW19 ....
Wimbledon School of Art
WIM/MER SW19 ....
Wimbledon School of English
WIM/MER SW19 ....
Wimbledon Stadium
TOOT SW17 ....
Wimbledon Theatre
WIM/MER SW19 ....
Windmill Trading Estate
MTCM CR4 ....
Winterbourne Infant School
THHTH CR7 ....
Woldingham Golf Club
WARL CR6 ....
Woldingham School
GDST RH9 ....
Wolsey Junior School
CROY/NA CRO ....
Woodbrook School
BECK BR3 ....
Woodcote High School
COUL/CHIP CR5 ....
Woodcote Park Golf Club
COUL/CHIP CR5 ....
Woodcotes Primary School
COUL/CHIP CR5 ....
Woodlea Primary School
CTHM CR3 ....
Woodmansterne Primary
School *BNSTD* SM7 ......
Woodmansterne Primary
School *STRHM/NOR* SW16 ..
Woodmansterne Sports Club
BNSTD SM7 ....
Woodside Health Centre
SNWD SE25 ....
Woodside Infants School
CROY/NA CRO ....
Worsley Bridge Junior School
BECK BR3 ....
Wrencote
CROY/NA CRO ....

Acknowledgements

st Office is a registered trademark of Post Office Ltd. in the UK and other countries.

s address data provided by Education Direct.

station information supplied by Johnsons

ay street data provided by © Tele Atlas N.V.   Tele Atlas

centre information provided by:

Centre Association   Britains best garden centres

le Garden Centres

Free Car Check worth £9.99 with AA Service Centres

Use yourself or give to a member of your family or a friend.

An AA Car Check could help you steer clear of costly problems by targeting the main causes of breakdown.

- The Car Check includes: tyre check — including spare; charging system/battery; drive belt tension; battery security; cooling system; fluid levels — engine oil and screen wash; lights; brake fluid; windscreen wipers/washers. This doesn't replace the need for regular servicing and maintenance.
- AA Service Centres have a national network of garages that are open 6 days a week, offering servicing, M.O.T., tyre replacement and mechanical repairs.

HOW TO CLAIM YOUR FREE CAR CHECK

- **Simply call 0845 609 0621 to book your car into an AA Service Centre.**
- Cut off the voucher at the bottom of this page and present it when booking your car in.
- **Offer ends 31st December 2005.**

Your FREE
Car Check voucher
(AA Street by Street Atlas 2005)

AASC PLANT NUMBER:

QUESTIONNAIRE

Dear Atlas User
Your comments, opinions and recommendations are very important to us.
So please help us to improve our street atlases by taking a few minutes
to complete this simple questionnaire.

You do not need a stamp (unless posted outside the UK). If you do not want to remove
this page from your street atlas, then photocopy it or write your answers on a plain sheet
of paper.

Send to: The Editor, AA Street by Street, FREEPOST SCE 4598,
Basingstoke RG21 4GY

ABOUT THE ATLAS...

Which city/town/county did you buy?

_____

Are there any features of the atlas or mapping that you find particularly useful?

_____
_____
_____

Is there anything we could have done better?

_____
_____
_____

Why did you choose an AA Street by Street atlas?

_____
_____
_____

Did it meet your expectations?

Exceeded ☐   **Met all** ☐   **Met most** ☐   **Fell below** ☐

Please give your reasons

_____
_____
_____
_____

Where did you buy it?

For what purpose? (please tick all applicable)

To use in your own local area ☐   To use on business or at work ☐

Visiting a strange place ☐   In the car ☐   On foot ☐

Other (please state)

LOCAL KNOWLEDGE...

Local knowledge is invaluable. Whilst every attempt has been made to make the information contained in this atlas as accurate as possible, should you notice any inaccuracies, please detail them below (if necessary, use a blank piece of paper) or e-mail us at *streetbystreet@theAA.com*

ABOUT YOU...

Name (Mr/Mrs/Ms)

Address

Postcode

Daytime tel no

E-mail address

Which age group are you in?

Under 25 ☐   25-34 ☐   35-44 ☐   45-54 ☐   55-64 ☐   65+ ☐

Are you an AA member?   YES ☐   NO ☐

Do you have Internet access?   YES ☐   NO ☐

Thank you for taking the time to complete this questionnaire. Please send it to us as soon as possible, and remember, you do not need a stamp (unless posted outside the UK).

We may want to contact you about other products and services provided by us, or our partners (by mail, telephone) but please tick the box if you DO NOT wish to hear about such products and services from us by mail or telephone. ☐

ML167z